Behold, Your House Is Left to You

Behold, Your House Is Left to You

The Theological and Narrative Place
of the Jerusalem Temple in Luke's Gospel

PETER H. RICE

☙PICKWICK *Publications* • Eugene, Oregon

BEHOLD, YOUR HOUSE IS LEFT TO YOU
The Theological and Narrative Place of the Jerusalem Temple in Luke's Gospel

Copyright © 2016 Peter H. Rice. All rights reserved. Except for brief quotations in critical publications or reviews, no part of this book may be reproduced in any manner without prior written permission from the publisher. Write: Permissions, Wipf and Stock Publishers, 199 W. 8th Ave., Suite 3, Eugene, OR 97401.

Pickwick Publications
An Imprint of Wipf and Stock Publishers
199 W. 8th Ave., Suite 3
Eugene, OR 97401

www.wipfandstock.com

PAPERBACK ISBN: 978-1-4982-8191-1
HARDCOVER ISBN: 978-1-4982-8193-5
EBOOK ISBN: 978-1-4982-8192-8

Cataloguing-in-Publication data:

Names: Rice, Peter H.

Title: Behold, your house is left to you : the theological and narrative place of the Jerusalem temple in Luke's Gospel / Peter H. Rice.

Description: Eugene, OR: Pickwick Publications, 2016 | Includes bibliographical references and index.

Identifiers: ISBN 978-1-4982-8191-1 (paperback) | ISBN 978-1-4982-8193-5 (hardcover) | ISBN 978-1-4982-8192-8 (ebook)

Subjects: LCSH: Bible. Luke—Criticism, interpretation, etc. | Temple of Jerusalem (Jerusalem).

Classification: BS2595.2 R45 2016 (paperback) | BS2595.2 (ebook)

Manufactured in the U.S.A.　　　　　　　　　　　　　　　　　　　　　10/06/16

To Abby, for her endless patience, her abounding love, her unwavering support, and her ineffable way of brightening the darkest of days

Contents

List of Tables | viii
Acknowledgments | ix

Part 1: Introduction | 1
1 Reading Luke: Narrative, Subtlety, and Echoes of Scripture | 7
2 Theodicy in the Ancient and Lukan Worlds | 30

Part 2: The Jerusalem Temple in Luke's Gospel—A Reassessment | 57
3 The Jerusalem Temple in Luke 1–2 | 59
4 The Jerusalem Temple in Luke 3–19 | 90
5 The Jerusalem Temple in Luke 19–24 | 121
6 Conclusion | 152

Appendix: Jerusalem and the Temple in Acts | 157

Bibliography | 165
Index of Ancient Documents | 179

List of Tables

Table 1: **The Rhetoric of Subtlety** | 18
Table 2: **The Songs of Hannah and Mary** | 64
Table 3: **"Anna" in 1 Kingdoms and Luke** | 67
Table 4: **Childhood Summaries** | 68
Table 5: **Echoes of Judgment** | 77
Table 6: **Priestly Blessings** | 146

Acknowledgments

THIS STUDY WOULD NOT have been possible without the help and guidance of many people. First of all, it hardly needs saying that this study would never have materialized without the steady, skilled, and tireless hand of my dissertation adviser, Mikeal Parsons, who was crucial both during the dissertation and during the publication phase of this project. This study is also steeply indebted to the careful, patient, and keen-eyed readings of Bruce Longenecker and Andrew Arterbury, during its earlier life as a dissertation. Chief of all, however, is my wife Abby, who has borne this burden along with me, who has celebrated with me in each victory, and to whom I dedicate this work. I owe thanks also to the editorial and production teams of Pickwick Publications for their assistance in turning this dissertation into a publishable monograph. Also deserving of mention are the many friends and family members whose love, optimism, and companionship were indispensable and unfailing aids in this otherwise largely solitary, sometimes lonely, task. To all of these, I cheerfully acknowledge an inestimable debt: I am grateful for your distinct contributions to this project; I am grateful for the blessing each of you has been in my life.

Part 1

Introduction

Although there has been "vast scholarly effort" to reexamine Luke's contribution to early Christian theology since Conzelmann's groundbreaking *Die Mitte der Zeit*, "at least one key Lucan theme still awaits thorough reassessment," namely, "the role of the Temple" in Luke's writings.[1] Francis Weinert made this observation more than 30 years ago, but the intervening decades have not remedied the lack: the role of the Temple—and Jerusalem with it—in the Lukan writings remains a subject in need of continued study. This is all the more surprising given that Luke references Jerusalem roughly twice as much as the rest of the NT combined and, moreover, that roughly one-sixth of Luke and Acts either occurs within or discusses the fate of the Jerusalem Temple.[2] The need for reassessment does not arise from lack of recent scholarly attention[3] but rather because recent methodological developments have yet to be brought to bear fully on the subject.

---

1. Weinert, "Abandoned House," 68.
2. Noted by, e.g., Walker, *Jesus and the Holy City*, 60.
3. See especially the following (primarily for Luke's Gospel): Bachmann, *Jerusalem und der Tempel*; Weinert, "Meaning of the Temple"; Weinert, "Abandoned House"; Weinert, "Luke, Stephen"; Giblin, *The Destruction of Jerusalem*; Klauck, "Die Heilige Stadt"; Esler, *Community and Gospel*; Brawley, *Luke-Acts and the Jews*; Chance, *Jerusalem*; Elliott, "Temple versus Household"; Elliott, "Household and Meals"; Dawsey, "Luke's Positive Perception"; Green, "Demise of the Temple"; Karris, "Luke"; Walker, *Jesus and the Holy City*; Taylor, "Jerusalem and the Temple"; Taylor, "The Destruction of Jerusalem"; Taylor, "Early Christian Eschatology"; Taylor, "The Jerusalem Temple"; Hutcheon, "'God Is with Us'"; Longenecker, "Rome's Victory"; Holmås, "'My House Shall Be Called.'"

Earlier important treatments include Baltzer, "The Meaning of the Temple"; and Gaston, *No Stone*.

Part 1: Introduction

In the present study, then, I aim to fill this lacuna at least partially, reassessing the role of Jerusalem and the Jerusalem Temple (JT)[4] in Luke's Gospel by:

1) use of a critical perspective that has been underemployed in many previous pursuits of this question, narrative criticism,

2) attending to Luke's pervasive and complex reliance on and use of the Jewish Scriptures in his Gospel,[5] and

3) accounting for an underutilized yet important aspect of Luke's context, namely, ancient theodicy.[6]

In the next two chapters, I will further clarify each of the three points above. But first, a further, brief word is required.

Some previous treatments of this question take what is from my perspective a reductive view of Luke as an author and thinker. Thus these treatments typically approach the topic of Jerusalem and its Temple in Luke's writings not as a pressing theological and scriptural problem—as I will argue it was for Luke and therefore also members of Luke's ideal audience—but primarily as a matter of the author's personal preferences and opinions. And so the question is reduced to a matter of a single, supposed

---

4. While the two entities, Jerusalem and the Temple contained within Jerusalem's temple mount, admit a certain degree of differentiability within the Lukan world, especially spatially—e.g., Jesus or the disciples can be in Jerusalem without being in the Temple—in terms of their ultimate fate and their chief significance for Luke, the two are inextricably linked, perhaps indeed to the point of being essentially coextensive—hence, my considering them together in this study. See Brawley, *Luke-Acts and the Jews*; Bachmann, *Jerusalem und der Tempel*, 134–70; Hutcheon, "'God Is with Us,'" 4; Karris, "Luke," 676; contra Walker, *Jesus and the Holy City*, 60.

5. Baltzer's early study ("The Meaning of the Temple") on this topic shines an illuminating light in this direction, particularly his examination of potential intertextuality with Ezekiel. Weinert, however, dismisses Baltzer's article as one that "interprets Lucan Temple texts from a non-Lucan standpoint," doing so with particular reliance on the OT ("Abandoned House," 69)—thus failing to understand, from my perspective, the extent to which the OT (in Luke's conception of it) impacts Luke's treatment of Jerusalem and the Temple in his works.

6. Very few of the major treatments of Jerusalem and the Temple in Luke's Gospel (or Acts) deal adequately, if at all, with the theodical crisis brought about by Rome's destruction of these structures in 70 CE. A striking exception to this is Longenecker, "Rome's Victory," anticipated by Hutcheon, "'God Is with Us,'" and Karris, "Luke." Keener notes that "Judea's function in his narrative [Acts] also includes an element of theodicy, explaining the holy city's destruction by showing the elite's rejection of Israel's rightful spiritual leadership" (*Acts*, 1:473).

perspective, in which Luke has either a "positive" or a "negative"—or, less often yet more helpfully, an "ambivalent"[7]—attitude toward these institutions. No doubt the opinions and preferences of the author play an important role in his presentation of Jerusalem and its Temple. These opinions and preferences, however, are significantly filtered through the theological and scriptural problem raised by the destruction of Jerusalem in 70 CE (see chapter 2). Conzelmann's groundbreaking work has helped Lukan scholarship think of Luke as, among other things, now also Luke the Theologian, an independent and thoughtful sculptor of his text(s).[8] In traditional consideration of Luke and the Jerusalem Temple, however, this common frame—and it is perhaps the dominant frame—for examining the question ("view/attitude/perspective") understands Luke to be a "theologian" only in the most reductive of senses: "Luke as theologian" simply means here that Luke has an agenda or perspective he inserts into the text as he retells the story of Jesus and the early church. Luke, within this understanding, differs little from, say, a vacuous, voluble blogger relating the latest news story with inevitably his or her own peculiar spin on the details. Against that, I follow other commentators in taking seriously the designation of Luke as a "theologian," one in line with Luke's deep knowledge of and concern for the Jewish Scriptures, as well as one that takes seriously the fact that *Luke* takes seriously what he perceives to be the faithfulness of Israel's God to God's promises—a theme abundantly on display in Luke's writings. Given, in other words, that Luke is indeed a theologian, we cannot assess the question of Luke's "attitude" or "perspective" on these matters until we first attend to the place these institutions occupy within his own theological landscape. In subsequent chapters, I will attempt to demonstrate that this landscape is far richer and more varied than some have supposed.

---

7. Aptly stating the apparent ambivalence present in Luke's writings is Holmås: "The crux of the presentation of the temple in Luke-Acts is the discrepancy between, on the one hand, the fact that the holy place is used consistently for positive religious ends by Jesus and his disciples and, on the other hand, the clearly critical comments in several key texts" ("'My House Shall Be Called,'" 396).

8. Not all of the treatments on this topic have given Luke even this much credit. Discussion of Jerusalem and the Temple in Luke's writings has frequently been marred by attempts to dig beneath the known text forms of Luke's writings in order to unearth putative Lukan sources (as in the reliance on a putatively reconstructed proto-Luke in Gaston, "No Stone"). This is often done with utter and, to my mind, unreasonable dismissal of the likelihood that Luke was actually in significant agreement with the views of whatever sources he chose to include, or else that he took considerable (and presumably largely successful) efforts to remove views quite at odds with his own.

Part 1: Introduction

Even if we avoid a simplistic picture of Luke as a thinker and theologian, other pitfalls remain.[9] Some who have approached the subject with proper attentiveness to Luke's theological and scriptural sensibilities have nonetheless failed to place the question of the Jerusalem Temple in the Lukan writings in the crucial context of post-70 CE theodicy. Yet, if we are to assess the place of Jerusalem and its Temple in Luke's writings, we must ask why it is that Luke gives these Jewish artifices such great prominence in the first place,[10] and the answer lies, I will suggest, in the theodical problem—keenly felt by many of Luke's contemporaries—of Jerusalem's destruction at Roman hands in 70 CE. Understanding the nature of the problem also sheds light on the nature of Luke's solution. Faced with a theological and scriptural problem, Luke gives, true to Lukan form, a theological and scriptural answer, as well as an answer not merely conditioned by his own biases, as such.

So much for the pitfalls, but now I must describe the path. What path should one follow in attempting to map the theological and narrative place of Jerusalem and its Temple in Luke's thought? Working from the insights of those who precede me, I believe the path is one requiring attention above all to Luke's narrative form and theological and scriptural acumen[11] as well as to his theodical context.[12] I aim in the pages that follow to pursue this

---

9. Among those who, to my mind, grant Luke a fitting degree of theological nuance and sophistication are Esler, *Community and Gospel*, Green, "Demise of the Temple," Taylor, esp. "The Jerusalem Temple," and Longenecker, "Rome's Victory."

10. Esler, *Community and Gospel*, faults numerous previous commentators for failing to account, in their assessments of the Temple in the writings of Luke, for the reason why Luke would have given it such prominence in the first place (133). Esler's socio-redactional reading offers important insights into the question, I believe, but still leaves unearthed some of the underlying theological dimensions that motivated Luke.

11. Especially helpful on the question of narrative are Green, "Demise of the Temple," Taylor, "The Jerusalem Temple," and Holmås, "'My House Shall Be Called.'" Yet I find myself in significant disagreement with Taylor, for example, on the question of context, specifically Taylor's claim that Luke must be read against widespread Jewish hopes of a restored Jerusalem. I see relatively strong evidence of a concern for theodicy in Luke's writings (see chapter 2) and comparatively weak evidence of a desire to temper expectations of a restored Jerusalem (Acts 1:6–8 being the likeliest evidence for this). Indeed Taylor himself adduces scant internal evidence for his claim but rather relies on an inference from external evidence, which he does not himself bring to the table.

12. The work of several scholars also suggests the relevance of sociological models for assessing the question (viz., Brawley, Esler, Green, often drawing on Eliade). I will attempt to incorporate some of the insights from these analyses in part 2 of this study, though I have been unable to incorporate them in any systematic way. This path, like many, requires that one pack only lightly, and I am already encumbered with the luggage

PART 1: INTRODUCTION

path—all the way to its first major vista, the breaking point between Luke and Acts. There, having surveyed the terrain of Luke's Gospel, I will offer an account of what Acts might hold in store (Appendix A). While I might wish to follow the path to its very end—and thus continue the trail through Acts—external circumstances (here the concrete realities of constructing and publishing a monograph) sometimes curtail journeys before their ideal end.

Many of course hold Luke and Acts to be inseparable halves of a two-volume work and thus may view my journey as not only partial but also incomplete. While I will not attempt to address the question of the literary relationship between the two works here, I will defend my procedure in the pages that follow by noting 1) the strong critique many have brought against the (ever stalwart) majority on this question[13] and 2) the very strong evidence that Luke's earliest identifiable (and admittedly second-century) audiences in fact read and encountered Luke and Acts as separate, if related, works.[14] In addition to this, 3) in Acts (and Acts 7 in particular) Luke the author goes beyond anything explicitly present in his Gospel in his criticism of the JT. While Luke's ideal audience (discussed in chapter 1) may ultimately hear aspects of Luke's Gospel in light of his eventual treatment of the city and its Temple in Acts, it is also valid to ask, as I will, how they would have understood Luke's Gospel in its own right. This is because, simply put, "Luke's Gospel is narratively intelligible on its own, apart from Acts."[15] If I thereby settle for the runner-up prize of arriving at (one reading of) the theology of Jerusalem and the Temple present merely in Luke's Gos-

---

pertaining to ancient theodicy, narrative criticism, and Lukan intertextuality.

13. See Parsons and Pervo, *Rethinking the Unity*; Gregory and Rowe, eds., *Reception of Luke and Acts*.

14. See Gregory, *The Reception of Luke-Acts*. Succinctly stating the relevant external evidence is Rowe: "No ancient author exhibits a hermeneutical practice that is founded upon the reading of Luke-Acts as one work in two volumes; no ancient author argues that Luke and Acts should be read together as one work in two volumes; and, there is not a single New Testament manuscript that contains the unity Luke-Acts or that even hints at this unity by placing Acts directly next to the Gospel of Luke" ("Literary Unity and Reception History," 451). I find Rowe's subsequent discussion of Acts's unique text-critical problems (viz., its longer, "Western" text) as strong evidence for its having a separate *Ausgangspunkt* from Luke's Gospel (see Rowe, "Literary Unity and Reception History," 453–54). This is a strong counter-response to Luke Johnson's otherwise on-target claim that "there is a gap between the authors cited by Rowe and the first readers of Luke-Acts, a gap not only of time, but also of circumstance and therefore of perspective" ("Is Reception History Pertinent?," 160).

15. Rowe, "Literary Unity and Reception History," 451.

PART 1: INTRODUCTION

pel, with only an appendiced overture toward Luke's thought as a whole,[16] I can only say that this is indeed a goal worthy of pursuit.

16. Thus I accede to Johnson's claim that a "literary-critical reading... of Luke's entire narrative [i.e., Luke and Acts] is best for one purpose, namely understanding his literary and theological voice" ("Is Reception History Pertinent?," 162). Hence, the appendix on Acts in this volume.

1

Reading Luke
Narrative, Subtlety, and Echoes of Scripture

READING LUKE'S NARRATIVE

As I approach Luke's Gospel, I follow in this study the insight of Joel Green, N. H. Taylor, J. Bradley Chance, Geir Otto Holmås, and others, that the question of Jerusalem and the Temple in Luke's writings must be asked and answered with respect to Luke's stated intention of providing auditors with a *narrative* (διήγεσις), and one that is orderly (καθεξῆς) at that.[1] As Luke Johnson aptly states the matter, referring to Luke's plan of presenting things καθεξῆς: "The exegetical implication is that, in Luke, we need to attend not only to *what* Luke says but also to *where* in the story he says it. Losing the thread of the story . . . means losing the thread of meaning."[2] Likewise, Joel Green has emphasized the importance of "exploring the particular shaping [Luke] has given his narrative" for grasping Lukan theology.[3]

I will thus undertake a narrative-critical reading, though making several departures from the norm, including from the usual emphasis on a first-time reading/hearing. There are several reasons for not limiting one's

---

1. On the "*narrato*-logical" ordering of Luke's works, see Moessner, "The Meaning of Kathexēs."
2. Johnson, "Kingship Parable," 142; emphasis original.
3. Green, *Theology*, 21.

Part 1: Introduction

approach to simply a first-time reading, including the fact that emphasis on a first-time reading is a virtually arbitrary convention within the field and also, more cogently, the strong evidence (discussed below) that Luke sometimes communicates subtly in a way not likely to produce ideal comprehension in his audience on a first reading.[4]

Although I will rely heavily on the insights of narrative criticism in my analysis of Luke's works, especially its keen focus on setting, plot, and characterization, I will not always foreground these theoretical undergirdings when discussing Luke's writings[5]—as doing so often has the ironic effect of removing auditors' focus from the narrative itself to the abstract apparatus being used to analyze the narrative—nor will I employ the full range of narrative-critical constructs and their linked verbage. Regarding the nexus of options for parsing out the authorial side of things, I not only make no distinction between "implied author" and "narrator," but I also generally avoid use of "implied author" in favor of simply "Luke," or "the Evangelist." I make the former decision, first, in recognition of Luke's writings as ancient works falling under the broad umbrella of "historical writing," the Third Gospel probably as a *bios* and Acts as some sort of non-elite historical writing.[6] Several have noted that the distinction between "narrator" and "author," which may be appropriate to works of fiction, applies far less readily to works of non-fiction.[7] Additionally, with precious few exceptions (viz.

---

4. I am hardly alone in maintaining that the import of Luke's writings are, at least on occasion, best felt by multiple exposures. The need for multiple exposures is, e.g., implicit in Longenecker's discussion of the narrative gap at Luke 4:30, especially in that the "norms and directives" or "field of reality" of Luke's texts in light of which the audience is invited to read Lukan gaps would hardly be accessible to an audience who had heard only the first four chapters of Luke's Gospel (*Hearing the Silence*)! Note Powell's claim that some texts appear to presume an understanding that arises only after multiple exposures (*Narrative Criticism?*, 20). Keener claims that likely repeated readings of Luke and Acts in house churches would have allowed "ideal hearers to pick up nuances and repeated themes not available to first-time hearers" and cites several ancient works, in various genres, that commend multiple exposures for catching a speech's or work's full meaning (e.g., Quintilian, *Inst.* 10.1.20–21; Keener, *Acts*, 1:18).

5. Here I am in line with Rowe, *Early Narrative Christology*, 9–10.

6. Increasingly since the work of Richard Burridge, there seems to be a broad consensus that the Gospels represent a form of ancient *bios*. I find the case for Acts as a historical work to be convincingly made in the thorough introduction to Keener's recent commentary on Acts (*Acts*, vol. 1, chapters 3–6), although I am not ready to endorse his more precise classifications of Acts as a popular-level historical monograph meant to tell the story of a people.

7. See the discussion in Merenlahti and Hakola, "Reconceiving Narrative Criticism":

Lucian of Samosata and Apuleius), ancient works simply do not employ the differentiation between implied author and (an "unreliable") narrator that is relatively endemic in the literature of recent centuries.[8] Thus distinctions between implied author and narrator are unlikely to be helpful in assessing Luke's works, especially in light of the genre differences between the Lukan writings and the minority report of satirists like Lucian and Apuleius.[9] My reason for eschewing "implied author" in favor of simply "Luke" (and, less frequently, "the Evangelist") is largely a stylistic decision.

It does also indicate, though, my agreement with the many narrative critics who increasingly recognize that narratival analysis need not be divorced from, and indeed can be greatly aided by, attention to the historical and social context in which a text was written.[10] As Jack Dean Kingsbury has noted, "Once one fully understands the 'world of the story,' one can then move to a reconstruction of the 'world of the evangelist.'"[11] And indeed, "[m]ore than ever, interpretations of the Gospel narratives are drawing upon our knowledge of the history, society and cultures of the first-century Mediterranean world *as a means to help us understand the story better.*"[12] This is precisely what I aim to do in this study. My study thus falls along the trajectory of narrative reading spearheaded by, among others, Charles H. Talbert.[13]

"In non-fictional narratives, therefore, the narrator represents the author . . . fictional stories . . . can be told from whatever point of view the writers finds best for his or her purposes. In other words, in non-fictional narratives, narrative structures are more transparent as to the aims and purposes of the author than in non-fictional [*sic*] narratives" (37–38).

8. Questioning the reliability of the narrator is sensible—even literarily savvy—when reading, say, Agatha Christie but yields far less fruit when reading an ancient writer of history.

9. In agreement with, e.g., Kurz, *Reading Luke-Acts*, 147–49; and Tannehill, *Narrative Unity*, 7; and with apologies to some narrative critics of Mark, e.g., Malbon, *Mark's Jesus*, esp. 232–44.

10. Cf. Merenlahti and Hakola, "Reconceiving Narrative Criticism," 34, 48: "In the case of the Gospels, the forms of narrative analysis that are more open to questions concerning the ideological *and historical* background of the text must be considered preferable, because they pay due attention to the nature of the Gospels as non-fictional narratives"; emphasis added.

11. Kingsbury, "Reflections on 'the Reader,'" 459.

12. Rhoads, "Narrative Criticism," 268; emphasis original. His essay appears to be somewhat programmatic on this point.

13. See especially Talbert, *Mediterranean Milieu*. I do not share Talbert's conviction that such readings must avoid, with surgical precision, any reference to authorial

Part 1: Introduction

The key contextual pieces that will shape my narrative reading are 1) the rhetoric-infused ethos of the Greco-Roman world,[14] 2) the late 1st century context in which Luke wrote, a context in which questions of theodicy were especially prominent (discussed in chapter 2 below), and 3) Luke's probable use of Mark. Thus my narrative reading of Luke, informed by the rhetorical models and praxis of the ancient world and attuned to redactional critical insights, has a strong genetic relationship to the narrative-rhetorical reading employed by Mikeal C. Parsons.[15] Unlike Parsons's commentaries, however, my study of course has neither the space nor the scope for tracing in detail the narrative flow of each of Luke's works and therefore stands under the mandate of keying in on those scenes that provide greatest grist for assessing the JT in Luke (and to a lesser degree Acts), even while not losing sight of the larger narrative dynamics at play in the work(s).

Emphasis on context also significantly informs my approach to the audience of Luke's writings. I am interested in how key segments of Luke and Acts might have sounded to a particular, "ideal" audience, namely, an audience sensitive to the conventions of ancient rhetoric in general, including the widespread use of subtle communication, sensitive also to issues of theodicy, and thoroughly knowledgeable of the Scriptures whose fulfillment Luke takes such great pains to show in the events surrounding the lives of Jesus and the early church. Although Luke's writings themselves suggest an audience attuned to such emphases,[16] I recognize that such an "ideal audience" to some degree arises from my own imaginary, though

---

intention; see Rowe, *Early Narrative Christology*, 4n12. I share broad sympathies with Rowe's methodology, including his reticence toward over-loading one's narrative reading with theoretical trappings and jargon (9) and his interest in producing a historically sensitive narrative reading (14–15).

14. Common to and pervasive in this rhetoric-infused ethos, particularly during the latter half of the first century, was the use of subtle communication, as in "figured speech," "emphasis," and even enthymemes. See Ahl, "Safe Criticism"; and see further below.

15. See, e.g., his *Paideia* commentaries on *Acts* and *Luke*. Rowe also allows for redactional critical insights in his narrative analysis of Luke (*Early Narrative Christology*, 16–17).

16. See the works of Parsons and others for Luke's use of ancient rhetoric at a middling but non-elite level (e.g., "Luke and the *Progymnasmata*"). See the discussion below for evidence of Lukan subtlety. See, e.g., Kurz, *Reading Luke-Acts*, 16, for the audience's presumed intimate knowledge of Scripture. See Luke's considerable emphasis on the destruction of Jerusalem and the JT compared to Mark and Matthew, as well as his theodical parables (all in chapter 2 below), for his sensitivity to issues of theodicy.

historically and contextually constrained, reconstruction.[17] Thus here I am in some ways simply expanding, in light of the increasing acknowledgment of ancient context as an appropriate informant for narrative criticism, Mark Allan Powell's description of an informed audience under his rubric of the "normative process of reading."[18] My "ideal audience" is also akin to the "Model Reader" described by Umberto Eco and as such arises from—or at least is constrained by—the text itself.[19]

A final point requires comment. My reconstruction of a likely hearing of the Third Gospel by members of Luke's ideal audience follows the majority of narrative-critical studies, particularly early ones, in assuming the thematic and narrative coherence of the work under examination—a position that a number of previous studies on Jerusalem and Temple in Luke's writings have found convenient to deny and that, furthermore, some from within even narrative-critical circles have recently challenged.[20] I agree with these latter critics that the coherence of Luke's Gospel remains a heuristic assumption, one in need of verification, and I acknowledge their concern that this assumption not take on a life of its own and thereby entice the interpreter into all manner of exegetical gymnastics for the purpose of maintaining what was only, at the beginning, a heuristic device—duly

---

17. As noted by Rhoads, "Narrative Criticism," 269.

18. See Powell, "Narrative Criticism?," 242–44. I also see myself somewhat in line regarding Luke's "ideal audience" with Craig Keener (*Acts*, e.g., 1:18).

19. Eco describes his "Model Reader" as one who has adequate cultural and textual knowledge for pursuing "interesting interpretive paths" when encountering a text. I also follow him in considering the whole of a text to be the indispensible basis for judging interpretations of that text ("How to prove a conjecture about the intention of a text? The only way is to check it upon the text as a coherent whole"), an idea he in turn attributes to Augustine's *De doctrina christiana*. Unlike Eco, however, I persist in thinking that the "empirical author" has a more than nominal say—and certainly more say than any other Model Reader—in constraining the meaning of a text, at least when examining ancient and sacred texts like those of Luke. The reason for our divergence here may be that Eco's theory applies specifically to "aesthetic text(s)" vis-à-vis their readers and author and to texts addressed to unknown audiences instead of to a single reader (and I will not take up the question of a possible "Lukan community" here). So I want to draw from Eco's notion of Model Readers (my "ideal audience") and his claim that conjectures must be judged based on the entirety of the work about which they are made, while sitting light to his views about the relative interpretive authority of authors, texts, and interpreters. See Eco, "The Author and His Interpreters."

20. See Merenlahti and Hakola, "Reconceiving Narrative Criticism," 13–48. For Luke, see, e.g., Metzger, *Consumption and Wealth*, 48, 189–90.

noted.²¹ Still, I believe it fair and circumspect to start by assuming the *relative* coherence²² of any work, while remaining open to the possibility that this assumption should, in the course of analysis, prove unlikely, even untenable.²³ In part I am guided here by Umberto Eco's contention that the only way to judge conjectures about texts (admittedly "aesthetic texts") is "to check it upon the text as a coherent whole."²⁴ My study will show, I hope, that on the subject of Jerusalem and the Temple Luke offers a coherent, if multifaceted, portrait.

SUBTLETY IN LUKE AND BEYOND

Lukan Subtlety: Seen as through a Veil?

Luke's use of subtle communication is a standard, if often tacitly acknowledged, feature of many interpretations of his writings, including especially many narrative ones. The burgeoning work on Lukan gaps, for example, certainly provides powerful illumination of a particular type of subtlety, one that requires significant audience involvement and that presupposes, on most readings, multiple audience exposures to Luke's works.²⁵ Discussions of Luke's use of Scripture also often presuppose a level of engagement and insight on the part of the audience that amounts to subtle communication on Luke's part—as seen in Baltzer's, Hutcheon's, and Taylor's readings of Jerusalem and the Temple in Luke.²⁶ Additionally, narrative critics

---

21. See especially the concerned parties cited by Merenlahti and Hakola, "Reconceiving Narrative Criticism," 28–29.

22. Merenlahti and Hakola ("Reconceiving Narrative Criticism," 31–32) rightly note the fact that ancient writers were generally less preoccupied with coherence than modern ones—hence the qualifying "relative."

23. Otherwise, one becomes involved in the comparatively greater danger of automatically writing off any apparent tensions or diversity within a work as mere incoherence.

24. Eco, "The Author and His Interpreters."

25. See comments above on Longenecker, *God in the Gap*.

26. This is also true, e.g., of Hays's recent work on intertextuality in Matthew's Gospel. Thus Hays claims that Matthew's carefully balanced genealogical structure, highlighting Jesus's Abrahamic and Davidic lineage and ascending from Abraham to David and then descending after David into exile and suffering its post-exilic "obscurity," "signals that the coming of Jesus portends the end of Israel's exile." He likewise claims that the appearance of the four women (all likely "ethnic outsiders") in the geneaology "encourages us to recall their stories and to reflect that they prefigure the mission to all nations that is announced in the Gospel's closing Chapter" ("Torah Reconfigured"). Whether

sometimes read the Gospels, especially since Culpepper's *Anatomy of the Fourth Gospel*, as containing occasional "implicit commentary." Though the specifics of such "implicit commentary" has become an occasion for debate, its general recognition among narrative critics of the Gospels serves as a further illustration of subtle communication, present in Luke as well as, it appears, the other NT Gospel writers.[27]

Much of the above work pointing toward subtle communication in Luke's writings (and among the other Gospel writers) has come from narrative critics, and these insights have yet to be placed fully within their ancient historical context. While I certainly will not attempt entirely to accomplish such a task here, I do hope to construct a bit of a makeshift bridge, especially by noting discussions of methods of subtle communication among select members of the elite Greco-Roman declaimers.[28]

A (Greco-Roman) World of Subtlety

Subtle communication, operating under a number of guises and terms, was a common feature of the ancient rhetorical milieu. Numerous among the elite rhetors of antiquity attest to its presence and indeed pervasiveness in their day, with varying degrees of (dis)approval.[29]

Hays's reading is a correct interpretation of Matt 1, it certainly pays Matthew's Gospel the compliment of assuming that significant import lies below the surface claims of the Gospel—i.e., that Matthew engages in what I have termed "subtle communication."

27. Culpepper argues for implicit commentary in John via misunderstanding, irony, and symbolism (*Anatomy of the Fourth Gospel*, 151–202). Commenting on Mark, Fowler criticizes Culpepper's definition of implicit commentary (*Let the Reader Understand*, 81–82). Kurz, on the other hand, largely embraces Culpepper's definition and applies his insights to Luke, though downplaying the importance of symbolism for Luke and claiming Luke's use of structure as an additional means of implicit commentary (*Reading Luke-Acts*, 135–55).

28. Arguing for Lukan subtlety (though not in such terms) on the basis on ancient rhetoric, particularly by use of enthymemes, is Robbins: "[T]he Gospel of Luke interweaves enthymemic networks in the text with social, cultural, ideological, and theological enthymemes that evoke contexts outside the work. In some instances, unexpressed premises or conclusions for enthymemes are expressed elsewhere in the work and create an explicit enthymemic network in the text. In the same portion of text, however, the premises or conclusions missing from the enthymemes may reside in social, cultural, ideological, and theology environments outside the text" ("From Enthymeme to Theology," 192).

29. For the discussion that follows in this section I am deeply indebted both to the work of and personal interaction I have had with Jason Whitlark (see esp. his "Figured

Part 1: Introduction

In his discussion of figures in Book 9 of the *Institutio Oratoria*, Quintilian refers to the related—or, as Quintilian himself suggests, perhaps even equivalent—techniques of *emphasis* and *figured speech*.[30] He describes *emphasis* as a figure in which "some hidden meaning is extracted from some phrase" (9.2.64). Along with a quote from Virgil's *Aeneid*, he cites the line from Ovid, "O Mother, happy in thy spouse!" as an example of *emphasis*, here indicating the sexual desire the daughter (Zmyrna/Myrrha) who speaks the line has for her father (9.2.64). This is subtle communication indeed.

Quintilian then describes *figured speech* as the technique

> whereby we excite some suspicion to indicate that our meaning is other than our words would seem to imply; but our meaning is not in this case contrary to that which we express, as is the case in *irony*, but rather *a hidden meaning which is left to the hearer to discover*. (9.2.65; emphasis added)

Quintilian goes on to discuss *figured speech* at some length, and several aspects of this discussion merit comment here. First, Quintilian gives several indications of the pervasive use of this figure in the late first-century rhetorical scene of which he was part.[31] It "is much in vogue at the present time" and "is of the commonest occurrence" such that he thinks he "shall be expected to make some comment" (9.2.65). Indeed, many over-used this technique in the early days of Quintilian's teaching (9.2.77) and employed the technique at all manner of inappropriate times (9.2.79). In light of the ubiquity of this figure Quintilian is, secondly, eager to place restrictions on it. Early in his discussion of it, Quintilian tells us that *figured speech* is only to be done under three circumstances: 1) when "it is unsafe to speak openly"; 2) when "it is unseemly to speak openly"; or 3) "when it is employed solely with a view to the elegance of what we say, and gives greater pleasure by reason of the novelty and variety thus introduced" versus expressing oneself more straightforwardly (9.2.66). Later, Quintilian, despite his initial list of three, gives what is indeed a fourth cause of using *figured speech*: suggestive power. Thus, "some things, again, which cannot be proved, may, on

---

Critique"). Although I take issue with several aspects of his discussion regarding *figured speech* in the ancient world, his essay has been an indispensable conversation partner.

30. "Similar, if not identical with this figure [*emphasis*], is another [*figured speech*]" (Quintilian, *Institutes* 9.2.65; LCL). I will follow Quintilian in treating these techniques together.

31. As rightly noted by Vegge, *2 Corinthians*, 129.

the other, be suggested by the employment of some *figure*. For at times such hidden shafts will stick, and the fact that they are not noticed will prevent their being drawn out" (9.2.75).

Even so, when it comes to *figured speech*, Quintilian positions himself as something of a moderate-liberal, one who would put constraints on the technique, though without—like some—forbidding it entirely (9.2.69). Among these moderating constraints are his advice that one not employ words of "doubtful or double meaning"—even though he later acknowledges that the great Cicero did so on occasion (9.2.99)—and, more importantly still, that the figure not hinge "on ambiguous collocations of words" (9.2.69). He also instructs his audience not to employ *figured speech* too frequently (9.2.72). In discussing the use of *figured speech* for elegance (9.2.96–99), Quintilian gives several examples for how this may be done, including through allusion, which is "by far the most artistic" use of *figured speech* (9.2.97). His example is "the case where a rival candidate speaks against an ex-tyrant who had abdicated on condition of his receiving amnesty: 'I am not permitted to speak against you. But a little while ago I wished to kill you'" (9.2.97). Thus the allusion is not to a text but to a well-known recent event.

Thirdly, Quintilian's advice on this figure is clearly shaped by the predominant setting in which he imagines it will be practiced—the court of law. Thus his advice pertains specifically to presenting before judges (e.g., 9.2.72, 76, 80) and to presenting against opposing counsel (e.g., 9.2.75). All of the (ample) examples he gives for the first two conditions (dangerous, unseemly) are in a forensic setting, save the last two examples, in which he discusses "those *figures* of which the Greeks are so fond, by means of which they give gentle expression to unpleasant facts" (9.2.92). In fact, his caution in employing figures (noted above) seems to be somewhat specific to the courtroom setting in which he imagines them to be employed and in which an injudicious use of *figured speech* may prove counterproductive, even damning (cf. 9.2.80, 95).

The key points of relevance that emerge from Quintilian's discussion of *emphasis* and *figured speech* are: 1) its pervasive use in first-century CE Latin, and probably also Greek, rhetoric; 2) that Quintilian and apparently other elite declaimers wish to put limits on it or else to squelch it entirely; 3) that this is partly so because of its danger in a forensic setting; 4) that Quintilian is not sure whether there is a dividing line between *emphasis* and *figured speech*, and any difference seems to be one primarily of setting, as he gives examples of the former from literary works and of the latter from forensic settings (real or preparatory); 5) that Quintilian discourages use of double-meaning words but commends use of allusions for *figured speech*. Before discussing the relevance of these points for interpretation of Luke, I must consider other discussions of these subtle methods of communication among the elite Greco-Roman declaimers, building from the above discussion of Quintilian.

Ps.-Cicero discusses *emphasis* in *Ad Herennium* Book 4, in which he states: "Emphasis is the figure which leaves more to be suspected than has been actually asserted" (4.53.67).[32] He gives five means of producing emphasis: hyperbole, ambiguity, logical consequence, aposiopesis, and analogy. The discussion of ambiguity is instructive, for, while warning against ambiguities "which render the style obscure," he commends exploiting the multiple meanings of words as a means of causing one's audience to suspect more than has been asserted: "It will be easy to find them [points of *emphasis*] if we know and pay heed to the double and multiple meanings of words." Thus he offers a dissenting voice on this score from the more cautious advice of Quintilian.

He goes on to describe emphasis by logical consequence with the example of addressing the son of a "fishmonger" with the line, "'Quiet, you, whose father used to wipe his nose with his forearm.'" The logical consequence plays to an apparently well-known stereotype regarding fishmongers and thus highlights the man's questionable pedigree through use of a hyper-truncated *enthymeme*.[33] Emphasis by analogy draws a parallel between one (presumably contemporary) event and a well-known situation or narrative and thus insinuates a connection between the two situations, as in: "'Do not, Saturninus, rely too much on the popular mob—unavenged lie the Gracchi.'" The point is that, just as the Gracchi, who enjoyed popular support, were publicly murdered, so Saturninus may suffer a similar

---

32. All quotes of *Ad Herennium* come from LCL. The entire discussion comes from *Ad Herennium* 4.53.67.

33. I am referring to *enthymeme* as a truncated syllogism here, which is how it has often been understood, although the term had numerous meanings in ancient rhetoric and although some challenge this understanding of the term (see Aune, "Enthymeme," 150–57). Here, what is stated is the conclusion, viz., that the man's father wiped his nose with his forearm, which leads via the unstated (general) premise that fishmongers wipe their noses this way to the unstated specific premise—and the basis of the jab—that the man is the son of a fishmonger. Thus instead of disclosing one premise and the conclusion, Ps.-Cicero here combines *enthymeme* with *emphasis*, giving a hyper-truncated *enthymeme* in which only the conclusion is stated.

fate and should not allow himself to become over-confident on the basis of popular support.

Compared with Quintilian, then, Ps.-Cicero does not show hesitancy in employing this figure but instead commends it: "This figure sometimes possesses liveliness and distinction in the highest degree." Likewise, *Ad Herennium* commends exploiting the multiple meanings of words, in direct opposition to Quintilian's proscription. The rhetors agree, however, in commending use of allusion when implying more than one states (under "emphasis by analogy" for Ps.-Cicero).

On the Greek side and in the first century BCE, Ps.-Demetrius, in his *On Style*, discusses the "covert allusion" (ἐσχηματισμένος ἐν λόγῳ), which pairs with the *figured speech* of Quintilian.[34] Like Quintilian, Demetrius believes this technique is wildly over-used (287)[35] and, like Quintilian, seeks to place constraints upon its use (288). The constraints he commends bear some similarity to those of Quintilian, though they are far from identical: "covert allusion" must be used only with "good taste (εὐπρεπείας)" and "circumspection (ἀσφαλείας)." As his examples demonstrate, "circumspection" and "good taste" incorporate not only situations in which it is dangerous for one to speak openly, because of being under a tyrant (289) or speaking to eminent persons (292–93) or even to fickle populaces (294), but also instances in which one might, e.g., censure companions in a way that is incisive though not openly reproachful (288).[36] Thus he agrees with Quintilian and Ps.-Cicero that a "covert allusion" may suitably be used for elegance and effect, apart from more pragmatic concerns (288, 290, 295–97). Ps.-Demetrius also agrees with Ps.-Cicero against Quintilian in commending the use of words with multiple meanings, especially as a means of subtle censure (291).[37]

---

34. See Whitlark, "Figured Critique," 164. All quotes from *On Style* come from trans. W. Rhys Roberts.

35. He concludes by saying of the "Socratic" manner of *figured speech*: "Such dialogues met with great success in the days of their first invention, or rather they took society by storm through their verisimilitude, their vividness, their nobly didactic character" (298).

36. Ps.-Demetrius is well-known for his commendation also of allegory (ἀλληγορία), over-against plain-speaking (ἁπλῶς), because of allegory's efficacy especially when threatening others (100). He explains: "Often the indirect expression is more impressive than the direct" (104). Even so, restraint must be practiced, lest one speak in riddles (102).

37. "This ambiguous way of speaking, though not irony, yet has a suggestion of it" (291).

Part 1: Introduction

Further discussions of *figured speech* appear after the time of Luke's writings, in the *Ars rhetorica* of Ps.-Dionysius (second century)[38] and Ps.-Hermogenes's rhetorical handbook (fifth century). These treatments have little bearing on my study and so are not addressed at any length here, beyond noting that *Ars rhetorica* assembles an impressive amount of examples of *figured speech* from classical Greco-Roman literature, showing that "not only did they [classical authors] use it [*figured speech*], but they used it self-consciously."[39] It is, then, both an ancient and a classical aspect of Greco-Roman communication. Thus, it is unsurprising that Frederick Ahl described figured speech as "the normal mode of discourse throughout much of Greek and Roman antiquity."[40]

In the table below, I summarize the most salient points from Quintilian, Ps.-Cicero, and Ps.-Demetrius for my study:

Table 1: The Rhetoric of Subtlety

Aspect	Quintilian	Ps.-Cicero	Ps.-Demetrius
Commends *figured speech*?	Yes, with constraints	Yes	Yes, with constraints
Approves use of *figured speech* for elegance, effectiveness?	Yes	Yes	Yes
Attests to ubiquity of *figured speech* in first century CE or earlier?	Yes	(unclear)	Yes
Approves use of allusion to achieve *figured speech*?	Yes	Yes	Yes
Approves polysemy to achieve *figured speech*?	No	Yes	Yes

---

38. I follow Whitlark in a second-century date for *Ars rhetorica*; see Heath, "Pseudo-Dionysius," 81–105, cited by Whitlark, "Figured Critique," 164n14. Though not dogmatic on the point, Russell prefers a date not earlier than the third century ("Figured Speeches," 156).

39. Heath, "Pseudo-Dionysius," 83. Russell, indicating his belief that Ps.-Dionysius at times overreaches, concludes that the writings attributed to Dionysius on rhetoric "may even seem to give countenance" to modern attempts "to uncover hidden agenda in so much ancient writing. More modestly, they may encourage us at least to identify examples of multi-purpose or schematized speeches of their own age" ("Figured Speeches," 168). Luke, too, is widely acknowledged as a composer of speeches.

40. Ahl, "Safe Criticism," 204, cited in Whitlark, "Figured Critique," 169.

The point of the above discussion has not been to attempt by synthesis to arrive at a standard nomenclature for and understanding of a putatively monolithic practice of *figured speech* in the ancient world[41]: such monolithic practice likely never existed, as the diversity of the sources attests. Rather, my purpose has been to demonstrate, first, the ubiquity of practices that may be grouped under the rubric of "subtle communication" in the rhetorical milieu in which Luke composed the Third Gospel and Acts. This ubiquity is seen not least in the efforts of members of the elite declaimers to proscribe or at the very least to constrain this practice.[42] Moreover, even these elite declaimers allow for use of *figured speech*, or subtle communication, for reasons other than sheer pragmatism (when dangerous or unseemly), especially for elegance and effectiveness.[43]

Given these factors, it is highly likely that Luke, too, would have employed subtle communication and might have done so for a number of reasons, not only because of, e.g., a putative fear of imperial recourse.[44] Although I will not here engage in lengthy consideration of Luke's purposes for employing subtle communication when discussing the fate of Jerusalem and its Temple (among other things), it is apropos to note that Luke may have done so from motives of seemliness (i.e., he did not wish to harp upon the painful fact for some members of his audience of Jerusalem's destruction, beyond the necessary Jesus sayings that spoke to such), of elegance,[45] and of efficacy, especially since, as Quintilian for one maintains, some arguments are most powerfully made not by open assertion but by leaving an insinuation that sticks into one's audience like a barb and eventually makes its meaning felt.

---

41. This is the error with which Whitlark flirts, I believe ("Figured Critique," 165); I view it as problematic that key parts of Whitlark's synthesis rely exclusively on the witness of Ps.-Dionysius and Hermogenes, both of whom write later than the NT period, by Whitlark's own accounting, and whose works may show common authorship or at least common tradition (see Heath, "Pseudo-Dionysius," 85–86).

42. Covert speech of the sort under discussion here seems to have flourished beginning with Nero's reign (see Ahl, "Safe Criticism"; Robinson, "In the Court of Time," 223–57).

43. For further discussion of the possible motives for subtle communication (or "implied speech"), see Vegge, *2 Corinthians*, 134–37.

44. Whitlark seems essentially to limit the "conditions" under which *figured speech* is called for to criticism of imperial power ("Figured Critique," 166–69).

45. Vegge notes as "a general attitude among Demetrius' contemporaries" that "implied speech is given a higher status than explicit speech" (*2 Corinthians*, 131).

Part 1: Introduction

Furthermore, these elite declaimers offer hints as to how Luke is likely to employ subtle communication. Each of the three rhetoricians whom we have examined allow for subtle communication by allusion, and two commend subtle communication through exploiting the polyvalent meanings of some words, while the third, who opposes this latter practice, nonetheless cites an example of such from Cicero, no less. The examples of allusion we have considered come usually from well-known events or stories within the shared narrative and literary milieu of the rhetor and audience. It is likely, then, that Luke's allusions will draw primarily from the Scriptures of Israel, especially as expressed in the Septuagint, since this represents the primary shared cultural script between Luke and his ideal audience.[46] Regarding the question of multivalent words, Luke is well-known for exploiting the several meanings of words,[47] even despite the warnings against such in rhetorical handbooks with which Luke may have been familiar.[48] This long-maintained recognition, plus the witness of both Ps.-Cicero and Ps.-Demetrius, suggests reading Luke with eyes and ears sharpened to attend to possible polyvalence of meaning and expression.

Summary

The practical and theoretical discussions of rhetoric by tradents both ancient and modern thus suggest the propriety of reading ancient works, including those of Luke, as containing subtle communication. Although the variety of witnesses do not readily yield a facile catalog of the repertoire of tactics or methods by which that subtle communication is likely to arrive, still some general summary comments may prove useful. Kurz suggests irony and misunderstanding and, to a lesser degree, symbolism and structure

---

46. Luke probably also refers to events from recent Judean history in, e.g., 13:1–5; 19:11–27. However, it is the LXX that is his primary source material for allusions. Jones considers the typological use of Babylon for Rome in works of the Pseudepigrapha as similar to figured speech (*Jewish Reactions*, 34); Luke, as I will explore, also employs typologies rooted in the sacred history of Israel, albeit with a less clearly defined motive than that of his contemporary Jewish apocalypticists.

47. See especially Marguerat's helpful discussion of Luke's "ambivalence sémantique," which he identifies with the rhetorical figure of "l'amphibologie," which "est en effet le support littéraire de la polysémie" ("Luc-Actes Entre Jérusalem et Rome," 79). His claim that Luke employs this figure in service of his theological aims (80) anticipates the present study, as well as, e.g., Rowe's work on narrative Christology.

48. E.g., Theon, *Progymnasmata* 81 (Kennedy, 31).

as means of Lukan subtle communication (i.e., "implicit commentary").[49] Numerous other Lukan commentators identify (even if only implicitly so) Luke's frequent and complex use of the Jewish Scriptures as a key source of subtle communication.[50] The ancient witnesses suggest that both allusion and irony or subtle meaning—especially through the exploitation of a word's multiple meanings[51]—were key and frequent means of subtle communication. Their witness, combined with the insight-bearing readings of previous scholarship on Luke, suggests that we should expect to find subtle meaning in Luke's writings both via allusion and use of polyvalent words.

INTERTEXTUALITY IN LUKE'S WRITINGS

Given the discussion above, this study must not neglect to consider more fully Luke's use of Israel's Scriptures.[52] Although the scope of this project does not allow for a full history of research on Lukan intertextuality, I will attempt to give some further indications of where this study falls within the larger world of scholarship on Luke's use of Scripture.

In one of the more recent monographs on Lukan intertextuality, Kenneth Litwak characterizes previous readings of Lukan intertextuality as operating with the schemas of 1) prophecy-and-fulfillment, 2) creation of continuity with Israel's past, especially through the use of imitation, or

---

49. Kurz, *Reading Luke-Acts*, ch. 9.

50. This is the case with Baltzer, "The Meaning of the Temple," and Karris, "Luke," but it is also ubiquitous in, e.g., Thomas L. Brodie's work on Lukan intertextuality. This fact is also suggested by Hays's work on echoes in the letters of Paul, especially his discussion of *metalepsis*: "When a literary echo links the text in which it occurs to an earlier text, the figurative effect of the echo can lie in the unstated or suppressed (transumed) points of resonance between the two texts ... Allusive echo suggests to the reader that text B should be understood in light of a broad interplay with text A, encompassing aspects of A beyond those explicitly echoed." Just later: "Metalepsis ... places the reader within *a field of whispered or unstated correspondences*" (Hays, *Echoes of Scripture*, 20; emphasis added).

51. Despite, again, the warnings against such in the *progymnastic* tradition (e.g., Theon, *Prog.* 81 [Kennedy, 31]).

52. In attempting throughout this study to analyze Luke's use of the Jewish Scriptures, I will rely upon the best-available critical versions of the LXX, assuming for heuristic purposes that those versions correspond accurately to the Jewish Scriptures as Luke knew and used them. Thus I employ Rahlf's edition, supplemented by the updated Göttingen editions, when available (e.g., Isaiah, Jeremiah, Sirach; the Göttingen edition is not yet available for 1 Kingdoms, unfortunately).

Part 1: Introduction

3) typology.⁵³ Litwak rejects the first and last of these schemas and endorses a modified understanding of the second, what he calls "framing in discourse."⁵⁴

Though I disagree with many of Litwak's conclusions, his study proves a helpful discussion partner. While he is correct in saying that neither prophecy-and-fulfillment nor typological readings accounts for the full range of Lukan intertextuality and is correct that Luke's use of Scripture has as at least its partial aim to show continuity between the people whose story Luke narrates and the sacred history of God's people told in the Scriptures of Israel, Litwak's "framing in discourse" nonetheless fails, I believe, to provide an entirely satisfactory lens for viewing Luke's use of Scripture.

First of all, Litwak rejects too much. For instance, it is clear to me, as it has been to many commentators, that Luke does at points employ Scripture in a manner that chiefly emphasizes the fulfillment of prophecy, especially in explicit quotations for the purposes of Christological explication in Acts. Additionally, Litwak's rejection of typological use of the Scriptures is premature. He seems to adduce two reasons for rejecting typological readings: 1) commentators employ it without precisely defining what typology means, and 2) typology cannot account for the full range of Lukan intertextuality.⁵⁵ As to the first criticism, that commentators often employ the language of typology without narrowly defining its meaning is perhaps less problematic than might appear on first glance.⁵⁶ Litwak short-circuits the discussion, however, by proposing his own unhelpful (and admittedly "narrow")

---

53. Litwak, *Echoes*, 9–30.

54. See Litwak, *Echoes*, 22, 31–34, 56–61.

55. See Litwak, *Echoes*, 59–60.

56. There are, after all, a number of arenas, particularly in the realm of what we generally label the aesthetic, in which intuitive recognition far outstrips the human capacity for precise formalization. To use a modern example, the caricatures that have been a mainstay of magazines and newspapers for centuries (from the low-brow *Mad Magazine* to the uptown *New Yorker*) are clearly recognizable to most human beings with the requisite cultural encyclopedia for reading them—and so this caricature with a diminutive jaw-line and rudely exaggerated ears is clearly meant to be Ross Perot, one-time presidential candidate, etc. The difficulty of formalizing the recognition that comes naturally to most humans finds vivid demonstration, however, in the fact that programming a computer to recognize these intuitively processed distortions has proven nearly impossible: what the human mind of normal readers does naturally, intuitively, the human mind of computer programmers has found nearly impossible to formalize. Human language is of course far less restrictive than the binary languages of computer programming, but still this illustrates the frequent difficulty of formalizing even basic and nearly universal facets of human intuition.

definition of typology: "a rubric by which a person, event or thing in the Scriptures of Israel is mapped on a point-by-point basis to some New Testament person, event or thing." He proceeds to reject a Moses typology for Jesus in Luke on the basis that, e.g., Moses never calls twelve disciples.[57] In doing so, Litwak demonstrates only the unsatisfactory nature of his own definition of typology and not its inutility as a theoretical schema for Lukan intertextuality. A more chastened definition, such as "typology is a rubric in which a person, event, or thing in the Scriptures of Israel is mapped to a person, event, or thing in the New Testament on enough recognizable points to establish a meaningful connection, one that is informed by, and that subsequently informs, its larger narrative context," would prove, I think, more useful.[58] This is precisely the kind of theoretical apparatus that might be adduced, e.g., from Luke Johnson's discussion of Luke's subtle framing of Jesus as a prophet both like and yet greater than Moses across the majority of Luke and the early parts of Acts. Moreover, denial of typological patterns in Luke's writings is simply untenable in light of Luke's own well-recognized proclivities for typologically linking characters also within his own works (Jesus and Paul, Jesus and Peter, Jesus and Stephen, etc.).[59]

An additional problem with Litwak's proposal is his driving concern to find a single schema that accounts for the entire spectrum of Luke's use of Scripture, despite Litwak's own recognition that Luke's presentation of Scripture varies widely throughout Luke and Acts, from subtle echoes to explicit quotations to citations with introductory formulae. Given the range of Luke's use of Scripture in his narratives, on what basis does Litwak assume that a single schema will account adequately for Lukan intertextuality? Indeed it seems to me, then, both on *a priori* grounds and on the basis of previous scholarship, that Luke employs Scripture to a multiplicity of ends

---

57. Litwak, *Echoes*, 59.

58. This more restrained definition of typology might be adequate to characterize, e.g., Hays's claims regarding Matthew's Gospel: "[W]e have to reckon with Matthew's use of typology, his deft narration of tales that Senior [in "The Lure of the Formula Quotations"] describes as 'shadow stories from the Old Testament.' . . . The story of Herod's slaughter of the innocents echoes Pharaoh's decree to kill the Hebrew children, and by so doing it suggests that Herod, who claims to be 'King of the Jews,' *is actually to be identified typologically* with Israel's ancient oppressor and that it is Jesus who is really the 'King of the Jews.'" Hays goes on to claim that "these sort of typological allusions" are ubiquitous in Matthew ("Torah Re-configured"; emphasis added).

59. See esp. Talbert, *Literary Patterns*; also, Keener, *Acts*, 1:556–58. This is sometimes referred to as "internal typology" (as in Bock, *Proclamation from Prophecy and Pattern*, 289).

PART 1: INTRODUCTION

such that multiple schemas, including both fulfillment-from-prophecy and typology, are apropos, especially if these typological readings account also for the larger narrative dynamics of Luke's works.[60]

In this regard,[61] it is apropos to note that when Luke explicitly quotes Scripture, usually with a formula, he generally does so to show the fulfillment of prophecy, especially Isaianic prophecy, in the events he or a major character narrates (Luke 3:4b–6; 4:18–19; 7:27; 8:10; Acts 8:32b–33; 13:33, 35, 41, 47), although sometimes characters, including Jesus, the devil, Stephen, and James, quote Scripture, or simply reference Scripture (Luke 6:3–5), for the purposes of instruction or debate (Luke 4:1–13; Acts 7:42–43, 49–50; 15:16–18). Additionally, at least once Luke quotes Scripture to show Mary and Joseph's piety and/or to clarify the movement of the narrative (Luke 2:23–24).

Luke's use of intertextual echoes is far more complicated still, and matters are exacerbated by disagreement as to what precisely constitute and how to identify "echoes."[62] On the question of identifying echoes, I generally follow Richard Hays's classic work *Echoes of Scripture in the Letters of Paul*,[63] but I join Brawley and Litwak in giving preeminence to two

---

60. It may be possible to collapse most or all of Litwak's "framing in discourse" into a narrative-sensitive typological reading (alternately, he might suggest collapsing my "narratively attuned typology" into his "framing in discourse"!). Though "framing in discourse" may in theory have a greater capacity for sorting for the abundance of intertextual echoes in certain Lukan passages (e.g., Luke 1–2), in practice Litwak's "choosing only those passages from Israel's Scriptures that qualify as intertextual echoes by [his] criteria ... and *which have interpretive value for my argument*" mitigates this potential theoretical advantage (*Echoes*, 69; emphasis added).

61. In the following (brief) discussion of Luke's use of Scripture, I consider Luke and Acts together, because recent attempts to argue for divergent authorship have hardly dinted the long-held consensus of joint authorship and because nearly all commentators view Acts as a sequel to Luke, even if not (ala Parsons) a sequel solely to Luke.

62. Also exacerbating matters is the fact that scholarly interests regarding intertextuality continue "to accord privilege to explicit quotations and obvious allusions," as Hays and Green remarked in 1995 ("The Use of the Old Testament," 237), yet this remains true today.

63. By this, I mean that I generally employ Hays's criteria, with the adaptations noted above, and that I am inclined to view "echoes" as intentional, or else subconscious but still informative, allusions by an author that he may have reasonably expected his audience to notice, at least on multiple exposures, and that, when heard, may contribute additional meaning to the obvious sense of the text. Thus "echoes" may be used with reference both to the author (the resonances that he intends or, less frequently, that he subconsciously includes) and to auditors (resonances that they were ideally able to detect).

of Hays's criteria (availability and volume),[64] though without jettisoning the rest of Hays's criteria (esp. recurrence and history of interpretation). I also follow Brawley in broadening Hays's "volume" criterion to measure volume not only on the basis of the "phraseological plane" but also in terms of replicated "form, genre, setting, and plot."[65] Luke's writings are of course replete with echoes of Israel's Scripture, particularly in Luke 1–2, and these echoes serve, in my estimation, to multiple ends. Sometimes Luke echoes Scripture for the same purpose that he often explicitly cites Scripture, i.e., in order to show the fulfillment of prophecy, as in the echoing of the Isaianic hopes of the Lord's salvation reaching to "the end of the world" in Acts 1:8 (cf. Isa 49:6; Acts 13:47). At other points, Luke echoes portions of Scripture for typological reasons, drawing a connection between a character in his story, usually Jesus, and OT figures, especially the prophets, for reasons that must be mapped across the narrative landscapes of both the source text and Luke's narrative(s). These uses of echoes also contribute—as does Luke's penchant for copying the style of the LXX as an end in itself—to Luke's creating a story that feels and sounds like the sacred stories of God's people.[66]

Because of the importance of Luke's typological use of echoes for my analysis of Luke's Gospel (Part 2), I must give this facet of Lukan intertextuality further attention.[67] As noted above, many commentators view the many echoes of Elijah and Moses respecting Jesus in Luke's Gospel as bearing typological import—that is, as establishing some manner of connection, the meaning of which is constrained by and specific to the characters being linked.[68] Thomas Brodie's work on Jesus as a prophet like Elijah/

---

64. See Litwak, *Echoes*, 61–65.

65. Brawley, *Text to Text*, 13.

66. I believe that, while simple imitation of Septuagintal style was on occasions an end in itself for Luke (as argued by Litwak and Green), it was not typically Luke's chief end in echoing the LXX.

67. The classic, though now dated, work on typology in the New Testament is Goppelt, *Typos*; see also Goppelt's article, "Typos," in *TDNT*; Davidson, *Typology*. Though some prefer to discuss typology as a Jewish/Christian "interpretive method" alongside allegorization, pesher, and midrash (so Evans and Novakovic, "Typology," 986–90), it may also be located—as in this study—under the rubric of intertextuality, here Luke's use, and especially his subtle use, of the Jewish Scriptures, with typology thus as a species within the broader genus of Lukan "echoes," which in turn falls under the larger heading of Lukan intertextuality. Locating typology within Lukan intertextuality makes especially good sense given Luke's penchant for employing typology between scenes and characters in Luke and Acts.

68. Bock prefers "typological-prophetic usage" instead of "typology"; while his

Part 1: Introduction

Elisha in Luke's Gospel is well-known,[69] and J. Severino Croatto has more recently explored a number of prophetic typologies employed for Jesus by Luke.[70]

To rehearse only briefly two of the most significant typologies, Luke portrays Jesus after the pattern of both Elijah/Elisha and Moses. The typological use of Elijah/Elisha occurs frequently in Luke 3–9: Jesus describes himself with reference to these therapeutic prophets (4:24–27), Jesus raises the widow's son (7:11–16; cf. 3 Kgdms 17:17–24), the fulfillment of the days of Jesus's ἀνάλημψις brings about his final turn toward Jerusalem (9:51; cf. 4 Kgdms 2:9–10), the sons of Zebedee earn Jesus's rebuke for seeking to destroy a Samaritan village on the pattern of Elijah (9:52–56; 4 Kgdms 1:10–12), and Jesus curiously refuses for his followers precisely the concession Elijah granted his own prophetic disciple (Luke 9:61–62; 3 Kgdms 19:19–21). Likewise, Luke's depiction of Jesus's Transfiguration "unmistakably refers" to the events on Mt. Sinai: "the mount, Moses, the glory, the cloud."[71] Add to this Jesus's speaking with Moses and Elijah about his ἔξοδος (9:31), and we hardly need Peter's testimony in Acts 3:22–26 to associate Jesus with the prophet like Moses. The Third Gospel in fact explores and offers a host of typological connections between Jesus and the prophets of old—some of which will receive additional attention in Part 2. Whether it is a theoretically necessary feature of typological connections in general,[72] in practice these typological links establish a connection that is synkritical in nature, specifically one that demonstrates Jesus's superiority

---

explanation has merit, it risks conflating salvation-historical with literary concerns (*Proclamation from Prophecy and Pattern*, 49, 291–92).

69. Brodie, "Towards Unraveling," 247–67; Brodie, "The Departure for Jerusalem," 96–109; Brodie, *Luke the Literary Interpreter*. See also Evans, "Luke's Ethic of Election," 70–83; Huddleston, "What Would Elijah and Elisha Do?," 265–82.

70. Croatto, "Jesus, Prophet," 451–66. See also, Keener, *Acts*, 1:714–15.

71. Croatto, "Jesus, Prophet," 461.

72. Probably following Goppelt, Bock claims this "progressive" sense as a necessary feature of typology generally (*Proclamation from Prophecy and Pattern*, 49); so does Davidson, despite noting this emphasis does not in fact appear in the very passage (1 Cor 10) from which he adduces it (*Typology*, 281). Regarding Lukan typology, this nuance works well when considering typological connections between Jesus and OT prophets but is problematized by Luke's use of "internal typologies" between characters within his works—clearly, e.g., Stephen, typologically linked to Jesus in Acts 7, is not supposed to be greater than his Lord!

over against the prophets whose lives and ministries provide the pattern for his own.[73]

It is important to note that the import of these typological connections may extend beyond linking the primary figures themselves, entailing further connections between the characters or groups—or even the broader narrative features—that surround the typologically linked characters. As an example, in presenting Jesus as in some ways parallel to Jeremiah, warning of imminent national destruction, Luke 13:34-35—despite the fairly unelaborated typological connection between Jesus and Jeremiah—nonetheless also implies a link between the nation of Israel who persisted in immorality during Jeremiah's day and Jesus's contemporary countrymen and -women.[74]

Luke is alone neither in his typological identification of NT figures with OT characters nor in his broadening these initial connections to entail further, often covert connections. Richard Hays sees a "typological" linking between Jesus and Jeremiah in the citation of Jer 7 in Mark 11:17, along with the sandwiching scene of Jesus's cursing the fig tree, which he takes to echo Jer 8:13. Hays goes on to argue that the typological link extends beyond even the characters Jesus and Jeremiah:

> Just as Jeremiah condemned the prophets and priests who spoke false deceptive words of peace and comfort while practicing injustice and idolatry, so Jesus takes up the mantle of Jeremiah to condemn the Temple establishment once again. The phrase "den of robbers" and the image of the barren fig tree provide the imaginative links; *for the reader who grasps the connection, the outward-rippling implications are clear.* As judgment fell upon Israel in Jeremiah's time, so it looms once again over the Temple.[75]

---

73. For example, whereas Elijah has to plead with God and then lie on top of the boy in order to revive him (3 Kgdms 17:17-24), Jesus does so with merely a word (Luke 7:14-15). For further examples of Luke's synkritical pairing of Jesus and Elijah, see Keener, *Acts*, 1:714-15.

74. As Bock notes (*Proclamation from Prophecy and Pattern*, 119).

75. Hays, "Can the Gospels?," 406-9; emphasis added. Another example from Hays's work on intertextuality comes from his claim that Matthew, when including the four (foreign) women in Jesus's geneaology, "is already, I think, *hinting* at a major theme in his Gospel, namely that the story of Israel is open to the inclusion of Gentiles . . . Matthew doesn't explain any of that. He doesn't quote any of the passages in which the women appear. But he includes them in the geneaology and *thereby encourages us to recall their stories*" ("Torah Reconfigured").

Part 1: Introduction

Typological connections thus open rich, and challenging, avenues of meaning.

Therefore, unraveling the import of Luke's typological use of echoes is certainly an art and as such admits a great deal of ambiguity. At each point, one must ask, How far does the Lukan text allow this connection to reach? Would Luke's ideal audience (or any first-century audience) be likely or able to draw such-and-such a conclusion, or are we over-reading the connection? These are persistent questions that are not easily resolved, and they certainly haunt the present study. Still, the risk of over-reading Luke's use of typology must be held in balance with the equally great risk of under-reading. We may hear too much in a series of echoes: we may also hear too little. The risk of hearing too little is heightened by the general unfamiliarity of most moderns, even biblical scholars, with the LXX—a limitation Luke's ideal audience, and certainly Luke himself, did not share.[76] As James A. Sanders cautions: "[Luke] knew certain parts of Scripture in such depth that unless the modern interpreter also knows the Septuagint . . . very well indeed he or she will miss major points Luke wanted to score."[77]

CONCLUSION

The pages above spell out the major features of my reading of Luke's writings: a modified narrative criticism and attention to Lukan subtlety, including Lukan echoes from the LXX. The departures I have taken from standard narrative-critical lines consist of an emphasis on multiple exposures to Luke's writings (instead of a first-time reading); a blurring of the traditional demarcating lines among "author," "implied author," and "narrator" because of considerations of genre and era and in order to locate my narrative reading within Luke's historical context; a reading toward what I characterize as "Luke's ideal audience" (including one well-versed in the LXX); and an operative assumption of the relative coherence of Luke's writings.

An analysis of ancient rhetoricians around the time that Luke wrote has shown the pervasiveness of subtle communication in Luke's ancient rhetorical milieu, especially through allusion and use of words with polyvalent meanings. While concerns for safety often governed use of subtlety, this was by no means the only motivation that spurred ancients to employ *emphasis, figured speech*, and other methods of subtle communication.

76. See Litwak, *Echoes*, 61.
77. Sanders, "Isaiah in Luke," 16.

Thus we need not surmise fear of reprisal as a necessary preliminary to identifying subtle communication in Luke's writings.

Finally, I have explored intertextuality in Luke's writings, drawing especially on the work of Litwak and Hays. Despite Litwak's objections, "typology" remains a viable and indeed elucidating category for exploring Luke's use of OT characters for mapping out the identity of Jesus—as well as for broadening his audience's understanding of the events and characters surrounding Jesus.

These pieces—narrative criticism, subtle communication, and intertextuality—are key lenses for reading Luke's narrative(s), and they will significantly shape and inform my discussion in Part 2 below. Before turning there, however, I must consider another important feature of Luke's context: the theodicy crisis that arose with the destruction of Jerusalem in 70 CE.

2

Theodicy in the Ancient and Lukan Worlds

THEODICY IN THE ANCIENT WORLD

Ancient theodicy is, as I have claimed, the final major contextual piece that is needed for proper evaluation of the place of Jerusalem and its Temple within Lukan theology. Thus I will here explore theodicy in the ancient world, and especially in Luke's post-70 CE milieu,[1] and then within Luke's own writings.

Despite its coining by the modern philosopher Leibniz, "theodicy" has found increasing applicability to ancient texts, both in term and in concept.[2] The term arose within the Christian tradition and thus originally adhered to the Christian monotheistic deity ("God"), but it has been applied also to

---

1. I follow the scholarly majority in identifying Luke's Gospel (and Acts) as written post-70 CE. However, neither am I dogmatic on this point nor does my thesis hinge on it. Whether Luke wrote post-70 CE, 1) his Gospel clearly shows interest in questions of theodicy, as I will explore in this chapter, and 2) Luke clearly knows the destruction of Jerusalem and the Temple as an unavoidable fact, and so the theodicy-centric angst of many within the post-70 CE world necessarily touches the Lukan world as well, though, if he writes prior to 70 CE, admittedly with moderately dampened intensity.

2. Consider, e.g., Brueggemann's bold statement that "'Theodicy' is the ultimate, inescapable problem of the Old Testament (although the term is never used)" ("Some Aspects of Theodicy," 253).

Theodicy in the Ancient and Lukan Worlds

polytheistic texts and cultures.³ Even so, because my interests here pertain to so-called "monotheistic" understandings of theodicy, I will employ the term "God" in discussing theodicy.

In general terms, theodicy is the human attempt to provide justification for God vis-à-vis the problem of evil and human suffering. The widely recognized conceptual pillars upon which the problem of evil and human suffering rest (within Jewish and Christian understandings) are: 1) God's sovereign power and 2) God's goodness, 3) in the face of evil and suffering, especially as experienced by human beings. Theodicy arises from the "existential need to explain suffering and evil"⁴ that arises in different communities and among different individuals across diverse cultures and eras. Therefore, when examining the theodical aspects of ancient texts, we need not limit our gaze to explicit or formalized discussions but should also be attuned to indications of the existential crisis that gives rise to theodicy in human experience.⁵

Helpful in this regard is Walter Brueggemann's language of a "theodicy settlement," in which a community's (or, I should like to add, an individual's) mental map about "the kinds of beliefs that produce . . . good outcomes . . . and bad outcomes" based on God's pleasure/displeasure correspond roughly to their lived experienced. Complementary to this is a "crisis of theodicy," in which the old settlement has been dislodged. Brueggemann rightly notes that the theodicy settlement is powerful even when implicit, as it often is.⁶ While I am skeptical of attempts to distill detailed maps of

---

3. For more on the history of theodicy, including Max Weber's broadening it to include "*any attempt to render suffering and evil sensible*," thus without the necessity of a monotheistic framework, see Laato and de Moor, "Introduction," x–xi.

4. This is the framing given for theodical analysis by Boase, who draws on the earlier article by Brueggemann ("Constructing Meaning," 454).

5. As Brueggemann aptly puts it: "Ancient Israel never engaged in the speculative activity of what the modern world has come to term 'theodicy.' It had no interest in rational, speculative adventurism to defend Yahweh's righteous sovereignty" ("Some Aspects of Theodicy," 264).

6. Brueggemann, "Some Aspects of Theodicy," 253. Brueggemann argues that a grand "theodicy settlement" runs across the entire Old Testament in which God's covenant people are blessed when they do good (retribution theology, in Green-Charlesworth terms) and that answers to the theodicy crisis that arises when this settlement is disturbed usually take the form of either "an enemy" (of many different shades) who intrudes to interrupt the normal good order of things or, less frequently and more daringly, of Yahweh's own breaking of the settlement. Brueggemann's synthesis, though helpful in many regards, omits several important pieces that are assembled by the Laato and de Moor volume (discussed below).

PART 1: INTRODUCTION

the events or claims that have given rise to theodical crisis from a given ancient text,[7] I do see profit and promise in attempting, through attention to context, to outline the general contours of the theodical milieu in which a given author operated.

Problems associated with theodicy were keenly felt by many Jews in the aftermath of Jerusalem's devastating destruction in 70 CE.[8] First-century Jews of course enjoyed a rich textual tradition to draw upon in pursuing questions of theodicy.[9] Though Jews were by no means unique among peoples of the ancient world in their asking and attempting to answer questions of theodicy,[10] Judaism shares with Christianity (and apparently also Islam) common theodical avenues and constraints that differentiate the great monotheistic religions from other religious traditions.[11]

One prominent synthesis has created a taxonomy for ancient monotheistic theodicy consisting of six "typologies": retribution theology, educative theodicy, eschatological theodicy, the mystery of theodicy (or "theodicy deferred"), communion theodicy, and human determinism.[12] A brief explanation of each is in order.

With its roots in ancient Near Eastern culture, retribution theology "is the prevailing type of theodicy in the Jewish Scriptures"[13]; it affirms evil as a punishment/response to human infidelity and wickedness. The second

---

7. I view this as a shortcoming of (or perhaps, rather, an over-extension within) James Crenshaw's article on theodicy in *Sirach*, in which he outlines the philosophical/theological "attack" leveled against the author's views by his putative ideological opponents ("The Problem of Theodicy in Sirach," 47–64).

8. Charlesworth claims that "Jews became increasingly concerned about theodicy from the third century BCE to the early second century CE" and goes on to note that, "[w]ith the loss of the Land and the Second Temple in 70 CE, one can imagine that theodicy reached one of its highest points in the history of Jewish thought," with *4 Ezra* as "the prime example of deep penetrating reflection on theodicy" ("Theodicy in Early Jewish Writings," 470–71); later, he specifies 63 BCE to 135 CE as the time of greatest existential angst for Jews (477).

9. The work of James L. Crenshaw has long provided insightful analysis of the theodicy tradition in the Jewish Scriptures. See his *Theodicy in the Old Testament*; *A Whirlpool of Torment*; "The Sojourner Has Come to Play the Judge," 83–92; "Theodicy in the Book of the Twelve," 175–91; *Defending God*.

10. See the essays on Akkadian, Ugaritic, Egyptian, and Hittite traditions of theodicy in Laato and de Moor, eds., *Theodicy in the World of the Bible*.

11. See the helpful discussion to this effect in Laato and de Moor, "Introduction," xxiv–xxx.

12. These are the Green-Charlesworth typologies, brought together by ibid., xxix–xxx.

13. Ibid., xxx–xxxii.

most prominent type of theodicy in the Old Testament, educative theodicy, has its roots, according to Laato and de Moor, in the wisdom tradition of the ancient Near East, in the experience of the exile, and later in Jewish martyr theology. It provides an understanding of at least some human suffering as educative, imparting an improved perspective or character to the one who suffers, as with Job and Jeremiah, especially as in Jeremiah's "confessions."[14] Eschatological theodicy, also known as "recompense theodicy," justifies suffering in the present with reference to benefits to be gained at the end of human history.[15] This is "the usual way to comfort and exhort the righteous ones to live according to the will of God in the Second Temple Judaism" and is presupposed in the New Testament.[16] "Theodicy deferred," which appears in the Wisdom Literature and the Psalms of the Old Testament, answers the problem of evil with a sort of non-answer: human beings (and sometimes super-human beings) simply do not know the answer to the riddle of suffering and evil. Key examples of this type of theodicy appear in Job (see esp. Job 28) and parts of 4 Ezra.[17] Communion theodicy emphasizes the role of suffering in drawing human beings closer to God, with the

---

14. Ibid., xxxix.

15. Ibid., xlii–xlv.

16. Ibid., xlv.

17. Ibid., xlvi–xlviii. Mention of 4 Ezra in particular necessitates acknowledgement that these theodicy categories are, especially when applied to concrete texts, heuristic categories, describing theodical approaches that in fact often intermingle and interact within a single work. This is certainly the case with 4 Ezra, in which the main character (perhaps mimicking the author's own experience) undergoes a transformation in his understanding of God's justice vis-à-vis Jerusalem's demise (see especially Longenecker, 2 Esdras, 96–98). This progressive aspect, as well as the generally dialogical nature, of 4 Ezra makes it especially elusive of single theodical categories (see the warning against just such a "harmonization" in Longenecker, 2 Esdras, 21). In general, the earlier episodes (I–III), in which Ezra resists and carps against Uriel's claims, including the central assertion that human beings (even members of the covenant community) cannot understand God's ways, seems to display a healthy dose of theodicy deferred. By contrast, the later parts of 4 Ezra (episodes IV–VII), in which Ezra has undergone his transformation, lean more firmly in the direction of retribution theology (since Ezra finally acknowledges God's justice in condemning sinners, even among Israel, despite Ezra's personal grief regarding this truth) and eschatological theodicy (since Ezra comes to find "consolation" in the visions of the future, heavenly sphere); on this, see especially Longenecker, 2 Esdras; also, Longenecker, Eschatology and the Covenant; Longenecker, "Locating 4 Ezra," 285–93. Note that, while theodicy deferred thus does not seem to be in line with the author's own (eventual) theodical preferences, the early chapters of 4 Ezra nonetheless offer a compelling tutorial in this theodical approach.

Servant Song of Isa 53 as perhaps the best example in the Old Testament.[18] Human determinism approximates understandings of Fate prominent in the Hellenistic world: humans are simply fated to attain this or that end. Elements of this "rather drastic" response to the problem of evil and suffering appear in *4 Ezra* and Qohelet.[19]

Omitted from the Green-Charlesworth typology is discussion of what Brueggemann calls "the enemy"—a character, whether human or super-human, who steps into the picture causing pain, suffering, and evil, most often Satan/the devil. Although Laato and de Moor correctly note the absence of "dualistic interpretive models" in Jewish theology such that Yahweh's presence always effectively dispels and prevails against "evil powers,"[20] they apparently overlook the fact that it is Yahweh's absence in the text that leaves room for the actions of these nefarious beings (whether human or beyond), even if only temporarily so. A tempting logical response to this fact might be something along the lines of: "Well, if God's absence is what allows these enemies to be effective, then they don't represent a theodical response since their presence still leaves unanswered the foundational question of, 'Why was God absent?'" The rational basis of this response likely does not override the existential relief many believers nonetheless gained (and gain) from attributing evil to the free will, or at least relatively unconstrained action, of other beings.[21] I suggest adding, then, "enemy theodicy" to the Green-Charlesworth typologies for Jewish-Christian theodical responses.

THEODICY IN THE JUDAISM(S) OF LUKE'S DAY

A full examination of the theodical lines traced in the various extant Jewish documents from the third century BCE to 135 CE obviously lies far beyond the scope of this study. Thus I will attempt here only to give some sense of the shape of the land, specifically by indicating the theodical "pride of place" occupied by the recent, horrifically realized, destruction of Jerusalem and

---

18. Laato and de Moor, "Introduction," xlviii–liii.
19. Ibid., liv.
20. Ibid., xxvii.
21. Indeed there is some evidence from the psychological sciences indicating that Christians who possess "robust notions of Satan" have more positive feelings toward God and are less likely to blame God for evil; see Beck and Taylor, "The Emotional Burden of Monotheism," 151–60. Beck and Taylor describe "robust notions of Satan" as enabling one to utilize "warfare theodicy."

its Temple for many Jews.[22] As I move into the era in question, I will note some of the theodical typologies employed by the texts and will comment upon each work's proclivity for orienting questions with respect to the two sides of God's character that are jeopardized when a theodicy settlement is disrupted, God's goodness and God's power.

According to Charlesworth, Jewish documents from the third and second centuries BCE (i.e., primarily the OT Apocrypha) show relatively little concern for theodicy and usually accept as satisfactory the dominant theodical line laid out in the OT, retribution theology, with the addition of eschatological theodicy[23] (which may be viewed, after all, as a variant of retribution theology, with a significant temporal twist).

Things began to change after 63 BCE, though only moderately so and though this was primarily true only for mainstream Jews residing in Palestine, at least prior to 70 CE.[24] Thus the Qumran documents reveal only modest concern for theodicy and usually work things out along the lines sketched for the OT Apocrypha (retribution theology, plus eschatological theodicy).[25] David Runia argues that Philo likewise evinces a theodical stance largely characterized by retribution theology and educative theodicy, especially in the wake of God's apparent vindication of the righteous (Alexandrian) Jews vis-à-vis Flaccus and Gaius in 38–41 CE, though there are also hues of "theodicy deferred."[26]

---

22. Though Stone maintains that "theodicy became the central issue" for Second Temple Jews dealing with the Babylonian (587–586 BCE), Seleucid (169–168 BCE), Roman (63 BCE), and second Roman (70 CE) desecrations and demolitions of the JT ("Reactions to Destructions," 196), he goes on to note the particularly anguished discussion in *4 Ezra* in response to the destruction in 70 CE (ibid., 200–204).

23. See Charlesworth, "Theodicy in Early Jewish Writings," 473–77. Stone seems to view retribution theology as more prominent in the wake of Antiochus Epiphanes's and Pompey's desecrations of the JT (e.g., 2 Maccabees, Judith, Psalms of Solomon) and eschatological theodicy as dominant subsequently (e.g., *2 Baruch*, *4 Ezra*), though this is probably because he views eschatological theodicy primarily in terms of a heavenly Jerusalem instead of emphasis on eventual (eschatological) rewards (Stone, "Reactions to Destructions," 196–200).

24. Charlesworth, "Theodicy in Early Jewish Writings," 477, 483.

25. Ibid., 477–82. Charlesworth adds also "Proleptic Fulfillment" as a theodical avenue pursued in the DSS (ibid., 481), but this falls within "eschatological theodicy" in the combined Green-Charlesworth typologies (see Laato and de Moor, "Introduction," xxix).

26. See Runia, "Theodicy in Philo of Alexandria," 576–604, esp. 599–604. Ultimately, Runia sees the pedagogic impulse trumping retributive impulses in Philo's theology (ibid., 604).

Part 1: Introduction

If representative of the views of Jerusalemite Jews after 63 BCE, the *Psalms of Solomon* indicate that the gradual tightening of the Roman "noose" around Judea's neck beginning with Pompey's desecration of the JT in 63 BCE increased theodical angst for Jews dwelling in the Holy Land.[27] The author of the *Psalms of Solomon*, reflecting on Pompey's sacrilege, solves the problem by reasserting retribution theology (*Pss. Sol.* 2, 8), an interpretation strengthened by Pompey's own eventual demise (reflected upon in 2:26–27).[28] Theodicy has been brought to the forefront in the composer's mind and, if he is at all representative, also in the minds of many Judean Jews, yet the old settlement (retribution theology) remains intact.[29] This settlement would withstand Roman aggression only so long, however.

Despite the detectable increase in theodical angst for Judean Jews following Rome's seizure of the Holy Land, the true watershed in ancient Jewish theodicy came with the events culminating in the destruction of Jerusalem and its Temple in 70 CE. It was the aftermath of that national tragedy that produced such theodically-tortuous works as *2 Baruch* and, above all, *4 Ezra*.[30]

---

27. See Charlesworth, "Theodicy in Early Jewish Writings," 483–84; Nickelsburg, *Jewish Literature*, 240, who sees clear allusion to the events of 63 BCE in Pss. Sol. 8:15–28.

28. Charlesworth, "Theodicy in Early Jewish Writings," 484–85; Nickelsburg, *Jewish Literature*, 239.

29. Indeed, "God's chief function according to the psalms [of Solomon] is that of judge, justly dispensing reward and punishment for human deeds" (Nickelsburg, *Jewish Literature*, 238).

30. Without question, Jewish responses to the national tragedy that culminated in 70 CE varied considerably—a fact I certainly do not intend to obscure here. Some works written shortly after and with reference to the destruction of Jerusalem and the decimation of so many facets of first-century Jewish identity show relatively little trace of theodical concern, such as those of Josephus. Other works seem more concerned about Judea's subjugation to Rome than about the destruction of the Temple specifically. This is what Jones claims regarding *4 Ezra* (*Jewish Reactions to the Destruction*, 57), though he may overstate matters (see *4 Ezra* 3:27, 28; 5:25; 6:19; and Vision 4). A clearer example of this attitude is found in *Sib. Or.* 4.24-30, 130-36, where, although God will punish the Romans for defeating the Jews, via the eruption of Mt. Vesuvius, nevertheless God's people will reject all temples (so Charlesworth, "Theodicy in Early Jewish Writings," 488–89). Those works that show a preoccupation with the Temple often envision an eschatological solution to the Temple's present desolate state, as in *Sib. Or.* 5.414-33; *2 Bar.* 4:2-7; *4 Ezra* 7:26-28; 9:38—10:59; 13:36 (see Chance, *Jerusalem*, 7), and not infrequently the appearance of the eschatological Temple coincides with the arrival of a messianic figure (e.g., *Sib.Or.* 5; *4 Ezra*; *Apoc. Ab.* 29–31; not so in *3 Baruch*, however). For a balanced assessment of the impact of this war on the various segments of Jewish society, see Levine, "Judaism from the Destruction of Jerusalem," 125–32.

Receiving its impetus from the Flavian era of Roman hegemony,[31] *4 Ezra* is something of a theodical *tour de force*,[32] with potent strains of theodicy deferred, retribution theology, and eschatological theodicy[33]—with, as noted earlier, theodicy deferred dominating episodes I–III and retribution theology and eschatological theodicy winning the day after Ezra's "transformation" (episodes IV–VII). Time and again in episodes I–III, the narrator's petitions and complaints regarding the inscrutability of God's justice in the midst of Jerusalem's destruction and Israel's subjugation to the nations are met with the stern response that God's ways are precisely that, inscrutable. A key example occurs in 4:1–21, where the angelic figure Uriel responds to the seer's query with riddles meant to show his inability to comprehend. The seer replies to the non-answer he receives with the claim that he seeks knowledge not of heavenly but of earthly things (4:22–25), and the cryptic answer the seer then receives from his angelic host (4:26–32) suggests the resolution lies in the eschatological future.[34] This is precisely what Ezra (and attentive auditors) discovers to be the case as *4 Ezra* unfolds into Ezra's visions of the eschatological future (episodes V–VI).

It is the failed calculus of classical retribution theology (3:28–36), combined with covenantal assurances (4:22–25; 5:21–30; 6:55–59), that has apparently given rise to the initial (and profound) theodicy crisis.[35] Thus questions seem to orient not around God's power but primarily around God's goodness—here expressed, unsurprisingly, in terms of faithfulness and justice. And so the narrator agonizes: Why did God not take away from Israel the evil heart inherited from Adam (3:20–27)? And how is God just in punishing Zion when its destroyers are equally wicked (3:28–36)? And how can God allow his chosen people to be tormented by the nations (5:23–30; 6:55–59)? And then, with Ezra broadening his theodical concern

---

31. So Myers, *I and II Esdras*, 129; also, Longenecker, *2 Esdras*, 13–14; and Stone, *Fourth Ezra*, 9–10, 361–65, arguing for *4 Ezra*'s composition at the end of Domitian's reign on the basis of Vision 5 (chapters 11–12). Not dissenting from the majority position, though allowing for a date as late as 120 CE is Metzger, "The Fourth Book of Ezra," in *OTP*, 1:520.

32. Putting the matter succinctly is Longenecker: "Whether in frustration or in confidence, [*4 Ezra*] is throughout a work of theodicy—that is, an attempt to understand and defend belief in the justice and sovereignty of God in view of the desperate condition of God's world" (*2 Esdras*, 12).

33. There are other traces of other ancient theodicy categories as well, e.g., educative as well as eschatological theodicy in 7:14–16.

34. See Stone, *Fourth Ezra*, 81–82.

35. Longenecker ascribes *4 Ezra* to "'crisis of faith' literature" (*2 Esdras*, 11).

Part 1: Introduction

to include all of humanity,³⁶ why should human beings be so unfortunate as to possess the vexing knowledge of their own mortality—a mortality that stands always and cognizantly under the sentence of future judgment (7.62–69)? Though it is possible to conceive of some of these questions as betraying a lack of confidence in God's power, they seem most naturally to point rather to foundering confidence in God's faithfulness and justice.³⁷

A number of similarities link 2 *Baruch* to 4 *Ezra*. Among these are the use of the Babylonian conquest of Jerusalem as the fictional setting, pseudonymous claim to have been penned by an ancient, well-known scribe, and shared use of apocalyptic genre.³⁸ In 2 *Baruch*, however, the logic of retribution theology more readily prevails (cf. 1–5), and God himself brings destruction on Jerusalem through the agency of four angels (6–8) and will ultimately punish the arrogant Romans (36, 38–40).³⁹ The author seems eager to assure auditors that, despite the destruction of God's city and God's house, God need not be attributed lack of power (5:1–4). Hence, surely, the destruction of Jerusalem by angelic agency⁴⁰ as well as the divine voice that invites in the conquering army.⁴¹ Indeed, God will eventually bring judgment on the arrogant nations by which he has destroyed his own people (13:8–11; 14.2), and the narrator confidently anticipates the eventual appearance of the true Jerusalem, the heavenly city (4.2–7). Thus, again, eschatology buttresses retribution theology.

Despite its ultimate confidence in retribution theology, 2 *Baruch* has its own moments of anguished theodicy, such as occur in chapters 10, 14,

---

36. On Ezra's shift of focus from the covenantal people of God to all of humanity in episode III, see Longenecker, *2 Esdras*, 46–55.

37. Thus Jones notes that, in response to 4 *Ezra's* painful and probing questions, "[o]ne might be tempted to doubt the justice of God" (*Jewish Reactions to the Destruction*, 123).

38. For these, and additional similarities, see Nickelsburg, *Jewish Literature*, 270, 283–85.

39. See Jones, *Jewish Reactions to the Destruction*, 97–100.

40. As Charlesworth notes, "By denying that the Romans destroyed Jerusalem and by stressing that it was accomplished through God's commands, the author endorses the power of 'the mighty God'" ("Theodicy in Early Jewish Writings," 493). Charlesworth derides this claim as "patently absurd" and has an overall poor opinion of 2 *Baruch* and its, for him, "rather too facile solution to theodicy" (492).

41. Jones notes that the voice of invitation suggests that otherwise the invading army would not have been able to enter the city and the Temple and that "the guardian" no longer "resided within"; in "this way efficacy is restored to God" (*Jewish Reactions to the Destruction*, 91, 92).

and 35. Thus can the narrator ask: "What have they profited who have knowledge before you, and who did not walk in vanity like the rest of the nations, and who did not say to the dead: 'Give life to us,' but always feared you and did not leave your ways?" (14:5, *OTP*). He goes on to ask why the deeds of Zion's many righteous people should not have offset the wicked deeds of other of its residents (14:7). In this passage, reminiscent of the early episodes of *4 Ezra*, *2 Baruch* probes the matter of God's justice and faithfulness. Even so, its overall confidence in retribution theology seems to override these (nonetheless poignant) moments of searching doubt, and its careful and elaborate depiction of God's angels as Jerusalem's true undoing indicate a comparatively greater concern for the other half of the theodical coin: God's power.[42]

Other apocalypses that likely come from this time and from a shared tradition also address the theodical problem created by the destruction of Jerusalem, though less desperately than do (at times) *4 Ezra* and *2 Baruch*. These are the *Apocalypse of Abraham* and possibly *3 Baruch*.[43] According to Nickelsburg's early analysis, these works follow *4 Ezra* and *2 Baruch* in attributing Jerusalem's demise to the people's sinfulness (retribution theology; see *Apoc. Ab.* 24–26) while anticipating punishment for Jerusalem's destroyers (retribution theology) and awaiting eschatological reward (eschatological theodicy).[44] While overall they demonstrate little of the agonized reflection that is characteristic of *4 Ezra* and that appears also in *2 Baruch*, the *Apocalypse of Abraham* does place a pained question in the patriarch's mouth upon his vision of the Temple's destruction: "Eternal, Mighty One! If this is so, why now have you afflicted my heart and why

42. See Jones, *Jewish Reactions to the Destruction*, 91–93.

43. Nickelsburg includes *3 Baruch* as an apocalypse from this period in the first edition of his *Jewish Literature* (280–81, 303, 304) but excludes it in the second edition. Gaylord Jr. is sure neither of *3 Baruch*'s dating nor to what extent it is a basically Jewish work with limited Christian interpolations versus a combination of an earlier Jewish and a later Christian work, though the Jewish parts may well be from the era in question ("3 Baruch," in *OTP*, 1:655–56 [653–61]). Charlesworth does not include *3 Baruch* in his discussion of Jewish works from this period ("Theodicy in Early Jewish Writings"). On the other hand, Bauckham places *3 Baruch* in this period (*Jewish World*, 114), and Jones locates both *3 Baruch* and *4 Baruch* within this period (*Jewish Reactions to the Destruction*, 112, 119–20, 156). Though including *3 Baruch*, I have given it minimal space, and none of my conclusions rest on its witness.

44. Nickelsburg, *Jewish Literature* (1st ed.), 303. Overall, the *Apocalpyse of Abraham*, though raising the question of theodicy, seems quite content with the classical theodicy settlement found in retribution theodicy, augmented with eschatological theodicy (27:1–12; 29:17–21).

will it be so?" (27:6, *OTP*). This pathos-laden exclamation, combined with God's immediate response that the suffering is due to the wickedness of Abraham's heirs, speaks to a concern for God's faithfulness and justice—what kind of a God would not only allow Abraham to see such a thing but also allow it to happen? The answer is that the God who does so, does so on just terms. The later, ekphrastic description of God's destruction of the "heathen" who harmed his people speaks to a concern for asserting God's power (31:1–8).

Though it begins with a weeping scribe lamenting Jerusalem's destruction (1.1–5), *3 Baruch* moves briskly away from such *pathos*-inducing imagery to breathtaking heavenly visions that demonstrate the awesome power of God and the justice of his universe (e.g., 2:7; 3:7–8; 9:7; 11:7–9; 15:2–4; 16:2–4). Thus *3 Baruch* affirms the justice but especially the power of God in the aftermath of Jerusalem's desolation.[45] It is also notable for its apparent concern regarding the proper maintenance of human-divine affairs in the wake of the Temple's destruction—a problem resolved by the heavenly ministrations of the angel Michael.[46]

At least two[47] of the *Sibylline Oracles* contain portions composed in the aftermath of the Flavian assault on Jerusalem (*Sib. Or.* 4.115–36; 5.397–429). *Sibylline Oracle* 4 affirms the destruction of Jerusalem as punishment for the sinfulness of God's people (4.117–18), but even so God will punish her destroyers with the cosmic destruction of Vesuvius (4.130–37)[48]—all perfectly in accord with the tenets of retribution theology.[49] Both God's justice and God's power are preserved. *Sibylline Oracle* 5 preserves these dual facets of God's character as well, though it leaves ripe avenues of doubt regarding God's power by attributing the catastrophe solely to Roman aggression (5.397–410). Only God's subsequent destruction of Titus (5.411–13) and eschatological subjugation of all of creation via a messianic figure (5.414–34) secure God's power and faithfulness.

---

45. Interpreting *3 Baruch* as preeminently concerned with the "efficacy"—i.e., power—of Israel's God is Jones, *Jewish Reactions to the Destruction*, 111–13, 121–23.

46. See Gaylord, "3 Baruch," in *OTP*, 1:659.

47. Charlesworth takes *Sib. Or.* 3.51–56, 75–92, 288–94 as referring to the recently realized destruction of Jerusalem in 70 CE ("Theodicy in Early Jewish Writings," 489), while Collins takes them to be second- and first-century BCE works of Egyptian provenance ("The Sibylline Oracles, Book 3," in *OTP*, 1:354–61).

48. See Charlesworth, "Theodicy in Early Jewish Writings," 488–89; Jones, *Jewish Reactions to the Destruction*, 178, 194.

49. Cf. Jones, *Jewish Reactions to the Destruction*, 204.

Even Josephus—albeit from a mixed pot of motives—heads off potential accusations against the power of Israel's God by claiming that the God of the Jews went over to Rome. While it is doubtful whether Josephus can be counted as showing genuine theodical concern in the aftermath of 70 CE, he may at least demonstrate an awareness of the fragility of the reputation of Israel's God in the wake of those events and so indirectly bear witness to the prominence of issues of theodicy among Jews in his day.

Collectively, the above works indicate the powerful pull toward theodicy felt by many pious believers in Israel's God in the wake of the disastrous events of 70 CE.[50] These works employ a variety of theodical avenues for resolving the challenge to God's character brought about by Jerusalem's destruction, and they give varying attention to the complementary sides of God's character brought into question by the theodicy crisis, God's power and God's faithfulness and justice.

THEODICY IN LUKE

Like several of his Jewish contemporaries, Luke seems to have felt the theodical angst of the post-70 CE world, whether as a matter of personal existential angst or, more likely, as a significant part of the general intellectual and cultural milieu of which he and members of his audience were part. I will explore the theodical emphases of Luke's Gospel below. Though much of the evidence centers around Luke's considerable interest in the fate of Jerusalem and its Temple, two theodical parables, both unique to the Third Gospel, also demonstrate a concern for theodicy apart from any obvious reference to Jerusalem or the Temple. After considering the theodical evidence in Luke's Gospel, I will examine the likely (and necessarily speculative) reasons for Luke's interest in theodicy, the contextual factors that may

---

50. While it is difficult to know to what degree these works should be "weighed rather than counted" in drawing a sketch of Jewish sentiments between 70 and 132 CE, it is remarkable how many of the extant works directly address issues of theodicy (each of the 4 apocalypses, in my view) and how many show some recognition of the need to shore-up God's reputation (the *Sibylline Oracles* and Josephus). Even if *4 Ezra* and *2 Baruch* display a literary relationship (so Nickelsburg, *Jewish Literature*, 284) or indeed even if all of the works addressed above were "written in some sort of dialogue with each others" (so Jones, *Jewish Reactions to the Destruction*, 156), it is noteworthy that these works, in spite of their many similarities, do theodicy so differently, thereby testifying to the diversity of those who were drawn to questions of theodicy at this time.

Part 1: Introduction

have shaped and given poignancy to questions of theodicy for Luke and for Luke's ideal audience.

It hardly needs saying that Luke spends considerably more time and effort probing Jerusalem's fate, including its role in the unfolding eschatological drama, than do the other canonical Gospels. I will place the evidence for such within the flow of Luke's narrative in chapters 3–5, and so here I will simply assemble (some of) such evidence as rough, semi-quantified "data." One of Luke's early (and unique) characters speaks to those "awaiting the redemption of Jerusalem" (2:38). Luke includes Jesus's initial lament over Jerusalem (Luke 13:34–35), found also in Matt 23:37–39, and adds to it the notice of Jerusalem's role as murderer of the prophets (13:33). Luke also includes another, unique lamentation of Jesus over the city (19:41–44), raises and obliquely responds to the question of whether Jesus's drawing near to Jerusalem entails the imminent arrival of the kingdom (19:11–27), makes the "Temple-cleansing" the climax of his Journey section (19:45–46; see comments ad loc. in chapter 5), makes Jerusalem's destruction—elaborated in rather vivid terms—a focal point of his "Eschatological Discourse" (21:20–22), and references Jerusalem's demise even during Jesus's march to the cross (23:27–31). Moreover, Luke begins Acts with what is probably a veiled reference to expectations of Jerusalem's political restoration (1:6).[51] Though further evidence will be forthcoming in my examination of Luke's Gospel in chapters 3–5, the hasty rehearsal above more than establishes Luke's surpassing interest in Jerusalem's fate.[52]

Luke concerns himself with Jerusalem more than any other New Testament writer—as seen even in the number of times he mentions the city's name (roughly two-thirds of the occurrences in the New Testament)—and so perhaps his including so much material about Jerusalem's fate reflects not a theodical concern per se but is simply a by-product of Luke's general interest in the city. This answer is unsatisfying, however, for the simple reason that, in Luke's milieu, to discuss Jerusalem—the (immediate) fate of which has been sealed in the Lukan (literary) world and almost certainly also in the (real) world of Luke's audience—is to court questions of theodicy. That Luke himself so frequently and so poignantly draws his auditors' attention not only to Jerusalem but also specifically to its fate serves as corroboration

---

51. Carroll reasonably claims that ἀποκαθίστημι "became a technical term [in OT usage] . . . for the political restoration of Israel by God" on the basis of passages like Ps 15:5; Jer 15:19; 16:15; 23:8; Ezek 16:55; Hos 11:11 (*Response to the End of History*, 146).

52. See also the helpful survey of the Lukan landscape in Holmås, "'My House Shall Be Called,'" 396.

of this truth. Whatever general interest Luke may have in Jerusalem, he clearly expresses a specific and pointed interest in its tragic demise and in questions of its role in salvation history. In so doing, Luke concerns himself with issues of theodicy.

At a number of specific points, Luke appears either to raise the question of theodicy or even to employ one of the expected Jewish-Christian theodical typologies. Without making any claims to being exhaustive and without attempting to situate the following episodes adequately in their narrative context (see chapters 3–5), I note the following.

Luke's theodical parables. Two uniquely Lukan parables employ the language and themes of theodicy. These are the Parable of the Friend at Midnight (11:5-8) and the Parable of the Persistent Widow (18:1-8). The parables share a number of similarities that frequently lead commentators to consider them together: the initial reluctance but eventual capitulation of the character of whom the request is made; their similar use of παρέχω (11:7; 18:5);[53] and Luke's explicitly framing each within the context of a discussion of prayer.[54] I will consider them together here as well.

Luke 11:5-8, which tells the story of a midnight visit and the reluctant "friend" who eventually responds to the petitioner's requests for provisions, occurs within "an extended presentation on prayer in 11:1–13" and at several points connects conceptually to that larger framing, especially the mention of bread (vv. 3, 5) and the shared emphasis on petitioning with vv. 9–10.[55] As such, most interpretations of the parable within its narrative context take it as a parable giving instruction regarding prayer.[56] Verse 5 introduces a hypothetical question, one that runs to the end of v. 7 and one that expects a negative answer: "Who among you if such and such happened would refuse your friend?"[57] Though the meaning of τὴν ἀναίδειαν

---

53. See Liefeld, "Parables on Prayer," 242); also, Snodgrass, *Stories with Intent*, 440; already in Jeremias, *The Parables of Jesus*, 153, 157.

54. Both in fact encourage persistence in prayer; see Fitzmyer, *Luke*, 2:910. John Nolland suggests a connection also based on the theme of shame/shamelessness in 11:8 and 18:5 (*Luke*, 2:868).

55. Liefeld, "Parables on Prayer," 241.

56. See the helpful history of research in Van Eck, "When Neighbours Are Not Neighbours," 2, whose own interpretation intentionally divorces the parable from its Lukan context, taking it as attributable to the historical Jesus, and reads it from a socio-scientific perspective. Whatever the value of considering this parable apart from its Lukan context, it is Luke's theology—and thus his framing here—which commands our interest at present.

57. See Jeremias, *Parables of Jesus*, 158; Green, *Luke*, 446–47; Snodgrass, *Stories with*

Part 1: Introduction

αὐτοῦ ("his shamelessness") in v. 8 is contested, it almost certainly carries a negative connotation[58] and probably refers to the shamelessness of the petitioner.[59] In this case, the point is that, even if the man in bed would not give bread on the basis of "friendship" and the mores of ancient reciprocity and hospitality, still, because of the petitioner's "shamelessness," the man in bed would not refuse his request.

Only later, in v. 13, does Luke supply the critical interpretive lens for the parable. There, commenting on the father who would not give his son undesirable gifts (vv. 11–12), Jesus states: πόσῳ μᾶλλον ὁ πατὴρ [ὁ] ἐξ οὐρανοῦ δώσει πνεῦμα ἅγιον τοῖς αἰτοῦσιν αὐτόν. This framing encourages the Lukan audience to read the earlier parable in a from-lesser-to-greater sense[60] and thereby discourages a reading that seeks a one-to-one allegory between every character and feature of the parable and believers'

Intent, 442; Marshall, *Luke*, 464.

58. See esp. Snodgrass, *Stories with Intent*, 442–45; and Snodgrass, "Anaideia and the Friend," 505–13, who notes that the word never has a positive meaning in the extant literature through the fourth century CE except in some Christian interpretations of Luke 11:8; also, Van Eck, "When Neighbours Are Not Neighbours," 8.

59. Following Snodgrass, *Stories with Intent*, 445; Fitzmyer, *Luke*, 2:912; Johnson, *The Gospel of Luke*, 178. *Contra* Green, *Luke*, 446–48; Van Eck, "When Neighbours Are Not Neighbours," 10–11; Huffard, "The Parable of the Friend at Midnight," 154–60. The attribution of ἀναίδεια to the man in bed seems largely to be based on the reconstruction of ancient village life by, among others, Herzog, which he somewhat famously summarizes with the line: "Bolted doors and sleeping children are minor obstacles easily overcome" (*Parables as Subversive Speech*, 202). While I am hesitant to shirk social-scientific reconstructions of the *realia* and values of the ancient world, I am even more resistant to allowing such reconstructions to override the evidence of the ancient texts themselves. Here, Luke's temporal indicator that it was midnight (μεσονυκτίου; v. 5), combined with the man's objections (v. 7), plus the more natural reading of τὴν ἀναίδειαν αὐτοῦ (v. 8) as a reference to the petitioner (see Fitzmyer, *Luke*, 1:912), collectively suggest that, at least for Luke's ideal audience, the petition is taken to fall potentially outside the bounds of normal friendship—and thus the "shamelessness" belongs to the man making the request. Admittedly, the passage admits a good deal of ambiguity, especially in its use of personal pronouns; see Marshall, *Luke*, 465, for a (cautiously) dissenting opinion. Even if I am mistaken in this and ἀναίδεια indeed refers to the shame the man in bed hopes to avoid, it has relatively little bearing on my larger reading of the passage, because the from-lesser-to-greater import of the passage still coheres. Alternately, Luke may leave the referent intentionally vague, thus allowing for a double-meaning in which the petitioner acts shamelessly and the man in bed responds in order to avoid the shame of failing to be hospitable.

60. Robbins's rejection of an argument from lesser to greater here in favor of an argument from analogy is not compelling ("From Enthymeme to Theology," 204–5).

religious lives.⁶¹ Rather, Luke seems here only to affirm the general truth, with an illustration from ancient village life, that God responds to believers' petitions.

Even so, the positioning of God vis-à-vis the man who is clearly, perhaps also culpably, hesitant to respond favorably to his petitioner opens up a common theodical vista: God the remote, God the hesitant, dilatory respondent. This theodical vista comes fully into view, however, only with a subsequent (related) parable: the Parable of the Persistent Widow.

Located near the end of Luke's Journey section, following upon a discussion by Jesus regarding eschatological trials that await his disciples (17:22–37), "The Parable of the Persistent Widow" (Luke 18:1–8) invites a surprising comparison between God and an unscrupulous judge.⁶² Like its counterpart in Luke 11, this parable offers a "how much more" argument—clearly implied by Jesus's words in vv. 6–7—one that absorbs much of the potentially unsavory comparison. Again, the point is precisely that God is *not* like the judge in the parable and so will answer the prayers of his people.⁶³ Even so, this parable again opens—and in fact opens further—the theodical vista from Luke 11:5–8: Will God answer his petitioners? Not only does it do so by comparing God to the judge—though, again, the nature of the comparison (*qal wahomer*) significantly mutes the potentially negative aspects of the comparison—but the fronting Luke gives to the parable also raises theodical concerns: Jesus told them the parable in order to show that it was necessary to pray continually and never to give up (v.

---

61. Because of this, to conclude that attributing ἀναίδεια to the petitioner implies "that it would be shameful to go to God with our needs" (Huffard, "Parable of the Friend at Midnight," 155) is unnecessary. Rather, "[t]he whole point of the parable . . . is that God is *not* like the sleeper. It is a parable contrasting God with the sleeper" (Snodgrass, *Stories with Intent*, 447; emphasis original).

62. "Jesus' choice of this brutal judge to illustrate God's helpfulness must have shocked his audience" (Jeremias, *Parables of Jesus*, 156).

63. Though he may be something of a needed correction to those who skip entirely over the parable's potential attribution of unsavory character-traits to God, nonetheless overplaying his hand is Metzger, "Where Has Yahweh Gone?"; and Metzger, "God as F(r)iend?" While he accuses New Testament scholars of "a proclivity to religionism" in failing to note the supposedly negative portrayals of God in Luke 11:5–8; 18:1–8; and elsewhere, Metzger's reading suffers from its own ideological biases, as seen especially in his denial of a "from the lesser to the greater" interpretation in these parables ("Where Has Yahweh Gone?," 51, 52–53), which is clearly implied by 11:13 and 18:6–7 (e.g., Fitzmyer, *Luke*, 2:1177, 1180). Still, he is on target in noting that these parables raise or at least hint at deeper issues in assuming the need for persistence in prayer ("Where Has Yahweh Gone?," 53).

Part 1: Introduction

1). The need for persistence in prayer cannot but simultaneously indicate the reality that prayers are sometimes (from a human perspective) slow in being answered.[64] This is true even if the parable teaches not only persistence regarding specific issues of petition but also as a holistic way of life, in anticipation of the kingdom's arrival and in the midst of suffering.[65]

The theodical vista these parables, and in particular 18:1–8, open is that which appears rather often in the Psalms (e.g., 42:9-11 [41:10-12]; 59:4-5 [58:5-6]; 74:1-11 [73:1-11]; 77:7-9 [76:8-10]; 88 [87] [LXX]) and in other Jewish works, including Luke's rough contemporaries, 3 Baruch and 4 Ezra.[66] Thus Ps 88 [87] urges, "O LORD, God of my salvation, when, at night, I cry out in your presence, let my prayer come before you; incline your ear to my cry" (vv. 1–2), and more bitterly still complains, "But I, O LORD, cry out to you; in the morning my prayer comes before you. O LORD, why do you cast me off? Why do you hide your face from me?" (vv. 13–14; NRSV).[67] And Ps 74(73):10-11 cries out: "How long, O God, is the foe to scoff? Is the enemy to revile your name forever? Why do you hold back your hand; why do you keep your hand in your bosom?" (NRSV). God's absence is, for the author, keenly felt. Much later, 3 Baruch bitterly reports the nations' mocking response to Jerusalem's destruction: "Where is their God?" (1.2, Greek version, OTP).[68] Relatedly, 4 Ezra protests the seeming disjuncture between God's righteousness and the injustice of the author's lived experience, a protest which, while going beyond complaint of

---

64. The question of how God relates to the judge, after all, does not exhaust the parable's import because "the attitude of the judge and the attitude of the woman . . . are tightly woven into the parable" (Marshall, *Luke*, 671); we must also consider the import of Luke's comparing the widow's need for persistence to the realities of discipleship (framed against the eschatological backdrop of Luke 17:20-35). This theodical angle is heightened if μακροθυμεῖν (v. 7) is interpreted as a reference to God's self-concealment, as argued by Haacker, "Lukas 18:7," 267–72.

65. See Green, *Luke*, 638–39; Marshall, *Luke*, 669–70; Fitzmyer, *Luke*, 2:1178. If this passage indeed counsels Christians to pray in the face of persecution, awaiting God's justice though unsure how or when God will make things right, then it leans in the direction of theodicy deferred.

66. Cf. 2 Pet 3:9.

67. This psalm also accuses God of tormenting the psalmist (vv. 6–8, 15–18) and thus falls under Brueggemann's minority of cases in which God himself has broken the theodicy settlement ("Some Aspects of Theodicy," 253). Such unsettling charges never appear in Luke's writing, to my knowledge, and so I will not pursue them further.

68. For an insightful discussion of this taunt as fundamental to the entire project of 3 Baruch, see Jones, *Jewish Reactions to the Destruction*, 111–42.

God's absence in the face of enemy aggression, rests upon the foundation of such complaint:

> [T]hose things which we daily experience: why Israel has been given over to the gentiles as a reproach; why the people whom you loved has been given over to godless tribes . . . and why we pass from the world like locusts, and why our life is like a mist, and we are not worthy to obtain mercy. (4.23–25, *OTP*)

Such passages reflect the disruption, in Brueggemann's terms, of the theodicy settlement, a disruption brought about by the actions of an enemy in God's apparent absence.

The situation envisioned in Luke's Parable of the Persistent Widow, who seeks vindication (ἐκδίκησόν με) against her opponent (ἀπὸ τοῦ ἀντιδίκου μου; v. 3), is akin to those described above. Thus the parable taps into the theodical angst expressed throughout Jewish tradition dating back to the Psalms, likely with reference to Jesus's earlier indication that suffering will be an inescapable reality for the faithful (17:33). When Luke's Jesus gives a strong affirmation of God's speedy (or, less likely, sudden) attentiveness to the elects' cries for justice (vv. 7–8), then, the Gospel writer is engaging in nothing less than an act of theodicy: he affirms that God will indeed prove faithful.[69] More specifically, this affirmation of God's faithfulness in granting justice affirms a general, even if partial, picture of retribution theology: God, who is powerful (as Luke here presupposes and elsewhere clearly affirms), will conduct the affairs of the cosmos such that justice ultimately prevails. If Luke indeed colors the passage "with a decidedly eschatological edge," which is likely in light of its positioning next to 17:22–37,[70] then it may be not only an expression of retribution theology but also of that subset of retribution theology, recompense theodicy.[71]

---

69. Cf. Herzog's comment: "While persistent prayer and the continuance of faith under persecution may be related to each other, they both raise a common question, not of eschatology but of *theodicy*" (*Parables as Subversive Speech*, 217; emphasis added).

70. So Green, *Luke*, 637; Klein, *Das Lukasevangelium*, 578; Johnson, *Luke*, 273; Marshall, *Luke*, 669, 676. Fitzmyer concludes that "mention of the Son of Man and his coming [in v. 8] clearly relates this allegorized parable to the preceding eschatological instruction about the day(s) of the Son of Man" (*Luke*, 2:1177; see also, 2:1175–76).

71. It is also unclear to what degree the "eschatological travails" described at the end of Luke 17 will find recompense in the form of eschatological reward versus grace in the present (or even in what sense the "eschatological" nature of such travails should be understood within Lukan theology—a question I will not attempt to resolve here). Luke likely expresses both retribution theology and recompense theodicy here. Given that Luke may be echoing the description of the judge and widow in Sir 35:11–24 (LXX)

Part 1: Introduction

Luke's theodical contribution here goes even beyond these reflections, however, for he ends this section with something of a twist, namely, the question Jesus poses: "But when the Son of Man comes, will he find τὴν πίστιν on the earth?" (v. 8). This question reorients the discussion from a focus on the faithfulness of God—which is at least partially called into question by the very act of becoming an object of discussion—to a question regarding the human response to God's faithfulness: Will τὴν πίστιν prevail on the earth?[72] Rather than simply affirm God's faithfulness, Luke turns the tables by questioning *human* faithfulness.

Luke 13:1–5. Here, in the midst of Jesus's circuitous journey to Jerusalem, unidentified members of the crowd speak to Jesus of an otherwise unknown incident: Pilate mixed the blood of certain Galileans with their sacrifices. Jesus's response is surprising: These Galileans, despite what members of his (and Luke's?) narrative audience might think, were no worse sinners than others; in fact, his audience will suffer the same fate, barring their repentance (vv. 2–3). Then Jesus cites the apparently well-known incident in which the Tower of Siloam fell, killing 18 people, and affirms that these were no more guilty than anyone else living in Jerusalem (v. 4); he follows this with a second exhortation to repent (v. 5).

Jesus's response to the initial prompt from his audience clearly places his comments here within the world of ancient theodicy; these Galileans, who suffered so cruelly, were presumed by members of the audience to be guilty of particularly heinous wickedness. This is retribution theology in its clearest and most stringent form: Suffering reveals immorality as a corollary to the immutable and universally applicable truth that God punishes evildoers. Jesus rebuffs this harsh position by affirming in v. 2 that these Galileans were no worse than other Galileans.

Jesus's answer grows more complicated and perplexing in the verses that follow, however. In v. 3, his audience—in a shocking turn of events—stands under the threat of a similar destruction, and moreover, so also do the residents of Jerusalem, as v. 4 implies. Particularly in light of the parable that follows and that clearly complements vv. 1–5, many interpreters take

---

(see Green, *Luke*, 638; Marshall, *Luke*, 675)—albeit with significant modifications—and that Sir 35:11–24 offers a clear affirmation of retribution theology, this line should probably not be seen to recede too far over against the eschatological moorings of the passage that precedes the parable.

72. Cf. Johnson, *Luke*, 273. The question also serves to reorient the larger discussion about the timing and placement of the kingdom of God, from 17:20–21; see Green, *Luke*, 642; Klein, *Das Lukasevangelium*, 581.

this passage as a call to national repentance (see discussion in chapter 4). Thus the Jewish nation as a whole—of which Jerusalem is the center and soul[73]—stands under the mandate of repentance: otherwise, doom awaits.

This reading of Luke 13:1–5 as a warning of the need for national repentance serves to place conditions on the earlier rejection of retribution theology: the Galileans and Jerusalemites who did not suffer were no less guilty than their compatriots who suffered so terribly in part because the entire lot of them is guilty! Thus Luke 13:1–5 clearly speaks to concerns of ancient theodicy yet does not speak clearly in doing so. On the other hand, it rejects strict retribution theology, given that, whatever their eventual fate, other Galileans and Jerusalemites did not in fact suffer as did the victims described in vv. 1, 4. Even so, on the other hand, the passage affirms the general truth of retribution theology by asserting a link between the nation's eventual (earthly) fate and its moral status (clearly implied by the mandate to repent). Thus Luke 13:1–5 both partially rejects and partially affirms retribution theology.

Acts 1:6-8. As noted above, when the disciples inquire "when God would restore the kingdom to Israel," they employ a term (ἀποκαθίστημι) that, for auditors familiar with the LXX, would conjure ancient hopes of Israel's political restoration, almost certainly conceived in terms of self-rule. The question of Israel's political restoration, relevant in the ca. 30 CE narrative setting, would have been all the more poignant and far more theodically pointed in Luke's probable post-70 CE context. A similar desire to know the timeline of Israel's restoration appears in theodically-oriented works of the period (e.g., *4 Ezra* 4:33—5:13; 6:7; *Apoc. Ab.* 28–29). The disciples' query and Jesus's response in v. 7 that it was simply not their place to know "the times and the seasons which the Father has set by his own authority" falls within the tradition of theodicy deferred.[74] Not only does Jesus *not answer* their query, but his immediately shifting to what appears to be another topic (the spread of the gospel) in v. 8 seems even to *invalidate* the question, leaving doubtful whether such a restoration will ever occur, at least as conceived by the inquirers.

Perhaps also belonging in this category of theodicy is Jesus's enigmatic claim that "Jerusalem will be trampled by the Gentiles until the times of

---

73. Hence, Luke's not incidentally choosing Jerusalem as the location of the second disaster example (v. 4).

74. Cf. *4 Ezra* 4:21, 33; 6:7–10; also, 3:14, in which God reveals the secrets of the end of time to Abraham alone, and at night.

PART 1: INTRODUCTION

the Gentiles are fulfilled" (Luke 21:24). Here, more clearly than in Acts 1:7, Jesus seems to indicate some sort of eventual restoration for Jerusalem specifically, but the puzzling reference to "the times of the Gentiles" seems to confound further (productive) inquiry. As in *Apoc. Ab.* 28–29 or the early episodes (I–III) of *4 Ezra*, the auditor is given some indication of future timelines and future events but in so cryptic a way as to be left effectively in the dark regarding these future events. To describe future events of import in such cryptic, mysterious language is a hallmark not only of apocalyptic writing in general but also of apocalyptic writings that embrace "the mystery of theodicy."

Explanations for Jesus's humiliation via crucifixion. Beginning in Luke 24 and then at numerous points in Acts, Luke interprets Jesus's crucifixion as a necessary part of God's plan—a concern already hinted at through Jesus's own use of δεῖ in Luke 9:22; 13:33; 17:25 (admittedly with reliance on Mark); and foreshadowed by Luke's reference to Isaiah' suffering servant in his Passion Narrative (Luke 22:37). The claim that Jesus, as Messiah, had to suffer in order to fulfill the Scriptures (Luke 24:25–27) and thus did so according to the plan and foreknowledge of God (Acts 2:23; 4:28), despite his innocence (Acts 3:14), and was vindicated by God's raising him (Acts 2:24; 3:15)—Luke makes this interpretation of, and explanation for, Jesus's death a key point in the early chapters of Acts and probably does so for several reasons. For one, this is simply the interpretation of Jesus's death that Luke himself believes to be true and that he attributes to the early Jerusalem Church. But this is not the whole of the story, for Luke takes pains not only to express this view but to give it something of center stage in Luke 24 and the early-going of Acts, also punctuating it, e.g., by stressing the culpability of the Jewish leaders who crucified Jesus, which by corollary emphasizes Jesus's innocence. Luke does this in Acts but especially via his changes to Mark's Passion Narrative.[75] These changes collectively demonstrate Luke's efforts to shape his interpretation of Jesus's death for further rhetorical purposes.

Likely among such rhetorical purposes is to offer a positive theodical argument. Here the problem centers not on God's power or faithfulness, but rather on the person of Jesus and specifically the shame and degradation his death by crucifixion would entail for many first-century auditors. Could this crucified, humiliated man really be "Lord," "Messiah," and "Savior"?

---

75. For these changes and an interpretation of their rhetorical import, see my article, "The Rhetoric of Luke's Passion."

Though this project could be more fittingly characterized as "Christodicy," it is closely akin to, and perhaps in Luke's theology even a subset of, theodicy. Interestingly, this type of "theodicy" would fall largely within the category of theodicy by "determinism," which is seldom employed by extant Jewish works from antiquity. In this case, however, we have a determinism shaped not by the governance of implacable Fate but by the plan of Israel's God, as foretold in Israel's Scriptures.[76]

Acts as "apologetic" literature. Claims that Acts evinces "apologetic" concerns are common among Lukan scholars.[77] Most argue only for apologetic intent, though some have gone so far as to suggest apology as a facet of Acts's literary genre.[78] The precise nature of Acts's supposed apologetic intent has proven difficult to pin down, however.[79] Perhaps the most plausible suggestion is Luke Johnson's claim that Luke addresses the large-scale rejection of Jesus by God's chosen people and defends "God's fidelity to his people and to his own word."[80] If this is the case, (Luke-)Acts "is . . . in the broadest sense a theodicy."[81]

Summary. There exists strong evidence, then, that both in individual pericopes and perhaps also in the macro-dynamics of Acts in particular, Luke concerns himself with matters of theodicy. These concerns seem to orient more toward questions of God's faithfulness than toward questions of God's power, as in the theodical parables and the macro-level theodical lines identified by Johnson.

Lukan Theodicy Crisis

This brief examination demonstrates Luke's interest in and concern for theodicy. This fact, viewed against both Luke's exceeding interest in

---

76. For a helpful discussion of Lukan theology in light of Greco-Roman understandings of Providence and Fate, see Squires, *The Plan of God*.

77. E.g., Munck, *Acts*, LV–LXI. Marshall rejects the claim that Acts's primary purposes was to provide a "political apologetic" but does not deny apology as one motive behind Acts (*Acts*, 21); similarly, Fitzmyer, 58; Johnson, *Acts*, xii, 7–9. Pervo argues for Acts as a "legitimating narrative," which he differentiates from "apologetic" works (*Acts*, 21).

78. Sterling, *Historiography and Self-Definition*, but see the critique of Sterling in Alexander, *Acts in Its Ancient Literary Context*, 191–93.

79. See the incisive discussion in Alexander, *Acts in Its Ancient Literary Context*, 183–206.

80. Johnson, *Acts*, 7–9, 476.

81. Johnson, *Acts*, 7. Cf. Alexander, *Acts in Its Ancient Literary Context*, 201–6.

Part 1: Introduction

Jerusalem and its Temple and the theodicy-saturated milieu in which Luke likely operated (70–135 CE), suggests that the utter devastation of Jerusalem and its Temple as a result of the failed revolt against Rome was a point of theodical concern for Luke.[82] In Brueggemann's terms, the events of 70 CE appear to have opened room for a theodicy crisis—or, more cautiously, a theodicy challenge—for Luke and/or for members of his audience.

But why should this be so, that the so-called "Gentile" Evangelist should consider the destruction of the Jewish holy city and Temple a cause for theodical reflection? I offer the following suggestions.

First of all, the events that culminated in 70 CE introduced room for both doubt and polemic regarding the efficacy of the Christian God over and against Roman might—the theodical problem Bruce Longenecker has effectively laid out.[83] Although Longenecker frames the problem in terms of a loss of honor, he addresses the "power" side of the equation, as I have framed things: since Roman might has destroyed the city and Temple that were the unique dwelling place of the God of Israel—the place where God chose to make God's name to dwell—then the power of God becomes suspect, which in turn threatens that God should also suffer a significant loss of honor. A (putatively) ontological problem (concerning God's power) becomes a social and political problem (concerning God's honor). Adding considerable fuel to this flame, as Longenecker argues, was Flavian propaganda that broadcast their victory over the Jews, especially through coinage—quite soon after Jerusalem's fall, Vespasian had "Judaea Capta" inscribed on coins minted both in Rome and elsewhere in the empire, including in Judea[84]—through triumphs and celebratory games, through literary works, and through triumphal architecture, including the well-known Arch of Titus in Rome.[85] Indeed, "the triumphal procession

---

82. As with any attempt to relate an ancient text to its usually only semi-accessible context, my reading of Luke's theodical concern participates in a certain amount of circularity: my reading of Luke's context as steeped in theodicy informs my reading of his Gospel, which in turn informs (along with other considerations) my identification of the theodicy-heavy period of the late first century as the appropriate context in which to situate Luke's Gospels. As Thiselton insightfully notes, a certain degree of circularity is simply inescapable in assessing ancient texts and ancient contexts: "We cannot arrive at a picture of the whole without scrutinizing the parts or pieces, but we cannot tell what the individual pieces mean until we have some sense of the wider picture as a whole" (*Hermeneutics*, 13–15 [14]).

83. See his essay "Rome's Victory."

84. See Zarrow, "Imposing Romanization," 44–55.

85. See, e.g., Price, "The Provincial Historian in Rome," 108: "The rebellion held an

adorned by the venerable vessels and sacred furniture of the temple cult seemed to boast of victory over God himself."[86]

This international and very public problem was exacerbated by an attendant quandary of a more localized nature: the jarring reversal of Scripture's many apparent indications that Jerusalem would be, not demolished, but beautified and restored. These hopes were painted especially and poignantly with the hues of Isaiah's palette; indeed an abundance of Isaianic passages and promises seemed to point firmly in the direction of Jerusalem's physical, political, and indeed eschatological glorification (e.g., Isa 2:2–3; 11:9–16; 52:7–10; 60; 61:1–7; 62; 65:17–25; also 56:7; 57:13; 65:11; 66:20). Isaiah had promised that "in the last days (ἐν ταῖς ἐσχάταις ἡμέραις)"—the very words Luke applies to Pentecost (Acts 2:17)—the mountain of God would appear and the house of God would be raised above the hills, causing all the nations to flock to Zion (Isa 2:1–4).

Within Second Temple Judaism, such passages could be taken to indicate a future restoral of Jerusalem's glory, as in texts like *Pss. Sol.* 11 and 17 and probably Sir 48:24–25 (admittedly written before Herod's rebuilding project).[87] This is in line with the tendency of many Second Temple docu-

---

extremely important place in the self-presentation of the Flavian house." Likewise, Zarrow notes: "The triumph over the Jews became a cornerstone of Flavian self-presentation," since this victory provided Vespasian "fundamental justification for his right to rule and his right to establish a new imperial dynasty" ("Imposing Romanization," 53). For an ancient description of Titus's Arch, see Josephus, *J.W.* 7.5.5. Simply put, "The Flavians emphatically celebrated Jerusalem's demise not only in Judea but in other provinces and in Rome" (Keener, *Acts*, 1:462n23).

86. Jones, *Jewish Reactions to the Destruction*, 109. Indeed the Flavians displayed seized vessels from the Temple during Titus's Roman triumph (Josephus, *J.W.* 7.161), as noted by Bauckham, *Jewish World*, 235.

87. Mallen, *The Reading and Transformation of Isaiah*, 36–41. Knibb argues as well that Sir 48:24–25 should be read in reference to the promise of Jerusalem's eschatological re-glorification in texts like Isa 61:1–7 ("Isaianic Tradition in the Apocrypha and Pseudepigrapha," 649). See also (though it may be late) *3 En.* 48A.10, which speaks of the gathering of Israel into Jerusalem in language evocative of Is 66:20 and 52:10 (per the marginal notes in *OTP*). As Le Donne, summarizing his work in *The Historiographical Jesus*, puts it: "In sum, there were multiple ways that Second Temple Jews envisioned the restoration of Israel, but almost all of them included the Lord's temple presence resting within the temple" ("The Improper Temple Offering," 350n23). Pokorný understands Jewish prophetic tradition to offer two eschatological visions in which Gentiles gather via pilgrimage to Jerusalem in order either to seek the Lord or to receive final punishment from the Lord (or both—as in Zechariah 14), and identifies numerous passages in Isaiah as demonstrative of the former ("Völkerwallfahrt") option (*Theologie der Lukanischen Schriften*, 45).

Part 1: Introduction

ments to read Isaiah eschatologically, as in some Qumran texts[88] and Sir. 48:22–25. In the period between the revolts, *Sibylline Oracle* 5 may also draw on Isaiah for its vision of the restored Jerusalem with its Temple.[89] Such hopes for Jerusalem's restoration, forged especially from the visions of Isaiah,[90] met a cataclysmic reversal with the failed Judean revolt, and while hopes for a new city and new Temple continued in the period between 70 and 135 CE, the dashing of these hopes likely helped raise theodical angst to its fever-pitch levels among some Jews.[91]

It is no stretch of the historical imagination to surmise that Luke felt, or at least could sympathize with, such angst regarding Jerusalem's dashed hopes, for he was himself an expectant reader of Isaiah, one whose thought and imagination was, by all indications, steeped in Isaianic phrasing, imagery, and hopes.[92] Additionally, Luke seems to have been aware of the wider

---

88. E.g., Brooke argues that 4Q174 undertakes an eschatological reading of Isaiah, for the purposes of communal self-definition ("Isaiah in the Pesharim," 613–15).

89. Note, for example, their shared belief in Jerusalem's being raised up to the clouds and the nations seeing its glory (5:424–25; Isa 2:1–4; 52:10; 62:2), the centripetal force this will have across the globe (5:426–28; Isa 2:1–4; 11:10–16; 52:10), bringing promise of a utopian cessation of hostilities and suffering (5.429–31; Isa 11:9; 65:20–23). Note also that this oracle earlier draws heavily on Isaianic imagery for Babylon to denounce Israel's new foe, Rome (5.162–78). On this, see Jones, *Jewish Reactions to the Destruction*, 225–26, although the oracle's obviously composite nature must factor here as well.

90. Blenkinsopp writes that "the destiny of Jerusalem-Zion" is "a central if not *the* central theme of the pre-exilic prophet [Isaiah of Jerusalem]" and that this theme becomes prominent again in so-called Trito-Isaiah (chapters 56–66) ("The Servant and the Servants in Isaiah," 174).

91. Besides the evidence presented earlier in this chapter, see also Bauckham, "Apocalypses," 160.

92. Luke's profound reliance on Isaiah is quite clear even on casual encounters with his Gospel. Not only does he quote Isaiah often and at length (Luke 3:4–6; 4:18–19; 8:10; 19:46; 22:37; Acts 7:49–50; 8:32–33; 13:34, 47; 28:25–27) and not only does he do so at key points in his writings (John's mission; Jesus's inaugural sermon; explanation of Jesus's parables; description of the JT; characterization of Jesus's crucifixion; criticism of the JT; characterization of Jesus's suffering; Paul's inaugural sermon [Davidic promise; worldwide salvation]; explanation of partial Jewish rejection), but Luke also alludes to Isaiah both at critical moments and quite frequently throughout Luke and Acts (Luke 2:25, 38; 7:22; 13:6–9; 23:29; Acts 1:8 [= Isa 49:6]; 3:8 [= Isa 35:6]; 8:26–39 [=Isa 56:3b]). Luke's profound and thoroughgoing reliance on Isaiah means that Luke does not simply read from a short, select list of Isaiah proof-texts—perhaps pre-assembled in existing Christian *testimonia*—but rather draws broadly from Isaiah, such that he is likely to have noticed and meditated over the portions of Isaiah that refer to the re-glorification of Jerusalem. See Mallen, *Reading and Transformation of Isaiah*; and Pao, *Isaianic New Exodus*, who emphasizes Luke's reliance on Isaiah's New Exodus theme in constructing

Jewish eschatological expectations regarding Isaiah[93] and indeed was himself disposed to reading Isaiah eschatologically—since he saw in the lives of Jesus and the early church the long-awaited fulfillment of Isaianic hopes. Thus Luke's Jesus inaugurates his own Galilean ministry with a reading of Isaiah followed by the affirmation: "Today this scripture is fulfilled before your eyes" (Luke 4:18–21). Thus Luke paints Jesus's ministry with further hues of Isaiah's envisioned release (Luke 7:22), such that "Jesus' gospel is essentially Isaiah's gospel."[94] Thus, too, does the salvation once envisioned by Isaiah come to startling fruition in the life of the early church.[95] Because of Luke's own profound reliance on and eschatological reading of Isaiah, the apparently failed vision of Jerusalem's restoration "in the last days" (Isa 2:1–4) would have had little less sting for Luke than for many of his Jewish contemporaries.

The Flavian propagandizing against the Jews and, by implication, their God and the reversed expectations regarding Jerusalem's glorification would have only exacerbated matters if Luke already felt the need to address potential or real doubts regarding God's fidelity in the face of the widespread Jewish rejection of Jesus, as Johnson claims. Luke thus likely faced something of a triple-headed monster, a hydra-esque threat to God's fidelity and power, and consequently to God's honor as well. While only two heads arose specifically from the Flavian conquest of Jerusalem, questions of God's fidelity to his people pair quite naturally with questions of God's fidelity to his city and house, since both questions ultimately arise out of concern that God should prove faithful to his own word, as given in Scripture.

Acts, though he probably overstates the case. Black argues that Luke intentionally pairs male and female disciples—as in Acts 1:13–14; 5:1–11, 14; cf. 2:17–18—in order to show the fulfillment of passages like Is 43:6–7; 49:22; 60:4 as part of his own theological agenda ("'Your Sons and Your Daughters,'" 193–206).

93. This general knowledge, which I have partially rehearsed above, comes through at a number of points in Luke's writings, including 2:38, the Kingship Parable (19:11–27), and Acts 1:6–8. Arguing that Luke knew and interacted with Jewish readings of Isaiah is Koet, "Isaiah in Luke-Acts," 97.

94. Evans, "From Gospel to Gospel," 671.

95. See Pao, *Isaianic New Exodus*; Mallen, *Reading and Transformation of Isaiah*.

Part 1: Introduction

CONCLUSION

The destruction of Jerusalem and its sacred Temple in 70 CE raised theodical angst to unprecedented levels among ancient Jews. Evidencing various levels of personal distress, pious Jews both agonized over the question of whether a faithful and just God could allow such (*4 Ezra* I–III; *Apoc. Ab.*27) and sought to reassert and reaffirm God's power (*2 Baruch*; *3 Baruch*; *Sib. Or.* 4, 5; *Apoc. Ab.* 29–31; possibly Josephus), in the process demonstrating the broad array of available theodical options—from deferred theodicy to the confident tandem of retribution theology and eschatological theodicy. In fact, in a single, rather remarkable work (*4 Ezra*), we see the author run this entire gamut!

Luke stands also within this world of theodical questions and concerns, as his writings show a concern for theodicy generally, especially on the side of questions regarding God's faithfulness (as in Luke's theodical parables), and for theodicy specifically with regard to the recent destruction of Jerusalem and its Temple. Likely standing behind Luke's interest in theodicy were several intersecting factors: the Flavian propaganda machine that trumpeted its conquest of Judea and, by implication, the comparative weakness of Israel's deity; eschatological hopes for Jerusalem and the Temple's restoration, most prominently expressed in Isaianic prophecy; as well as, finally, Luke's own concern to show the faithfulness of Israel's God in the face of widespread Jewish rejection of Christianity.

In order to look ahead, it is helpful first to look backwards momentarily. George Nickelsburg offers a helpful summary of *4 Ezra*, *2 Baruch*, and the *Apocalypse of Abraham* as raising two questions: "Why?" and "Whither?," the first speaking to the issues of theodicy raised by the razing of Jerusalem and the second dealing with "reconstruction," viz. "what will take the place of the temple as the people attempt to pick up the broken pieces of their life and their religion?"[96] Though he likely would not frame things in quite this manner, Luke also will offer answers to these questions, however obliquely so. I will explore these answers in the chapters that follow.

---

96. Nickelsburg, *Jewish Literature*, 270.

PART 2

The Jerusalem Temple in Luke's Gospel
A Reassessment

My study turns now to a reassessment of Jerusalem and its Temple in the Gospel of Luke, followed by a brief consideration of Acts (Appendix A). Undergirding the analysis that follows are recognition that Luke has composed a *narrative* as well as attention to the various contextual factors I have explored, especially Luke's rhetorical milieu, teeming with sundry methods and means of initiating subtle communication, and the widespread and multifold angst among believers in the Jewish God following the destruction of Jerusalem and the attendant Flavian celebration. In this latter regard, Luke, like his Jewish contemporaries, faces a theological, and in particular a theodical, problem, and so we should expect him to provide theological avenues for addressing the problem—as, I hope to show, indeed he does. Consideration of the narrative dynamics of Luke's Gospel has prompted me to break my analysis into chapters that correspond to the Gospel's typical dividing lines: Luke 1–2 (chapter 3), Luke 3:1—9:50 and 9:51—19:16/27 (chapter 4), and 19:17/28—24:53 (chapter 5).

In my treatment of individual portions of Luke's Gospel, I strive to be neither exhaustive nor even equitable: some scenes are simply more important for my thesis than others and will be treated as such. Luke 2:22–40—which serves, as I will argue, to set up so much of Luke's handling and presentation of Jerusalem and the Temple—is as an example of the former case, and I will give it appropriately disproportionate attention.[97] My deci-

---

97. A non-exhaustive list of the pericopes that, though discussed, receive short shrift

Part 2: The Jerusalem Temple in Luke's Gospel

sions regarding relative length and depth of examination should thus be taken neither as reflective of my assessment of a scene's relative importance within Luke's oeuvre nor as a virtual dismissal of its significance for my thesis. Each pericope that I discuss might well deserve monograph-length consideration even only for the purposes of my thesis.

The major strands of this Lukan tapestry painting the future, past, and late-first-century present of the Jerusalem Temple are, as I will attempt to show: 1) an interpretation of Jerusalem and its Temple in terms of the abandoned οἶκος of Shiloh (Luke 1–2; 13:35a); 2) a progressively realized eclipsing or transmuting of the JT's sacerdotal functions with the arrival (Luke 2:22–40, 41–52) then ministry (Luke 5:12–16; 17:11–19; 19:45–48) and finally death (23:45) of the Lord Jesus; 3) an accent on Jesus's status as a prophet, indeed the prophet *par excellence*,[98] and the fateful collision this entails with the city that is (in Luke's thought) the murderer of the prophets (11:49–51; 13:31–35; 19:41–44; 23:27–31); and 4) related to Luke's emphasis on Jesus as rejected prophet, an indictment of Jerusalem's leadership for resisting God's will, by rejecting the prophet and his message and through their general and persistent wickedness. These four strands Luke deftly weaves together, providing a theologically informed and theodically oriented answer to the riddle of Jerusalem's demise.

---

in the pages that follow would include Jesus's temptation (4:1–13), the Transfiguration (9:28–36), Jesus's first lamentation for Jerusalem (13:31–35, minus v. 35a), the Kingship Parable (19:11–27) along with the Entry scene (19:28–40), 2nd lamentation (19:41–44), Jesus's taking possession of the Temple (19:45–48), and the Parable of the Tenants (20:9–18).

98. Luke of course makes clear that Jesus is much more than merely a prophet, even the greatest of all prophets—and emphasizes this point even before the Lord's birth (see Luke 1:43).

3

The Jerusalem Temple in Luke 1–2

INTRODUCTION

From a narrative-critical perspective, how an author begins a work, quite simply, matters.[1] This is true not only of Luke's famous Prologue (Luke 1:1–4), but also of the Infancy Narratives that comprise (with a little semantic flexibility regarding 2:41–52) the rest of Luke 1–2.[2] Robert Tannehill has described these chapters as "previewing" or "foreshadowing" Luke's larger purposes in Luke and Acts, especially regarding the theme of salvation.[3] Such insights into the significance of narrative beginnings—already important for my discussion of methodology in chapter 1[4]—will also guide my discussion of Luke 1–2 below. Suffice it to say here that these scenes hold significance not only for the rest of Luke's Gospel (and perhaps beyond) in general but also specifically for the city and Temple that figure in them so prominently,[5] and so I consider them at some length below.

---

1. For this point, along with a host of interpretive strategies, see Parsons, *The Departure of Jesus*, 151–86. Also, Powell, "Toward a Narrative-Critical Understanding," 125–31; Resseguie, *Narrative Criticism*, 209–13.
2. Green makes this point quite well in his article "The Problem of a Beginning."
3. Tannehill, *Narrative Unity*, 1:20–21, 32.
4. Note esp. my reliance on Moessner, "The Meaning of Kathexēs," 1513–28.
5. As noted by Tyson, "The Birth Narratives," 113.

Part 2: The Jerusalem Temple in Luke's Gospel

THE SAMUEL CHILDHOOD THEME IN LUKE 1-2: STRUCTURE AND ECHOES

Luke 1-2 tells, with occasional and inspiring lyricism, the story of the announcements, births, and, with varying degrees of taciturnity, early lives of Jesus and John. Virtually all commentators see intentional parallelism, sometimes labeled as a "diptych," between Jesus and John as a dominant overarching structural feature of Luke 1-2, although the precise dividing lines are a point of debate.[6]

Before throwing my own hat into the arena of opinions on the matter, I will first consider Luke 2:22-52, the verses that concern me most in this study. This section of Luke's opening chapters participates in the Jesus-John parallelism and synkrisis[7] that is so prominent throughout Luke 1-2, although here, too, commentators are divided as to exact boundary lines. Some see 2:41-52 (or, less often, 2:40-52) as the parallel Jesus section to John's depiction in 1:80,[8] while probably the majority of commentators view 2:41-52 (typically along with short segments of Luke 1) as an intrusion without parallel in the John material that thus breaks up the Jesus-John diptych.[9] Another minority view maintains that the diptych is in fact broken by the entirety of 2:22-52, which thus form a final, Jesus-only capstone to the birth narratives.[10] I side with the majority of commentators in seeing 2:41-52 as the major break in the Jesus-John parallelism,

---

6. For a layout of some of the major options, see the very helpful charts in McComiskey, *Lukan Theology*, 15-17; and Brown, *Birth*, 248-49.

7. Throughout this section, I will refer to Luke's pairing of Jesus and John with the language of "parallelism," "diptych," and "synkrisis," for reasons both of style (in accordance with ancient rhetorical practice, modern ears generally find word variation more pleasant than repetitiveness) and of meaning: "parallelism" emphasizes the structural similarities, "diptych" reminds us of Luke's skillful artistry, and "synkrisis" speaks to Luke's intention—viz., to compare Jesus and John. In creating this Jesus-John synkrisis, Luke surely does not mean to denigrate John but rather employs a double-encomium in which one character is shown to be great through his superiority to another character worthy of great esteem; see Pseudo-Hermogenes, *Progymnasmata* 19 (Kennedy, 84).

8. See Talbert, *Literary Patterns*, 44; Green, *Luke*, 50. Thus there is no break in the parallelism, though Jesus remains superior to John, since he receives considerably greater narrative attention.

9. Martin Dibelius is an early proponent of this view; see also Laurentin, *Structure et Theologie*, 32-33; Brown, *Birth*, 251-52; Fitzmyer, *Luke*, 1:313-14; Nolland, *Luke*, 1:34-35; Bovon, *Das Evangelium*, 1:46-47; Wüthrich, *Le Magnificat*, 69.

10. Serrano, *Presentation*, 226-27. See also Gaechter and Lyonnet; cited by Brown, *Birth*, 249.

although I lean toward the minority reading of Serrano and others in one regard: I view the end of 2:22-40, viz. Anna's appearance (vv. 36-38), as a sort of break in the diptych in a manner that is proleptic of the more formal break brought about by 2:41-52. Anna's witness to Jesus (2:36-38) thus constitutes both a break in the Jesus-John parallelism and yet a strong marker in the Jesus-John synkrisis by clearly indicating Jesus's superiority, since he is witnessed to by a male/female pair, whereas John receives witness only from his father.

Overall, my preferred breakdown of the Jesus-John synkrisis for the whole of Luke 1-2 follows roughly the lines mapped out long ago by Dibelius[11]: John's annunciation (1:5-25) paired with Jesus's annunciation (1:26-38), with 1:39-56 as a sort of interlude (although it may also be taken as an extension of Jesus's annunciation)[12]; then, John's birth (1:57-66) paired with Jesus's birth (2:1-21), and John's vocation and growth (1:67-80) paired with Jesus's vocation and growth (2:22-40, with the dissenting vv. 36-38), with 2:41-52 as a second interlude, in some ways parallel to 1:39-56.[13]

Another important, and widely noted, feature of Luke 1-2 are the Septuagintal echoes that pervade this section of Luke's writings, both in terms of content and style. Among the most prominent of these echoes is the Samuel Childhood story. Besides their native, deep resonances in this portion of Luke (discussed below), making these echoes especially prominent (and increasingly so on multiple readings of Luke's Gospel and Acts) is the dearth of such echoes elsewhere in the Lukan corpus. Luke employs Samuel typology as a method of characterizing both John and Jesus in these early scenes.

---

11. See Nolland's (*Luke*, 1:20, 34-35) similarly high assessment of Dibelius's structure. Many commentators give a breakdown that is roughly equivalent to Dibelius's (e.g., Bovon, *Luke*, 1:29; Fitzmyer, *Luke*, 1:313-14).

12. Arguing for the entirety of 1:26-56 as parallel to 1:5-25 is Meynet, "Dieu Donne Son Nom à Jésus."

13. The "interludes" are parallel especially in terms of function: both demonstrate the superiority of Jesus over the estimable John. The first interlude (1:39-56) is the only scene in which Mary and Elizabeth (and thus the *in utero* Jesus and John) interact, and here Elizabeth's unborn son leaps for joy at the sound of the voice of the mother of his "Lord" (1:41, 43), spurring Mary's Magnificat. The second interlude (2:41-52) shows Jesus's superiority via his proximity to God (his "Father"), the remarkable wisdom he displays in the scene, and by the scene's breaking of the Jesus-John diptych such that Jesus corresponds more fully than John to the type of Samuel.

Part 2: The Jerusalem Temple in Luke's Gospel

The first reference to Samuel's childhood comes at the end of the initial description of Elizabeth and Zechariah in Luke 1:5–7.[14] Verse 7's mention that Elizabeth was "barren" of course recalls a number of OT parallels, including Abraham/Sarah and Samson's mother (Judg 13:2–7) as well as Hannah, mother of Samuel,[15] but the ideal audience, having had multiple exposures to Luke's Gospel, would take special notice of this as the beginning of the Samuel typology that produces so many deep resonances throughout Luke 1–2.[16] Long before John himself enters the scene, then, Luke's ideal audience has 1 Kgdms 1–4 firmly in sight (and within hearing). Given this initial framing, coupled with the prevalence of the Samuel childhood typology throughout Luke 1–2 (and thus in a sort of positive feedback loop), Luke's ideal audience would be invited to detect even faint echoes of Samuel's childhood in these early scenes and to interpret these as typological markers for John (and later, for Jesus).

This positive feedback loop suggests the propriety of a maximalist reading of Samuel resonances here, which seems to be in fact how many commentators read this scene.[17] Thus Evans hears an echo of Hannah's "words of devotion" in 1 Kgdms 1:11 and Mary's self-description as the "Lord's handmaid," Brown notes the similarity between the Nazirite command in Luke 1:15–16 and Hannah's Nazirite promise regarding Samuel in 1 Kgdms 1:9–15,[18] and Green hears an echo of Hannah's conception of Samuel (1 Kgdms 1:19–20) in the similar account regarding Elizabeth and

---

14. Other echoes may in fact occur earlier than v. 7, for Green (*Luke*, 73) notes that, while the language of remembrance is "absent from this immediate literary co-text [in Luke 1]," a remembrance motif is in fact present, especially given Zechariah's name ("God remembers"), thus echoing 1 Kgdms 1:11, 19–20. Nolland (*Luke*, 1:26) also notes a verbal similarity between the dative name introduction of Elkanah (1 Kgdms 1:1) and Zechariah (Luke 1:5).

15. This is widely noted in the commentaries—e.g., Evans, *Luke*, 24; Fitzmyer, *Luke*, 1:317. C. F. Evans characterizes Hannah as "the scriptural model" for the righteous yet barren (*St. Luke*, 146).

16. This need not mean the other echoes, of Abraham/Sarah and Samson's parents, would be drowned out. Here Litwak's notion of an "echo chamber" is helpful (*Echoes*, 31–32).

17. Alternately, those commentators who note a myriad of faint parallels between the stories may simply be participating in that learned "parallelomania" that some have lamented! Even if so, however, the parallels that they perceive, when valid and when plausibly audible to a first-century audience, work to support my typological reading.

18. Brown, *Birth*, 273.

John (Luke 1:24–25).[19] I find these commentators correct both in specifics and in their general maximalist approach to Samuel echoes here. There are likely a number of further echoes, albeit quite faint, that are generally overlooked by commentators.[20] The most important of these is an echo related to setting. Despite the fact that a number of commentators note parallels between the cultic contexts of each text,[21] few have paid adequate attention to the extent of these parallels. Especially important is the fact that in both narratives the indication by a divine representative (Eli and Gabriel) that an otherwise barren couple will have a child comes while the member of the couple who has been praying for a child is worshiping in a cultic setting—the Shiloh tabernacle in 1 Kingdoms, the Jerusalem temple in Luke. As I will argue, this pairing of the holy sites at Shiloh and Jerusalem is a subtle but important feature of Luke's use of Samuel typology in Luke 1–2.

Luke 1:26–38, the annunciation of Jesus, clearly parallels that of John (Luke 1:5–25)[22] and contains relatively few echoes of Samuel's childhood. In fact, Luke begins to craft Jesus's story with significant echoes of

---

19. Evans, "Prophecy and Polemic," 173; Brown, *Birth*, 273; Green, *Luke*, 81. Less persuasively, Laurentin connects Mary's visit to Elizabeth (Luke 1:39–44, 56) with David's attempt to return the ark to Jerusalem (2 Kgdms 6:2–11); Laurentin, reading these echoes typologically, likens Mary to the Ark of the Covenant, the means by which Jesus arrives in "son lieu," the Temple (*Structure et Théologie*, 79–81).

20. Further echoes that perhaps warrant mention include the following. First, both couples receive a child in response to prayer, though 1 Kingdoms and Luke work the prayers into the narrative very differently. Hannah's prayer receives explicit focus (1 Kgdms 1:10–11), while in Luke, Zechariah prays, and this fact is not narrated but is announced later as an accomplished fact by Gabriel (Luke 1:13). Another echo lies in the verbal confusion associated with both Hannah and Zechariah: the former is thought to be blabbering-drunk (1 Kgdms 1:13–14), while the latter, because of his unbelief, is rendered mute until his son's birth (Luke 1:18–20). St. Bonaventure (*Commentary*) notes further parallels: he links Elizabeth's statement that her reproach had been removed following the conception of John (Luke 1:25) to the reproach "Hannah" suffered from her rival in 1 Kgdms 1:6, among other parallels in the Jewish Scriptures (1:39); he also connects the people's recognition that Zechariah had seen a vision in Luke 1:22 with the people's acknowledgement of Samuel's status as faithful prophet in 1 Kgdms 3:20. He also likens Luke 1:24 to 1 Kgdms 1:20 (1:37) and hears an echo of 1 Kgdms 1:6 in Luke 1:25 (1:39).

21. Nolland (*Luke*, 1:28) notes that both texts report the relatively rare phenomenon of a revelation in the temple. C. F. Evans (*St. Luke*, 145) notes the decided emphasis on "temple piety" in both texts.

22. Indeed, many commentators rightly note a brief but strong synkritical positioning of Zechariah and Mary in these scenes, much to the latter's favor, especially regarding the aftermath to each parent to be's questioning of Gabriel in response to the promise of the seemingly impossible birth.

Part 2: The Jerusalem Temple in Luke's Gospel

Samuel's childhood only in the next scene, the first interlude (1:39–56), in which Elizabeth and Mary (and thus John and Jesus) meet.[23] The Samuel echoes in this scene are even more pronounced than in the scene of John's annunciation and thus warrant consideration at some length.

Virtually no scholar contests Luke's placing in Mary's song explicit allusions to Hannah's song (1 Kgdms 2:1–10).[24] Luke Johnson claims that Hannah's song supplies the framework for the Magnificat, although Luke fleshes out the song with allusions to various psalms.[25] Others see the Magnificat as at least "modeled" on Hannah's Song.[26] Interestingly, Litwak downplays the significance of Hannah's song, arguing that Pss 19, 85, 101, and others are "a far better, and more likely source" because 1 Kgdms 2:1–10 has few verbal agreements with the Magnificat.[27] He notes only a single verbal parallel (πεινοντες [1 Kgdms 2:5]/πειναντες [Luke 1:53]), along with the fact that 1 Kgdms 2:4–5, 7 parallels Luke 1:52–53 "in thought."[28] Numerous additional verbal parallels in fact exist. Not only do both songs begin with a formulaic καὶ εἶπεν (1 Kgdms 2:1; Luke 1:46), but there is also strong parallelism between the opening lines of the songs[29]:

Table 2: The Songs of Hannah and Mary

1 Kgds 2:1	Luke 1:46–47
Ἐστερεώθη ἡ καρδία μου εν Κυρίῳ, ὑψώθη κέρας μου ἐν Θεῷ μου, ἐπλατύνθη ἐπ' ἐχθρούς μου τὸ στόμα μου, εὐφάνθην ἐν σωτηρίᾳ σου.	Μεγαλύνει ἡ ψυχή μου τὸν κύριον, Καὶ ἠγαλλίασεν τὸ πνεῦμά μου ἐπὶ τῷ θεῷ τῷ σωτῆρί μου.

---

23. With skillful artistry, Luke sets up this meeting in the scene of Jesus's Annunciation, when Gabriel tells Mary of Elizabeth's unlikely pregnancy (1:36).

24. See, e.g., Brown, "The Annunciation to Mary," 256–57; Nolland, *Luke*, 1:68.

25. Johnson, *Luke*, 41.

26. See C. F. Evans, *St. Luke*, 172–73; Green, *Luke*, 101.

27. Litwak, *Echoes*, 108 n. 174. With this assessment, Farris agrees; he claims that the Magnificat contains a wealth of themes not found in Hannah's song, paralleling 1 Kgdms 2 only in the theme of divine reversal, which was nevertheless "a rather common motif in the ancient world" and which differs in the two hymns (*The Hymns*, 116).

28. Farris, *Hymns*, 108. C. F. Evans sees a reverse-ordered parallel between the Magnificat's themes of a) replenishing the hungry and b) depriving the rich, and 1 Kgdms 2:5–8 (*St. Luke*, 176).

29. St. Bonaventure (1:88) notes the parallel between these verses (*Commentary*, 94), though doubtless working without the benefit of a Greek text. He also likens Luke 1:52 to 1 Kgdms 2:7–8 (1:97).

These noteworthy similarities indicate that Luke here adopts both the style and the content of Hannah's song, while shortening it by deleting the middle two clauses, though perhaps adapting a phrase from the third to include in his second line (italicized above). The parallel structures are all the more striking in that Luke has retained virtually none of the original wording—and that even though in the very next verse (1:48) Luke quotes from an earlier prayer by Hannah almost verbatim. Thus Mary proclaims that God has "looked on the humble state of his servant" (ἐπέβλεψεν ἐπὶ τὴν ταπείνωσιν τῆς δούλης αὐτοῦ; Luke 1:48), which matches nearly verbatim Hanna's her earlier prayer requesting a son (ἐὰν ἐπιβλέπων ἐπιβλέψῃς ἐπὶ τὴν ταπείνωσιν τῆς δούλης σου; 1 Kgdms 1:11).[30] Further similarities appear as Mary's Song progresses: Hannah praises God's salvation (σωτηρία σου; 1 Kgdms 2:1), while Mary praises God her Savior (σωτῆρί μου; Luke 1:47); Hannah's song twice uses the verb ὑψόω (1 Kgdms 2:1, 10), which occurs also in the Magnificat (Luke 1:52), with a similar meaning in context to the first use in Hannah's song; both refer to the equalization of the poor/humble with rulers (δυνάστης) and their thrones (θρόνος; 1 Kgdms 2:8 vs. Luke 1:52); both use related words to refer to those with riches (πλουτίζω in 1 Kgdms 2:7 vs. πλουτέω in Luke 1:53). There are, then, a significant number of echoes between Hannah's Song (and earlier prayer) and the Magnificat, which collectively demonstrate the range of Luke's intertextuality, from direct verbal allusion to parallels that operate on the levels of theme and content[31] (as in John's annunciation).

After the Magnificat and a summary notice that Mary stayed three months with Elizabeth, Luke shifts to the next scene, John's birth (1:57–80). This scene, which finally sees the reversal of Zechariah's stilled tongue—and dramatically so in his prophecy of John's (1:68–79), but also Jesus's surpassing (1:76) greatness—again mutes echoes of Samuel's childhood. Indeed the old narrative of the great child-prophet at Shiloh is entirely lost to sight and sound[32] until the final verse of the scene (Luke 1:80), which

---

30. See Nolland, *Luke*, 1:68; Farris, *Hymn*, 24–25; C. F. Evans, *St. Luke*, 174; Brown, *Birth*, 358.

31. Green notes two prominent motifs in Mary's song—God as warrior and God as "the merciful God of the covenant," who lifts up the lowly, feeds the hungry, and remembers his promises (*Luke*, 102). These motifs both resonate roundly with Hannah's song. For potential echoes from other passages of Scripture, see Brown, *Birth*, 358–60.

32. Unless, that is, the "horn of salvation" in the house of David (v. 69) refers to 1 Kgdms 2:10. The expression matches the language and images of Ps 131:17 (LXX) more closely, however; see Strauss, *The Davidic Messiah*, 99–100, who also cites *Shemoneh*

Part 2: The Jerusalem Temple in Luke's Gospel

summarizes John's early career in clear imitation, though of style and content rather than wording, of the several summaries of Samuel's early life (1 Kgdms 2:21, 26; 3:19). This verse plays the important role of solidifying a typological connection between John and Samuel while also providing grounds for further comparison between John and Jesus, again to the latter's advantage, especially in its providing a clear structural link between John's and Jesus's early lives (cf. Luke 2:40, 52), in the telling of which Luke shows Jesus to be superior. Here, then, Luke employs structure and intertext as coordinated and interwoven components in achieving his rhetorical purposes.[33]

After leaving John in the desert (1:80), Luke narrates the birth of the Lord Jesus Christ (2:1–21; cf. v. 11). As in John's birth account, chords from Samuel's childhood find little resonance here.[34] They return emphatically in the scene that follows, however—and here we come to the focal passage(s) for this part of my study.

I will discuss this scene, the Presentation of Jesus in the Temple (Luke 2:22–40), at greater length below, so it is necessary here only to highlight the vivid Samuel childhood echoes that enliven this penultimate episode of Luke 1–2. Several reliable commentators descry a connection between Luke's upright Simeon and 1 Kingdom's Eli, especially because both are (emphatically) old men who, in the house of God, bless the parents of the child of promise being then dedicated to God (1 Kgdms 2:20; Luke 2:28).[35] An even stronger, and complementary, connection exists between the prophetess Anna, who appears in Luke 2:36–38, and Samuel's mother, Hannah.[36] Not only do they share identical Greek names (a fact curiously overlooked by a number of commentators[37]), but Luke composes his Anna

---

Esreh 15 and Sir 15:12 as "striking parallels" to Luke 1:69.

33. Among these purposes are, again, establishing a typological connection between both Samuel and John and Samuel and Jesus while also creating a double-encomiastic synkrisis of Jesus and John.

34. The likeliest echo is the appearance of κατάλυμα in Luke 2:7 (cf. 1 Kgdms 1:18); see C. F. Evans, *St. Luke*, 200.

35. E.g., Brown, *Birth*, 450; Fitzmyer, *Luke*, 1:429; C. A. Evans, *Luke*, 40; also, Danker, *Jesus and the New Age*, 62. Bock's diminution of Samuel echoes here proves slightly tone-deaf, in my estimation (*Proclamation from Prophecy and Pattern*, 84–85).

36. Brown ("Presentation," 5–6) notes that Simeon/Anna follow Zechariah/Elizabeth in their paralleling Eli/Hannah.

37. Among the scholars who note this connection are C. A. Evans, *Luke*, 46; Danker, *Jesus and the New Age*, 70; Brown, "Presentation," 2–3, 5–6, passim; Marshall, *Luke*, 123. Evans cites Lach, pp. 32–33, as noting that Hannah was considered to be a prophetess in

with many of the thematic chords that sound in the Ἅννα of 1 Kingdoms. Indeed, both women worship, fast, and pray in the House of God (cf. 1 Kgdms 1:7–8, 10–13, 16), with overtones of grief.[38] After the story of Jesus's presentation, Luke gives a summary of Jesus's upbringing (Luke 2:40) that echoes both that of John (1:80) and those of Samuel in 1 Kingdoms. Once again, Luke reflects upon the story of Samuel's childhood, though by copying themes and concepts rather than directly borrowing vocabulary, as this table makes clear[39]:

Table 3: "Anna" in 1 Kingdoms and Luke

Aspect	Ἅννα (1 Kgdms 1)	Ἅννα (Luke 2:37)
Fasted	οὐκ ἤσθιεν (1:7; cf 1:18)	νηστείαις
Prayed	προσηύξατο (1:10) ηὔξατο εὐχὴν (1:11) προσευχομένη (1:12) αἴτημά (1:17)	δεήσεσιν
Worshiped	(προσκυνεῖν—1:3)[A]	λατρεύουσα
In Temple	οἶκον Κυρίου (1:7) ναοῦ Κυρίου (1:9)	ἱεροῦ
Grief	(various)	(implied)

A This word is used for Elkanah, Ἅννα's husband, though the context implies the same for Elkanah's wives.

In the last episode of Luke 1–2, Jesus's parents, after journeying to the JT to worship, mistakenly leave Jesus behind (2:41–52). Here Luke again draws on the Samuel childhood story thematically but with little verbal repetition: in 1 Kgdms 2:11, 18–21, as in Luke 2:41–51 the parents leave behind their oldest son at the Lord's Temple, where he ministers,[40] though obvious differences adhere (the intentionality of leaving the child; the nature

---

Jewish traditions, specifically b. *Megilla* 14a (*Luke*, 46).

38. For a discussion of grief as it pertains to Luke's Ἅννα, see Green, *Luke*, 151. The grief of Samuel's Ἅννα is apparent throughout 1 Kgdms 1:6–16.

39. Another similarity that might profitably be added to the list is the absence of the women's husbands. Luke explicitly portrays his Ἅννα as a widow (i.e., a woman who no longer has a husband), while Samuel's Ἅννα suffers the dubious and rivalry-plagued fate of being married to a polygamist, whose absence is often highlighted in the text (cf. 1 Kgdms 1:9–18, 21–23).

40. Though Luke does not state Jesus's ministry, vv. 49–50 clearly imply that Jesus's behavior here is linked to his larger vocation, even if not clearly understood by his parents.

Part 2: The Jerusalem Temple in Luke's Gospel

of the service; etc). Luke ends the account with a summary statement of Jesus's growth (2:52) that especially parallels that of Samuel in 1 Kgdms 2:26.[41] Here, parallel phrases are aligned (the other summaries are given for comparison):

Table 4: Childhood Summaries

1 Kingdoms	Luke
Καὶ τὸ παιδάριον Σαμουὴλ ἐπορεύετο, καὶ ἐμεγαλύνετο καὶ ἀγαθὸν καὶ μετὰ Κυρίου καὶ μετὰ ἀνθρώπων. (2:26)	Καὶ Ἰεσοῦς προέκοπτεν ἐν τῇ σοφίᾳ καὶ ἡλικίᾳ καῖ χάριτι παρὰ θεῷ καὶ ἀνθρώποις. (2:52)
Καὶ ἐμεγαλύνθη τὸ παιδάριον Σαμουὴλ ἐνώπιον Κυρίου. (2:21) Καὶ ἐμεγαλύνθη Σαμουὴλ, καὶ ἦν Κύριος μετ' αὐτοῦ. (3:19)	Τὸ δὲ παιδίον ηὔξανεν καὶ ἐκραταιοῦτο πνεύματι. (1:80) Τὸ δὲ παιδίον ηὔξανεν καὶ ἐκραταιοῦτο πληρούμενον σοφίᾳ. (2:40)

Also to be noted is Luke's initial framing comment that Jesus's parents would go annually to the Temple to worship (2:41)—a fact frequently highlighted regarding Samuel's parents also (1 Kgdms 1:3, 21; 2:18). Bonaventure, in his commentary on Luke, looks back here on 1 Kgdms 2:18 and imagines Samuel to have been 12 years old when he began ministering before the Lord (2.99). Fitzmyer also notes that Jesus's age (12) matches that of Samuel at the start of his prophetic ministry according to the tradition reported by Josephus (*Ant.* 5.10), but does not observe that this tradition (of which Luke is probably aware) plays into Luke's painting of Jesus and John in terms of Samuel.[42] Though faint, these echoes grow more audible when heard against the stronger chords of Samuel's childhood that sound throughout Luke 1–2. Moreover, they gain deeper resonance in light of the fact that there are very few stories in the LXX relating a boy's presence in the Temple of God. Thus, with ears previously attuned to Samuel's story and with virtually no interference from competing scores, ideal readers/auditors can easily detect echoes of Samuel's childhood here.

---

41. Although many modern commentators fail to draw a parallel between these scenes (but see Craddock, *Luke*, 42), at least one older commentator made this connection: St. Bonaventure links Jesus's being left at the temple here to Elkanah and Avva's leaving Samuel (*Commentary*, 2.94).

42. Fitzmyer, *Luke*, 1:440–41, n. 42.

From the fact that Luke recalls the childhood story of Samuel in narrating various parts of the announcements, birth, and upbringings of both John and Jesus, some commentators infer that Luke does not intend, and presumably does not invite, identification of these characters with Samuel in any sort of typological way.[43] Thus Raymond Brown claims, with the shift of the Samuel references from John in Luke 1 to Jesus in Luke 2 particularly in focus: "Luke's method is not one of identifying figures in the infancy narratives with OT characters; rather he uses the pigments taken from OT narratives to color in the infancy narrative."[44] In light of the burgeoning recognition of, and considerable insights produced by, typological identification of Jesus with OT characters, particularly other prophets, elsewhere in Luke's Gospel (see chapter 1), this conclusion may be premature.[45] In fact, Luke's shift of Samuel echoes from John to Jesus serves his broader synkritical purposes in Luke 1–2: it not only reinforces the structural parallels between their announcements, births, and upbringings (e.g., 1:80 and 2:40)—the basis of any comparison between the two—but also suggests Jesus's superiority via his more thoroughly attaining to the pattern of Samuel, especially with the narration of the precocious beginnings of his ministry in the Temple (2:41–52), which parallels the inception of Samuel's pro-

---

43. There is no need to maintain—as I do not—that Luke's typological use of Samuel for John and Jesus necessitates positing a typological relationship of equal communicative and symbolic weight between each of the minor characters in Luke's story who corresponds to a minor character from Samuel's childhood. Very often in Luke's writings, the minor characters simply help establish the typological connection between major characters, as with Anna/Hannah, Zechariah/Eli, Simeon/Eli, etc. Perhaps importantly, Luke does at times employ minor characters to correspond typologically to people groups, especially people groups that are significantly impacted by the eschatological horizon of Jesus's ministry, as he does with the Gentiles/Naaman and hometown residents/Israelites in the Jesus/Elijah-Elisha typology of Luke 4:25–27. Along these lines, C. A. Evans argues that Luke employs echoes of Elijah-Elisha (along with Deuteronomy) especially in order to treat the theme of election and thus to clarify who are included and excluded from the kingdom, often with surprising reversals of fortune ("The Elijah/Elisha Narratives," 75–83).

44. Brown, *Birth*, 451.

45. The fact that Luke casts both John and Jesus as latter-day Elijahs, after all, does not bar most interpreters from taking this dual characterization as typological, and surely Luke does intend a typological connection (cf. Luke 4:24–27 and 9:51 for Jesus; 7:24–28 for John). Even though there are divergent Elijah traditions in scripture, as argued by Croatto ("Jesus, Prophet," 454–58) and even if Luke mutes aspects of Mark's typological portrayal of John as Elijah (see Fitzmyer, *Luke*, 1:215), still this does not vitiate the point that Luke presents both John and Jesus after the pattern of a single prophet and yet intends a typological association between the prophet and both characters in his Gospel.

phetic vocation in the house of God at Shiloh (1 Kgdms 3:1–19)—all while John remains in the desert (1:80, albeit in accord with its own prophetic precedence). Just as Luke shows Jesus's superiority through the parallel yet disproportionate structure of Luke 1–2,[46] so he shows Jesus's superiority by the parallel yet disproportionate comparisons with Samuel. When read with narrative and typological sensitivity, then, the dominant Jesus-John parallelism tracks with and illuminates the function of the pervasive Samuel childhood echoes in Luke 1–2, which on the one hand pair Jesus and John but on the other show Jesus to be superior. So the shift of Samuel echoes from John (Luke 1) to Jesus (Luke 2) does not argue against, but rather strongly indicates, the appropriateness of a typological reading of the Samuel echoes in Luke 1–2 for both John and Jesus.

Moreover, and once again, one need not define (as Litwak does) typological readings as comprehensive correspondence between intertextually linked characters (such as John and Samuel, or Jesus and Samuel)—which is surely impossible for Luke 1–2—but rather may and, in light of my analysis, *should* define typology only as a comparison on certain levels (see chapter 1). If this introduces an ambiguity into interpretation that some find distasteful, I suggest that the ambiguity is a product not of sloppy categories but rather of the multivalence of Luke's own writings and, in particular, of his use of the Jewish Scriptures. This more chastened (and useful) definition of typological use of OT characters means that we must think not in terms of a strict dichotomy between mere aesthetic use of OT prototypes and, on the other side, comprehensive typologies in which characters correspond at every imaginable point, but rather of a spectrum, with varying modulations depending on the case, between these untenable extremes.

When understood typologically, Luke's recalling of Samuel childhood in depicting the births and early lives of Jesus and John have, in my judgment, three primary functions. First, they likely alert the audience to the momentous shift in salvation history brought about by the arrival of John and Jesus—hence, Luke's using them at the start of his Gospel. Luke himself seems to understand and elsewhere casts Samuel as a pivotal figure, the first of the prophets after Moses, who, not himself being the prophet like Moses, nevertheless points to the days of that prophet, Jesus himself (see Acts 3:22–26, esp. v. 24). This function corresponds to the casting of both

---

46. See Serrano, *Presentation*, 224n60: "Jesus' superiority over John is reflected in the structure itself"; Green, *Theology*, 55: "Without disparaging the eschatological significance of John, then, Luke communicates in this imbalanced set of parallels [in Luke 1–2] the superiority of Jesus." Cf. Kingsbury, *Conflict*, 38–39.

Jesus and John—who together signal the shift in salvation history, John as forerunner, Jesus as Messiah—with notes from Samuel's early years.[47] Yet Jesus is greater than John, as Luke makes abundantly clear, and this emphasis points to the second primary function of the Samuel Childhood Typology.[48] Indeed, this typology also begins to reveal the identity of Jesus, an identity that partially consists of his being like yet even greater than the prophets of old, yes, even Moses himself, and also begins to reveal the implications this supra-Mosaic identity has for God's people.[49] I will continue to explore this function below, after which I will disclose what I consider to be the final major function of this Samuel typology.

JESUS PRESENTED IN THE TEMPLE (LUKE 2:22-40)

It is significant that these Samuel childhood echoes reach something of a crescendo in Luke 2:22–52 (now considered more fully), for here Luke begins to distance Jesus from John the Baptist—as seen in the architectonics of the passage, viz. the breaking of the John/Jesus diptych, realized in 2:41–52 but foreshadowed in 2:36–38—and thus begins to emphasize Jesus's unique identity. This presentation of Jesus in the Temple is both a presentation of Jesus before God and a presentation of Jesus to the audience.[50] Here, then, structure (the early cracks in the diptych) and content (the presentation of Jesus in the Temple) correspond and reinforce one another, each reveal-

---

47. The Samuel echoes may also indicate John and Jesus as ushering in a new era of prophecy, especially in light of texts like 1 Macc 4:46 and 9:27, and also Jer 15:1 and Ps 99:6, where Samuel is paired with Moses, the first and greatest prophet (see Johnson, *Luke*, 18–19; cf. Acts 3:22–23). Militating against this reading, however, are the many other characters in Luke 1–2 who prophesy, prior to John's and Jesus's ministries, especially Simeon (2:26, 34–35; but see also the discussion of Zechariah in Vanhoye, "L'Interete de Luc"), though each of these characters enjoys some connection to the two boys.

48. I do not claim that these echoes are strictly limited to the three functions that I specify above, although I do view these as the primary functions. They also of course serve to cast Luke's story as a continuation of sacred history, as Brawley, Green, and Litwak have noted, but that function is very plausibly subsumed under the more specific functions I am highlighting. Thus I find myself thinking more along the lines of Kingsbury, who notes that Luke composes these scenes with abundant OT "atmosphere" for the purpose of showing that God is "undertaking a *new* action in the history of salvation" (*Conflict*, 37; emphasis added).

49. On Jesus as the prophet like Moses, see Fitzmyer, *Luke*, 1:213.

50. See Serrano, *Presentation*. Brown also views the sacrificial rationale as secondary to the real emphases of the scene (*Birth*, 450–51; "Presentation," 2–3, 5–6).

Part 2: The Jerusalem Temple in Luke's Gospel

ing and punctuating Jesus's unique identity. The Samuel childhood echoes thus constitute a significant dynamic at play in Luke 2:22–40[51] (and also 2:41–52), and I will discuss them more fully after considering other important dynamics in this passage.

Serrano rightly notes that Luke 2:22–39/40 begins with one plot arch but then shifts noticeably to another. In Serrano's language, this scene begins with a "plot of resolution," in which Jesus must receive purification at the JT in accordance with the Law, but shifts, upon the introduction of Simeon in v. 25, into a "plot of revelation," in which Jesus's identity is revealed.[52] Thus the original driving force of the scene—the need for purification—takes a decided backseat to the revelations made about Jesus by Simeon and Anna (vv. 25–38), only finding resolution, and summarily so, in v. 39's notice that they finished everything required by the "Law of the Lord." And indeed, within the flow of the narrative, Simeon's Spirit-guided revelation (v. 27) serves as a sort of intervention that actually interrupts Mary and Joseph's fulfillment of the legal customs: Upon the family's entrance into the JT to fulfill their sacerdotal obligations (v. 27), Simeon intercepts the family, simply taking Jesus into his arms (v. 28), and offers his song of praise and promise, the *Nunc Dimittis* (vv. 29–32).

Two features of Simeon's song are of particular importance for my study. First of all, it is the first clear mention in Luke's writings of the message, so important within Lukan theology, that Jesus's arrival means salvation for all peoples (vv. 31–32). In fact, the universality of Simeon's *Nunc Dimittis* (ὃ ἡτοίμασας κατὰ πρόσωπον πάντων τῶν λαῶν, φῶς εἰς ἀποκάλυψιν ἐθνῶν καὶ δόξαν λαοῦ σου Ἰσραήλ; vv. 31–32) stands in contrast with the relatively ethnocentristic tenor of Zechariah's *Benedictus* (Luke 1:67–79). The contrast is probably not coincidental, given that Simeon's Song parallels that of Zechariah's within the Jesus-John diptych of Luke 1–2[53] and that in the figure of Simeon Luke recalls another priest also, now from sacred history, Eli.[54] Also important to note is the strong Isaianic language of the *Nunc Dimittis*, which here serves to characterize Jesus's Messianic vocation[55] and

---

51. Note that Brown (*Birth*, 450) explains Luke's apparent confusion in 2:22–24 regarding the two separate rites, which he threatens to conflate into one, as largely a result of his desire to present the baby Jesus at Jerusalem in parallel to the presentation of the baby Samuel at Shiloh.

52. Serrano, *Presentation*, 202–7.

53. E.g., Brown, *Birth*, 443.

54. Brown, "Presentation," 5–6.

55. Croatto ("Jesus, Prophet") notes that "the soteriological function of this 'Messiah'

the appearance of which is hardly surprising given Luke's heavy reliance on Isaiah elsewhere for articulating the universality of salvation.

Curious on multiple grounds is what follows Simeon's Song. After, and perhaps in response to, Mary and Joseph's understandable bewilderment (v. 33), Simeon blesses the family and then addresses Mary somewhat ominously: Ἰδοὺ οὗτος κεῖται εἰς πτῶσιν καὶ ἀνάστασιν πολλῶν ἐν Ἰσαρὴλ καὶ εἰς σημεῖον ἀντιλεγόμενον—καὶ σοῦ [δὲ] αὐτῆς τὴν ψυχὴν διελεύσεται ῥομφαία—ὅπως ἂν ἀποκαλυφθῶσιν ἐκ πολλῶν καρδιῶν διαλογισμοί (vv. 34b–35). Croatto, probably rightly, sees this as a shift from the emphasis on Jesus's Messianic vocation in the *Nunc Dimittis* back to his role as "controversial prophet."[56] Among the traditional *crux interpreta* for this passage are the meaning of "the rising and falling of many in Israel" (πτῶσιν καὶ ἀνάστασιν πολλῶν ἐν Ἰσαρὴλ), as well as the proper interpretation of the piercing of Mary's heart. Perhaps the least unsatisfactory interpretation of the latter is that this is the sword of division that separates those who rise from those who fall and that demonstrates the reality that the demands of God on Jesus as divine Father supersede even those of his earthly family,[57] sometimes to painful effect. Following Brown, I favor this reading especially in light of its applicability to the scene that immediately follows in Luke 2:41–52. This anticipated division within Jesus's own family mirrors the division within all Israel his life and vocation will bring about[58]; this seems to be the general referent of the "rising and falling," as well as "the sign that will be opposed" (σημεῖον ἀντιλεγόμενον; v. 34). Whether one can determine more specific referents of this rising and falling (for there are "many") is another question.

[i.e., in the *Nunc Dimittis*] is the same as that which describes Yahweh's Servant in Isa 42:1–7 and 49:1–9a" (452).

56. Croatto, "Jesus, Prophet," 452. Helpful for understanding the relationship between the two oracles of Simeon is the comment by Koet that, with the second oracle, Mary "wird gewarnt, dass der angesagte Segen nur unter Schmerzen Wirklichkeit werden kann" ("Simeons Worte," 1558).

57. See Brown, *Birth*, 463–64; Brown sees the Lord's discriminating sword of judgment from Ezek 14:17 as the relevant intertext here, as do Fitzmyer, *Luke*, 1:429–30; and Danker, *Jesus and the New Age*, 69. Serrano's objection to this reading has merit but is not decisive (*Presentation*, 188n140).

58. In this regard, Luke is following his usual pattern of letting sayings material interpret the narrative for his readers/auditors; see Johnson, "Kingship Parable," 142. Simeon's prophecy of division will resound again and again in the narrative of Luke's Gospel and as such is thematically foundational for Luke's Gospel.

Part 2: The Jerusalem Temple in Luke's Gospel

The language of rising and falling of course conjures up the theme of divine reversal so prevalent in Luke's Gospel (e.g., 6:20–26), and already featured in Mary's Magnificat (1:48, 51–53), and so Luke probably intends his audience to hear at least a general reference to, and indeed a somewhat paradigmatic statement of, this favorite theme. Still, the context of the phrase implies further meaning. First, it comes immediately after the decidedly more positive *Nunc Dimittis* announcing Jesus's crucial role in bringing salvation to all. Second, the framing of the "rising and falling" as primarily intra-national in scope,[59] the note of opposition in v. 34, and the fact that Mary, who has already extolled God's penchant for reversing the fortunes of low and proud alike, will not herself emerge unscathed in this "rising and falling," suggest a meaning more than the straight-forward divine reversal featured elsewhere in Luke's Gospel. Rather, the rising and falling seems to center around divided responses within Israel to Jesus's (universal) mission. Note also that πτῶσις is commonly used in the LXX to refer to God's judgment, sometimes on God's own people.[60]

Auditors familiar with Luke's Gospel (or other early Christian interpretations of Jesus's death, for that matter) will already know that among those who oppose Jesus most vigorously are the Jewish authorities in Jerusalem, most of whom had a power base centered around the Temple itself.[61] Auditors hearing Luke's Gospel post-70 CE will know that these same opponents subsequently suffered, as a collective, a most decisive downfall. That Luke's narrative at this moment places the baby Jesus at the very epicenter of that downfall is not coincidental. Rather, it is likely that he intentionally places, with a keen sense of irony, this prophecy of rising and falling precisely at the location where Jesus's fiercest and most lethal opponents will finally (the auditor knows) meet their collective doom.[62]

59. Though some suggest a scope of division beyond Israel itself (e.g., Tannehill, *Narrative Unity*, 1:42–43), I side with those who view the division as exclusively or at least primarily intra-national (e.g., Johnson, *Luke*, 57; Marshall, *Luke*, 122; Fitzmyer, *Luke*, 1:422).

60. πτῶσις as term of judgment: Isa 17:1; Ezek 26:15, 18; 27:27; 31:13, 16; 32:10; Nah 3:3; Zech 14:12, 15, 18 LXX. πτῶσις with reference to judgment on God's people: Isa 51:17, 22; Jer 6:15 LXX.

61. This is of course a special emphasis in Luke's Gospel, as I will discuss later.

62. As his Gospel unfolds, Luke employs διαλογισμός and its related forms with reference to the Jewish leaders' opposition to Jesus (5:21–22; 6:8), most trenchantly in the Parable of the Vineyard (20:14), and also with reference to his own disciples (9:46–47; 24:38); Tannehill, *Narrative Unity*, 1:43–44. See also the Parable of the Foolish Rich Man, in which God exposes the greedy man's vain reasoning (12:17).

This interpretation is strengthened, I believe—and indeed elaborated—by the appearance of an additional, subtle reference to the Samuel Childhood story, one not yet noted and one that points to the final function of this Samuel typology. Perhaps because of a myopic focus on verbal allusions, commentators often overlook the narrative of Samuel's childhood itself, which is, in its telling, thoroughly interwoven with another quite vivid story: the downfall of the house of Eli. Indeed, so interwoven are the two stories that the first prophetic act of the boy Samuel is to foretell doom for Eli's house (1 Kgdms 3:11–15). From Hannah's song of praise (1 Kgdms 2:1–10), after a summary of Samuel's ministry (2:11), the text moves immediately to the sordid tale of Eli's sons (2:12–17), back to Samuel's ministry (2:18–21), then to Eli's rebuke of his wicked sons (2:22–25)—interrupted by a summary of Samuel's childhood (2:26)—and the prophecy of doom on Eli's house (2:27–36), on to Samuel's advancing ministry (3:1—4:1), the first act of which is to prophesy doom on the house of Eli, and concluding with the fulfillment of that prophecy with Eli and his sons all dying in a single day (4:2–18). Thus the two stories comprise a virtual fugue in the text of 1 Kingdoms—a fact surely not lost on Luke and certainly accessible to Luke's ideal audience—and Luke, rather remarkably, alludes to every single section of narrative depicting Samuel's rise in 1 Kingdoms.[63]

Attention to these facts makes audible an additional, though faint, echo from the early pages of 1 Kingdoms in this section of Luke 2.[64] Simeon's dour prophecy of "rising and falling" (πτῶσιν καὶ ἀνάστασιν) employs language common to the LXX. The verb forms of these nouns occur in close proximity as part of the announcement by the anonymous man of God of the imminent demise of Eli's house: καὶ πᾶς περισσεύων οἴκου σου

---

63. Luke alludes to 1 Kgdms 2:1–10 (and earlier) in the Magnificat and elsewhere (see above); 2:11 in the various growth summaries of John and Jesus (Luke 1:80; 2:40, 52); 2:19 in Luke 2:41–52; 2:21 and 2:26 again in the growth summaries; and 3:1—4:1 in Luke 2:41–52.

64. As Brawley sagely observes: "explicit allusions are often signals for readers to listen for more expansive voices from the context of the explicit allusions," and "[o]vert references to scripture prompt readers who know the Septuagint to consider covert allusions to the larger context of scripture" (*Text to Text*, 5, 124). Also helpful is the notion of "internarrativity," as elaborated by Jonathan Huddleston: "But internarratival allusion [in distinction from intertextuality] sends interpreters back, not to the source text, but to the source *story*, with a different set of questions: What is the overall shape of the wider narrative, beyond the alluded-to narrative—and how does this narrative profile influence the alluding text?" ("What Would Elijah and Elisha Do?," 267). I would not characterize Luke's appeal to the story of the fall of the house of Eli as internarrativity, however—for he does, as I will show, provide numerous actual verbal links in 2:33–35.

Part 2: The Jerusalem Temple in Luke's Gospel

πεσοῦνται ἐν ῥομφαίᾳ ἀνδρῶν. . . . καὶ ἀναστήσω ἐμαυτῷ ἱερέα πιστόν (1 Kgdms 2:33b–35a).[65] Given the shift of forms (from the LXX's verb to Luke's noun), as well as the frequent use of the nominal and verbal forms of these terms in the LXX,[66] most auditors could hardly be expected, despite the abundance of Samuel echoes throughout this and its surrounding sections, to hear resonances of the prophecy against Eli's house on the basis of these two words alone.

Amplifying these echoes, however, are four supporting chords. First is Luke's strange use of the archaic ῥομφαία ("sword") in 2:35, outside of Revelation used only here in the NT. By verbal cue, this curiously archaic word would quite intentionally transport Luke's ideal audience once more into the world of Israel's Scripture. Among the swirling chorus of echoes such language might conjure is another equally dour prophecy, that of 1 Kgdms 2, in which the man of God prophesies that Eli's house will fall (πεσοῦνται) by the sword (ῥομφαία) of men (v. 33).[67] Strengthening this impression, secondly, in 1 Kgdms 2:35 the anonymous prophet's pronouncement takes what would be for an early Christian audience a strongly christological turn: καὶ ἀναστήσω ἐμαυτῷ ἱερέα πιστόν, ὃς πάντα τὰ ἐν τῇ καρδίᾳ μου καὶ τὰ ἐν τῇ ψυχῇ μου ποιήσει· καὶ οἰκοδομήσω αὐτῷ οἶκον πιστόν, καὶ διελεύσεται ἐνώπιον χριστοῦ μου πάσας τὰς ἡμέρας (2:35).[68] Given the obviously christological nature of Simeon's pronouncement, as well as its location in the JT, the promise of a faithful house and the ambiguous use

---

65. πίπτω occurs at the end of v. 33; ἀνίστημι, at the start of v. 35—a span of twenty-seven words, including ῥομφαία and σημεῖον between them. Though it is perhaps more a matter of modern scholasticism than exegetical relevance, there may be something to the fact that the words for "fall" and "rise," whether in nominal or verbal form, occur in close proximity with ῥομφαία infrequently in traditional LXX text forms and never more closely together than here: Judg 4:14–16 (eighty-one words); 7:13–15 (fifty-seven words); 1 Kgdms 17:47–49 (sixty-three words); 3 Kgdms 1:50–52 (fifty-one words); Amos 9:10–11 (twenty-nine words); Jud 8:18–19 (forty-five words); cf. Josh 6:15–21; 1 Kgdms 21:9–14. Only in 1 Kgdms 2:33–35 do ῥομφαία, σημεῖον, and "rise" and "fall" occur together in close proximity.

66. C.F. Evans claims that these verbs are seldom paired together in the LXX (*St. Luke*, 218), but their pairing is hardly rare (see, e.g., Deut 22:4; Josh 7:10; 2 Kgdms 22:39; Isa 51:17; Amos 9:11; etc.).

67. To "fall" (πίπτω) by the "sword" (ῥομφαία) is a common idiom in the LXX (e.g., Judg 4:16; 2 Kgdms 3:29; Jer 51:12; Ezek 5:12; 6:11, 12; 11:10; 17:21; 24:21; 25:13; Hosea 7:16; Amos 7:17; 1 Macc 4:15; 7:38, 46) and occurs literally in 1 Kgdms 31:4–5.

68. This passage may be recalled, with reference to Jesus, in Heb 2:17. Albeit centuries later, the early Church Fathers interpreted the passage christologically (e.g., Eusebius, *Dem. ev.* 4.16.44–45; Didymus, *Comm. Zach.* 1.243.5; Hippolytus, *Comm. Dan.* 4.30.9).

of χριστός provide a strong connection with Simeon's words. Thirdly, Luke invites an informed audience to hear an echo of the downfall of the Elide house through his suggestive use of πτῶσις, since this downfall reached its climax with the literal and quite memorable neck-breaking fall of Eli himself[69]—again narrated with the verb πίπτω (1 Kgdms 4:18). Solidifying the connection, finally, is the prophet's promise that Eli will receive the sign (σημεῖον) of the death of his two wicked sons (1 Kgdms 2:34) and the use of διελεύσεται in 1 Kgdms 2:35. These chords, faint in themselves, play together in harmony to conjure forth resonances of the prophecy against Eli's house.[70]

In sum, with allowances for noun-to-verb shifts in two instances, five words, including the quite rare ῥομφαία, appear in close succession in both Simeon's ominous words and the prophecy of Eli's ruin in 1 Kgdms 2:33–36; the latter passage ends with a promise bearing strong christological resonances (vv. 35–36), and Luke's use of "rising and falling" finds vivid illustration in the particular method of Eli's demise. In light of the prominence of Samuel echoes in close proximity to Simeon's prophecy in Luke 2:34–35 and the interweaving of the Samuel-rise and Eli-fall narratives in 1 Kingdoms, Luke's ideal audience could be expected to detect the thematic and verbal links between Simeon's words and 1 Kgdms 2:33–35 and so draw a connection between Eli's rejected house and the Jerusalem priesthood of Jesus's day.

Table 5: Echoes of Judgment

1 Kgdms 2:33b–35	Luke 2:34b–35
καὶ πᾶς περισσεύων οἴκου σου πεσοῦνται ἐν ῥομφαίᾳ ἀνδρῶν. καὶ τοῦτό σοι τὸ σημεῖον, ὃ ἥξει ἐπὶ τοὺς δύο υἱούς σου τούτους Οφνι καὶ Φινεες· ἐν ἡμέρᾳ μιᾷ ἀποθανοῦνται ἀμφότεροι. καὶ ἀναστήσω ἐμαυτῷ ἱερέα πιστόν, ὃς πάντα τὰ ἐν τῇ καρδίᾳ μου καὶ τὰ ἐν τῇ ψυχῇ μου ποιήσει· καὶ οἰκοδομήσω αὐτῷ οἶκον πιστόν, καὶ διελεύσεται ἐνώπιον χριστοῦ μου πάσας τὰς ἡμέρας.	ἰδοὺ οὗτος κεῖται εἰς πτῶσιν καὶ ἀνάστασιν πολλῶν ἐν τῷ Ἰσραὴλ καὶ εἰς σημεῖον ἀντιλεγόμενον—καὶ σοῦ δὲ αὐτῆς τὴν ψυχὴν διελεύσεται ῥομφαία—ὅπως ἂν ἀποκαλυφθῶσιν ἐκ πολλῶν καρδιῶν διαλογισμοί.

69. Both Josephus and Pseudo-Philo follow the scriptural account in specifying the mode of Eli's death by falling (*Ant.* 5.359; *L.A.B.* 54.5).

70. The appearance of καρδία in each passage may be the icing on the cake—or it may be simply coincidental, given its commonness (seven hundred-plus uses in the LXX; forty-plus in Luke's writings).

Part 2: The Jerusalem Temple in Luke's Gospel

Though something of an aside, it is instructive to note how Luke's recalling of 1 Kgdms 2:33–36 (and the surrounding context) in Simeon's prophecy provides further illustration and clarification of his typological use of the OT in this section of his Gospel (and likely elsewhere).[71] The echoes serve to suggest a typological connection between major characters in 1 Kingdoms and the Third Gospel (Eli's house = Jerusalem's religious authorities), though without pairing together the referents of the specific verbal cues. Thus the "sign" in 1 Kgdms is the death of Eli's sons, whereas Jesus himself is (it appears) the "sign" to be opposed in Luke 2:34. Similarly, while a "sword" will pierce Mary's heart, it is the sons of Eli who will perish by the "sword"—and surely Luke does not intend to pair the mother of the Lord with the wicked sons of Eli! It is important to note that these facts do not obviate a typological reading here but instead merely preclude a typological reading that seeks an immediate and corresponding referent for each word echoed from 1 Kgdms 2. Rather, the passage must be heard in light of the larger intertextual connections of Luke 1–2, in which Luke pairs major characters such as Jesus and Samuel, intending a typological connection, while echoing minor characters in order to establish the typological connection of major characters but without necessarily intending a similarly typological connection (as with Simeon and Eli).[72]

Here Luke uses these verbal clues to direct his audience to the context of 1 Kgdms 2:33–36. On the basis of the rest of Luke 1–2, the audience

---

71. Luke's recalling 1 Kgdms 2:33–35 here does not necessarily preclude his also referencing other parts of the LXX as well. Bovon claims that Isa 8:14–18 lies in the "background" of Simeon's prophecy, especially his language of rising and falling, use of "sign" imagery, and employment of κεῖται, which Bovon links to the stone of offense from Isa 8 (*Luke*, 1:104; cf. Fitzmyer, *Luke*, 1:429; Danker, *Jesus and the New Age*, 68). Fitzmyer and others see Ezek 14:17 as standing behind v. 35a (*Luke*, 1:429–30), with the sword thus as a "divine instrument for testing and refining [God's] people" (Bovon, *Luke*, 1:105; cf. Danker, *Jesus and the New Age*, 69). These echoes may work in tandem with the echoes from 1 Kgdms that I have identified, with, e.g., the "sign" of opposition from Isa 8 adding depth to the potentially christological "sign" language in 1 Kgdms 2 and the sword as a divine instrument for refining adding nuance to, while not overpowering the meaning of, the sword of destruction from 1 Kgdms 2. Note that the verbal links to 1 Kgdms 2:33–35 are far stronger than the links proposed for Isa 8:14–18 and are far more encompassing than the links to Ezek 14:17.

72. Still, he does sometimes invite a typological association between characters from Scripture and groups who are affected by the salvation-historical implications of Jesus's life and ministry. As noted earlier, this is especially clear from the typological connection between those who received aid from Elijah/Elisha and Jesus's ministry to those outside of his hometown (Luke 4:24–27).

will already associate Jesus and Samuel and on the basis of the text of 1 Kingdoms itself will know the interrelatedness of the stories of Samuel's rise and the fall of Eli's house. In fact, this passage clarifies and pushes the connection further: it is the Lord's faithful priest, who is ambiguously but inescapably linked to his anointed, who stands to gain at the great expense of the house of Eli (1 Kgdms 2:35–36). The audience familiar with Luke's Gospel will know, as argued above (and see also below), that on opposite sides of the division within Israel brought about by Jesus's life and ministry are Jesus himself and the religious authorities whose seat of power is in Jerusalem. By recalling this scene from 1 Kingdoms, then, Luke invites, even teases, his auditors to contemplate a typological connection between the rejected priesthood of Eli and the religious authorities (including the priesthood) of Jesus's day. Just as Samuel's ministry corresponded to the end of Eli's house, so Jesus's ministry, Luke hints, will bring to an end the priesthood of Jesus's day.[73]

The historical similarities of the two group's positions would further strengthen the connection: Just as Eli's house and the cultic center around which it was based (Shiloh) stood on the precipice of a great fall in the early chapters of 1 Kingdoms, so the Jerusalem authorities and cultic structures of Jesus's childhood would soon meet their end, as Luke's post-70 CE audience knows quite well.

In this regard, it is important to consider that Luke, as well as his ideal audience, would have little difficulty drawing a connection between Eli's downfall and Shiloh's demise, since Shiloh's downfall had long-since become axiomatic (Jer 7:14; 33:6, 9 LXX) and since the two were firmly connected as a centerpiece of Samaritan theology,[74] regarding which Luke appears to be both knowledgeable and interested.[75] One should note also

---

73. Here I am in line with, again, Hays's reading of echoes of Jer 7–8 in Mark 11. According to Hays, the typological connection between Jesus and Jeremiah extends beyond those figures and includes also "outward-rippling implications" ("Can the Gospels Teach Us?," 408). Here the primary "outward-rippling implication" is a typological linking between Eli's house at Shiloh and the religious authorities at Jerusalem.

74. It is widely accepted that ancient Samaritan theology considered Shechem to be the original and still-legitimate cultic site, though it was in practice eclipsed when Eli established the illegitimate and schismatic cultic site at Shiloh. See MacDonald, *The Theology of the Samaritans*, 16–17; Coggins, *Samaritans and Jews*, 120; Pummer, *The Samaritans*, 3.

75. Consider especially Luke's pointed interest in Samaritans in the central section of his Gospel (e.g., Luke 9:52–56; 10:30–37; 17:11–19), his insinuations (discussed in the next chapter) that the Jerusalem cult was an obstacle to the proper in-gathering of God's

Part 2: The Jerusalem Temple in Luke's Gospel

the explicit connection drawn between Shiloh and Eli's house in 1 Kgdms 14:3 and 3 Kgdms 2:27. Moreover, the Jerusalem-Shiloh link continues and gains additional force in Luke 2:41–52—discussed below.

Before moving on, we must attend to Anna and especially to her "speaking about Jesus to all those who were awaiting the redemption of Jerusalem" (2:38). The apparent use of either *synecdoche* or *metonymy*[76] here of course parallels the earlier description of Simeon as one who "was awaiting the consolation of Israel" (2:25b), and the straightforward meaning is simply that of 2:25b. Still, the mention of a woman spending her life in the JT awaiting "the redemption of Jerusalem" redounds with irony for a post-70 CE audience, in a way not easily felt by modern commentators. While we possess cognizance of the fact that Jerusalem was destroyed roughly 70 years after the time being depicted, for Luke's ideal audience, this was a jarring, vivid recent event—far more world-shattering for some

---

people, especially Samaritans, and his affinities for Samaritan traditions in Acts 7—when discussing the Temple, no less!

Examples of Samaritan tradition or theology in Acts 7 include: (1) Luke's assertion that Abraham did not leave Haran until the death of his father Terah (v. 4), which agrees against the MT and LXX with the rendering of Abraham's age in the Samaritan Pentateuch (Gen 11:32), among other Jewish traditions (viz., Philo, *De Migratione* 177); see Bruce, *Commentary on the Acts of the Apostles*, 147; Bruce, "Stephen's Apologia," 41; Fitzmyer, *Acts*, 371. And (2) Luke's unprecedented claim that the patriarchs were buried not in the cave of Machpelah but in Shechem (v. 16; cf. Gen 23:17–20; 33:19; 50:13)—thus placing the patriarch's burial place at the Samaritan holy site! Discussing—and attempting to refute—further points at which Acts 7 may rely textually on the Samaritan Pentateuch are Mare, "Acts 7"; and Richard, "Acts 7." Though Bruce also warns against overplaying the evidence here (esp. Luke's locating the tomb at Shechem, "Stephen's Apologia," 41), one should also be wary of underplaying the connection. The point is not that Luke has relied textually on the Samaritan Pentateuch (Richard's concern) or that Acts 7 discloses the historical Stephen to be a Samaritan or that Luke is putatively endorsing Samaritan theology wholesale (Bruce's concern: "Stephen's Apologia," 40), but rather this: acknowledging that Luke seems to drop hints of Samaritan tradition at the precise moment when he, through Stephen, levels his strongest critique against the Temple (see Appendix A), we must consider whether these hints may be intentional and, if so, what are Luke's possible motives for giving such hints. One plausible motive is that Luke views the JT, and indeed the entire Jerusalem power center, as a key obstacle to reconciling the Samaritans with the rest of God's people—an obstacle removed by Jesus's life and ministry (see comments on Luke 9:51—19:27; 23:45)—and wants to conjure up this dynamic in Stephen's speech.

76. Commentators usually opt for *synecdoche* (thus viewing Jerusalem as part of the larger whole, presumably Israel; e.g., Bovon, *Luke*, 1:106; Marshall, *Luke*, 124; Green, *Luke*, 152)—but it may also be characterized as *metonymy* (reference to a related but distinct entity).

among his likely audience than even September 11 or the assassination of John F. Kennedy for many American contemporaries. Moreover, this event was depicted widely and propagandistically, in Luke's day, on the boastful *Judea Capta* coins of the Flavian emperors and eventually on the Arch of Titus (see chapter 2 above). Finally, λύτρωσις itself had a powerfully political meaning for many Jews of this time, implying freedom from foreign oppression—as seen, above all, in its use on Jewish coins during the Bar Khokba revolt.[77]

Therefore, although most commentators pass by the phrase with little hint of pausing,[78] if Luke, writing after 70 CE and otherwise sensitive to issues of theodicy, does not use *metonymy/synecdoche* here purposefully, and with deeper meaning, then this turn of phrase is an infelicity of jarring proportions.[79] Furthermore, that it comes shortly after Simeon's dolorous prophecy about divisions and rising and falling within Israel—which, unlike in 2:25, is now divided, even if only rhetorically (i.e., via *synecdoche/metonymy*)—suggests a potential meaning more ominous than the plainest sense of the phrase. I view this, then, as a further, and even paradigmatic, example of Lukan subtlety, along the lines mapped below.

Though widely recognized, Luke's use of Isaianic language both in introducing Simeon and in the *Nunc Dimittis* itself is perhaps worth

---

77. On this see Fitzmyer, *Luke*, 1:432.

78. On the relatively short list of those who, to my knowledge, note the terrible irony of Anna's comment to a post-70 CE audience are Gaston, *No Stone*, 256; Tannehill, "'Cornelius' and 'Tabitha,'" 352; Llewellyn, "The Consolation of Israel," 9; Walker, *Jesus and the Holy City*, 59-60. This is, in fact, precisely one of the reasons why Gaston takes Luke 1-2 as composed of "an earlier tradition": "After A.D. 70 such a proclamation [viz., that of 2:38] would have *seemed a bitter mockery* . . . Such statements could not have been written at any time after the fall of Jerusalem or to anyone but Jews" (*No Stone*, 256-57; emphasis added); in contrast, most scholars find it likely that such statements *were* written (or at the very least were copied into new form) post-70 CE and likely to an audience that included at least some Gentiles. We must find, then, other methods of solving the quandary than Gaston's somewhat facile positing of a non-Lukan source. (Surely it is no longer possible to view Luke as having been as sloppy as that!) Green, looking back on 2:38 in his discussion of 21:5-38, clearly senses the tension but does not adequately resolve it (*Luke*, 741). Garland, in discussing this phrase, notes that "Jerusalem's consolation is tied to its reception of Jesus" and points the auditor to Jesus's condemnation of the city in Luke 19:41-44—without observing the obvious irony this entails for Luke 2:38 (*Luke*, 137)!

79. Hopes of seeing a politically restored and liberated Jerusalem/Israel continued after the fall of Jerusalem in 70 CE (see Fitzmyer, *Luke*, 1:432), and Luke may here be warning against the vanity of resurrecting or persisting in such hopes, though this is by no means clear.

Part 2: The Jerusalem Temple in Luke's Gospel

recounting, even in abbreviated form, here. Luke's initial description of Simeon as one "awaiting the consolation of Israel (προσδεχόμενος παράκλησιν τοῦ Ἰσραήλ)" (2:25) loudly and definitively strikes the chords of the latter half of Isaiah, including Isa 40:1 and 66:12–13.[80] The tones are even stronger in the *Nunc Dimittis*, which is a "pastiche" of passages from Isaiah (Isa 40:5; 42:6; 46:13; 49:6; 52:9–10).[81] The *Nunc Dimittis* also employs the neuter form σωτήριον (v. 30), which is common in Isa 40–66 (cf. Luke 3:6).[82]

Further strengthening the Isaianic flavor of the entire scene is Isa 59:9, which sets "consolation" and "redemption," in their verbal forms, as parallel.[83] Thus the parallel descriptions of Simeon, awaiting the consolation of Israel, and Anna, awaiting the redemption of Jerusalem, form not only a Lukan but also an Isaianic pair. Given the Isaianic flavor of the scene as a whole, and the jarring comment regarding Anna in particular, members of Luke's audience seeking a deeper meaning than the brutally ironic straightforward sense of Anna's and others' "awaiting the redemption of Jerusalem" might look to Isaiah, particularly what we now know as Deutero- and Trito-Isaiah, for interpretive clarity.[84]

Among the interpretive options there is Isa 63:4, in which occurs the only use of the noun form of λύτρωσις in (Rahlf's) Isaiah (although the verb occurs somewhat frequently). Here, God as divine warrior speaks of having exercised judgment on the nations during the "year of redemption (ἐνιαυτὸς λυτρώσεως)." "Redemption," then, allows for multiple and divergent meanings, and Luke may be exploiting this fact.[85] Although

---

80. See Brown, "Presentation," 6–7; also, Rusam, *Das Alte Testament*, 78–85. Note that Isa 40:1 and 66:12–13 specifically reference Jerusalem, strongly inviting informed auditors to hear Anna's later description (esp. v. 38) in Isaianic terms.

81. See Brown, "Presentation," 7. Isaiah 51:17–23, which speaks of Jerusalem's calamities, may serve as a partial background for Simeon's language of "rising and falling" (see esp. Koet, "Simeons Worte," 1559–64), in which case this supplies an obvious point of contact to Anna's speaking of the "redemption of Jerusalem." The possible double-allusion to Isa 51 and 1 Kgdms 2 in Simeon's second oracle suggests a further linking between Jerusalem and Shiloh here.

82. As noted by Tannehill, *Narrative Unity*, 1:40.

83. See Nolland, *Luke*, 1:123.

84. Members of Luke's ideal audience would know the text of Isaiah better than most modern readers, including many New Testament scholars, and would certainly know it in Greek. They would also know the key significance of Isaiah for interpreting Luke's writings and, via Lukan theology, Jesus's life and ministry as a whole.

85. As discussed in chapter 1, exploiting the double meanings of words was a

the theme of judgment on the nations might seem to offer little hope for re-interpretation of the irony-laden expectation of Jerusalem's "redemption" in Luke 2:38, the larger context of the passage, which pleads for God to renew and rescue his people, also speaks of God's fighting against his own people because of their rebelliousness (Isa 63:10). Isaiah 63, then, indicates that "redemption" may mean bloodshed rather than peace and that God the warrior does himself fight against his people in the face of their rebellion[86]—a meaning Luke may imply, via metalepsis, in 2:38.[87]

Whether Luke had in mind or intended his audience to hear reference to Isa 63 here is probably beyond all knowledge, and the connection to the sole noun occurrence of λύτρωσις in Isaiah is no unassailable basis for a positive conclusion, despite the deep reverberations of Deutero- and Trito-Isaiah in Simeon's prophecies. Still, the unbearable irony of the description of Anna stands as a cue to the audience that Luke intends in the surrounding scenes more than meets the eye, teasing his hearers into contemplating precisely what sort of "redemption" this might be. It also alerts Luke's audience, more generally, to his use of subtle communication as a facet of his treatment of Jerusalem and the JT. Only by attending to this irony-forged cue and noting the parallelism between Samuel-Jesus and thus also Shiloh-Jerusalem is the audience prepared for the later, otherwise surprisingly harsh pronouncements against Jerusalem beginning in Luke 13.[88]

---

common means of subtle communication in the ancient world.

86. The theme of God as opponent to his own people of course occurs in much of the prophetic tradition and features prominently in Jeremiah and Ezekiel. As I will argue below (following C. A. Evans), Luke frames Jesus's march to Jerusalem with strong overtones of judgment via allusion in Luke 9:51 to traditions in Jeremiah and Ezekiel of God's opposing his own people. An audience aware of those echoes would be even more likely to hear in Anna's "awaiting the redemption of Jerusalem" an echo of the similarly-themed Isa 63.

87. Potentially strengthening the connection between the passages are the several mentions of God's trampling (καταπατέω) the nations in Isa 63 (v. 3 [twice], 6) and then the description of the nations' trampling God's Temple (v. 18); Luke (uniquely) employs a variant form of the verb (πατέω) to describe the Gentile's trampling Jerusalem (Luke 21:24). This raises the likelihood, however slightly, that Luke points toward Isa 63 for understanding the events of 70 CE.

88. See, e.g., Walker, *Jesus and the Holy City*: "In light of Jesus' reference to the Temple as 'his Father's house' (2:49), the next two references to the Temple [4:9 and 13:35] come as a dramatic surprise" (61); and 13:35 "is a solemn first pronouncement intended to shock. The story takes a violent twist, rudely disrupting the placid atmosphere created in the opening Chapters." While appealing, this interpretation simply ignores not only the discordant notes of Luke 1 and 2 but also the other menacing storm clouds in the first

Part 2: The Jerusalem Temple in Luke's Gospel

A final point requires comment. It is significant that this scene is the first time in Luke's writings that Jesus appears in the JT.[89] Earlier in this Gospel, Luke has not shied away from acknowledging, even emphasizing, the sacerdotal activities of the JT, especially with Zechariah (1:8–11)[90] and, to a lesser degree, in the early-going here (2:22–24, 27).[91] A marked shift occurs in Luke's Gospel, however, (and continues into Acts) away from presenting the JT as a sacerdotal cultic center.[92] The shift consists not of an outright denial of the legitimacy of priest-led worship in the JT but rather in a pointed and consistent de-emphasis on that aspect of temple life within the Lukan narrative(s), and the shift begins, at least most emphatically, in this very scene—with Simeon's interruption of Joseph and Mary's intention to fulfill the customary rites in 2:27–28.[93] Thus, when the present

---

half of Luke's Gospel, including the agonistic dynamics I will highlight below. Alternately, the "dramatic surprise" of subsequent episodes, esp. 13:31–35, might point less-than-ideally-informed auditors back to the earlier episodes of Luke's Gospel in search of answers.

89. As Serrano rightly notes (*Presentation*, 219, 276–77).

90. Although I will not discuss the Zechariah scene at length, note that Zechariah is administering the twice-daily *Tamid* service (see Marshall, *Luke*, 54; Green, *Luke*, 68; Nolland, *Luke*, 1:28, 33; *m. Tamid* 5–7), and that Gabriel's rendering Zechariah silent thus prevents him from completing the service by speaking the blessing over the people upon exiting the sanctuary (see *m. Tamid* 7; Nolland, *Luke*, 1:33). So the interruption of the Temple's sacerdotal function, while most clearly elaborated with Simeon's appearance, finds a precursor in the Zechariah scene.

91. The difference between the emphasis in the scenes consists mainly, it seems to me, in 1) Luke's free use of ναός in the Zechariah scene (but absent here), and 2) Luke's actually narrating cultic activity in the Zechariah scene (1:8–10), while merely mentioning the need for such here and then passing over the narration of that activity summarily in 2:39.

92. Throughout, I will speak of the JT's "*sacerdotal* cultic functions" in order to differentiate this aspect of the Temple's cultic role from the other kinds of worship that in Lukan theology (as I read it) remain relevant to the Temple following Jesus's birth, ministry, and finally death. The "sacerdotal cultic functions" I have in mind are any activities in the Temple that require the ministration of a priest or priestly class—as opposed to the prayer and instruction that come to characterize Jesus's and his disciples' activity in the JT. Prayer and instruction are "cultic" in the sense that they express religious devotion.

93. Taylor ("Jerusalem Temple," 472) identifies this shift away from the JT as a cultic center as beginning in Luke 1, with the arrivals of John and Jesus, as evidenced in the Third Gospel's move away from ναός as a description of the JT's cultic function: after featuring in 1:9, 21, 22, it occurs again in Luke's Gospel only at the rending of the veil in 23:45, and then appears in Acts 17:24 and 19:24, both times in reference to idols! I agree that the shift in some senses begins with the births of John and Jesus and with the interruption of the *Tamid* offering in 1:9–22 but Luke gives his strongest cue via the interruption of the flow of the narrative in the Simeon and Anna pericope. Thus Luke

pericope shifts from "plot of resolution" (centered on the need to fulfill the cultic service) to "plot of revelation," it undergoes a shift that carries across throughout the rest of Luke's writings, away from the JT as sacerdotal cultic site.[94] As the Lukan narrative unfolds, the proper function of the JT is no longer sacerdotal, or even cultic, beyond its utility as a place of instruction and prayer; rather, it serves, when properly used, as a means of pointing to Jesus himself—as it does in the present scene.[95] This shift provides context, for those in the know, for Luke's puzzling use of ναός—positively in the opening scene with Zechariah and thereafter only in contexts that reject identifying the divine presence within a particular locale (Luke 23:45; Acts 17:24; 19:24).[96]

Thus, regarding the present scene, the cultic requirements, the initial driving force behind this little story, receive only cursory mention as fulfilled (2:39), and likewise the following pericope, despite mention of the family's observance of Passover (v. 41), features the JT primarily as a place of instruction (2:46–50).

JESUS'S PRESENCE IN THE TEMPLE (LUKE 2:41–52)

The final scene of Luke 2, the twelve-year-old Jesus's surprising appearance in the Temple, offers a number of exegetical challenges, including the meaning of Jesus's curious response in v. 49. A full analysis is neither possible nor desirable here, and I must instead focus on those aspects of the scene that are most pertinent to my study.[97]

---

gives multiple indicators of the shift (including the simple de-emphasis on the cultic role of the JT starting here and the shift in his use of ναός after the Zechariah scene) that are complementary and that surround the births of John and Jesus. In this regard, Luke 1–2 once again preview and interpret the narrative that is to follow.

94. Serrano (*Presentation*, 202n190) seems potentially to detect, and resist, this implication.

95. So Holmås, "'My House Shall Be Called,'" 406–9.

96. See Taylor, "The Jerusalem Temple," 465–66.

97. Some will object, perhaps rightly, to my foot-noted treatment here of Jesus's ambiguous expression in v. 49: ἐν τοῖς τοῦ πατρός μου. If commentators are correct in preferring "in my Father's house" over the less-specific "about my Father's affairs" (so Marshall, *Luke*, 129; Fitzmyer, *Luke*, 1:443), then it likely has bearing on my thesis, although I confess to being unsure how much (and precisely what kind of) weight to grant it. Reading v. 49 as "in my Father's house" hardly dislodges any major aspects of my reading, especially since God abandons the JT only gradually as Luke's narrative progresses, and in fact the puzzling absence of the noun "house" here may foreshadow God's

PART 2: THE JERUSALEM TEMPLE IN LUKE'S GOSPEL

Note, first of all, that, despite the notice that Jesus's parents went yearly to Jerusalem to attend the Feast of Passover (v. 41) and despite the fact that this supplies the context for the present scene (v. 42), Luke otherwise gives no attention to the Passover—i.e., he does not specifically attend to or elaborate the sacerdotal or other cultic activities that this would have entailed.[98] This muting of the sacerdotal and cultic aspects of the Passover stands in stark contrast to the activity of the boy Jesus in the Temple—questioning, learning, teaching (vv. 46–47). Thus a Passover pilgrimage is, in Luke's narrative, co-opted for other purposes, namely in order to reveal Jesus's precocious wisdom and unique relationship to the Father (v. 49). Much like in the previous scene, then, a sacerdotally-oriented cultic imperative provides the backdrop for the scene, yet it is other, non-sacerdotal activity to which Luke gives center stage. Thus to speak generically of "Temple piety" here is off the mark[99]: such language obscures Luke's use of sacerdotal cultic worship as a plot device (perhaps even as a foil) while giving actual attention to the non-sacerdotal activity within the Temple, specifically to revelations regarding Jesus's identity.

Also important for this study is to note how this passage strengthens the above reading of the prophecies of Simeon and Anna. As noted previously, there are strong, if subtle, typological connections between Jesus's presence in the JT and Samuel's early ministry in the Shiloh house of God. Even Luke's mention of Jesus's age likely strengthens the connection, as there was Jewish tradition, known to Josephus at least, which understood Samuel to be twelve years of age when beginning his ministry at the Shiloh holy place.[100] Yet ominous tones everywhere surround Samuel's presence there, since his first received prophecy, in the house of God no less, announces the end of the house of Eli, which, as argued above, was easily linked to Shiloh's demise as cultic site. Indeed, following the capture of the ark, which occurs in concert with the overthrow of Eli's house, Shiloh enters the narrative of Kingdoms only twice more—once tangentially (1 Kgdms 14:3), the second time in fulfillment of the prophecy against Eli's

---

eventual abandonment of the Temple in Luke's narrative (see my comments on 13:35a below). Note, moreover, that in Luke's Gospel Jesus does not claim to be the active cause of, and certainly does not celebrate, the eventual demise of the Temple—which is, rather, a result of its abandonment by God, granted partially in response to the treatment of Jesus by the Temple's powerbrokers.

98. For such details, see Fitzmyer, *Luke*, 1:439–40.
99. As in Brown, "Finding of the Boy Jesus," 480.
100. Fitzmyer, *Luke*, 1:440–41.

house (3 Kgdms 2:27)—before the establishment of the Jerusalem cult. Shiloh is remembered elsewhere in Scripture as a place made desolate, rejected by the Lord.[101] Most significantly, Jeremiah prophesies doom for Jerusalem and its cult, promising it will be made like Shiloh (Jer 7:14; 33:6, 9 LXX). Thus, the typological connection between Samuel's incipient ministry at Shiloh and Jesus's presence in the JT here would bring into view for a post-70 CE audience the truths both that the JT—here populated by the surprising twelve-year-old Jesus—no longer in fact remains and that, just as Luke has paired the two cultic sites via the Jesus-Samuel connection, so also Jeremiah long before interpreted Jerusalem's fall in light of Shiloh's hoary demise.

This unstated, insinuated typology is best viewed as a rather skillful example of what Richard Hays terms *metalepsis*, in which "a literary echo links the text in which it occurs to an earlier text" and yet "the figurative effect of the echo ... lie[s] in the unstated or suppressed (transumed) points of resonance between the two texts."[102] Although Luke clearly alludes to Samuel's childhood in depicting the childhoods of Jesus and John and although he also alludes, more subtly, to Eli (in the figure of Simeon), he gives only the faintest of references to the fall of Eli's house and never so much as mentions desolate Shiloh, despite its dominant role as the setting of Samuel's childhood. Even so, he dances all around this side of the story—by alluding to every pericope of its complementary piece, the Samuel childhood story, by conjuring up (so faintly) the prophecy of Eli's fall, and now by placing the twelve-year-old Jesus in the Temple, precisely the point in the corresponding Samuel narrative at which the two sides of the story merge: Samuel's rise meets Eli's fall.

On my reading, then, Luke 2:22–52, which continues the Samuel childhood echoes from Luke 1, takes the typological implications of those echoes in a surprisingly ominous direction, by establishing links between the Jerusalem priesthood of Jesus's day and Eli's house and, correspondingly, between Jerusalem and the fallen Shiloh. Although modern commentators have roundly overlooked them,[103] these typological implications

---

101. See Ps 77:60; Jer 7:12, 14; 33:6, 9 LXX.

102. Hays, *Echoes of Scripture*, 20.

103. That scholarship has overlooked (or perhaps, "under-heard") the typological import of these echoes is likely attributable to a series of interrelated limitations: 1) the relatively late scholarly acknowledgment of Luke's status as a theologian or even independent sculptor of the text, coupled 2) by the relatively recent efforts to unravel his complex and multifaceted use of the Jewish Scriptures (including the only partial recognition of

are consonant with, and in fact anticipate, the first explicit discussion of Jerusalem's fate in Luke's Gospel, Luke 13:33–35, which otherwise—i.e., on a purely favorable reading of the JT in Luke 1–2—comes out of the blue as a dire warning with little apparent precedent in Luke's narrative (cf. 11:49–51). Faint echoes of Shiloh's demise, moreover, may also haunt Jesus's pronouncement in Luke 13, as I explore in the next chapter.

SUMMARY OF ANALYSIS ON LUKE 1–2

Above I have argued that Luke draws a typological connection between first John and then Jesus and the great prophet of old, Samuel, and does so in a way that emphasizes Jesus's superiority over John, while still elevating the latter. I have also argued that in the final two pericopae of this section, Luke begins to drop ominous hints of the future demise of Jerusalem and the JT: 1) by subtle communication via his ironic description of Anna as "awaiting the redemption of Jerusalem" (2:38), 2) by subtle allusion to the story of Eli's fall and thus, via metalepsis, by insinuation of Shiloh's fall, and 3) by effecting, in these scenes so dominated by the presence of the JT, his de-emphasis on that structure as a sacerdotal cultic site and re-presentation of it as, properly used, pointing toward Jesus. The reason for this shift may be, as some have claimed, that Luke has shown in these early scenes what the proper function of the Temple is—viz. to lead and point to Jesus—and yet, as Luke's Gospel unfolds, opposition to Jesus becomes concentrated within the power structure of the Temple—i.e., they misuse the Temple.[104] This view is, I think, partially correct, as Jesus's opponents do have the Temple, and indeed Jerusalem more broadly, as their base of power, but this view nevertheless makes the mistake of downplaying the deeply rooted immorality Luke also places on the heads of the Jerusalem leadership. Although from here Luke leaves behind the Samuel typology that was the basis for an association between Shiloh-Jerusalem and Eli-Jerusalem's religious authorities in Luke 1–2,[105] echoes of Shiloh, as well as Luke's use of

---

Samuel Typology by previous studies), along with 3) the crucial post-70 CE context in which Luke wrote and the theodical questions that were endemic to that context, as well as 4) the frequent use of subtle communication among those with at least moderate rhetorical education in the first century.

104. See, above all, the incisive discussion in Holmås, "'My House Shall Be Called,'" 406–9.

105. Fitzmyer claims that the connection between Jesus and Moses, Elijah, and Elisha helps establish Jesus as "an eschatological prophet" who "pours forth" the eschatological

subtle communication and his de-emphasizing of the sacerdotal functions of the JT, continue as important features of his Gospel as the story of Jesus's life, ministry, and passion unfolds.

---

giving of the Spirit (*Luke*, 1:214–15). This explains, in my view, why Luke drops the Samuel echoes after Luke 1–2, as they would potentially obscure the other prophetic typologies that Luke wishes to highlight with Jesus's adult ministry. The Samuel connections are appropriate to Jesus's childhood precisely because it was Samuel's childhood and not adult ministry that was associated with the fall of the Elide priesthood, so by linking the childhoods of John and Jesus with Samuel Luke draws a typological connection between Jerusalem-Shiloh and the Jerusalem authorities-Eli's house, while not interfering with the typological associations that he wishes to employ regarding Jesus's (and John's) adult ministry.

4

The Jerusalem Temple in Luke 3–19

INTRODUCTION

Here I examine the place of Jerusalem and its Temple in the two middle sections of Luke's Gospel: John's ministry and Jesus's Galilean ministry (3:1—9:50) and the Jerusalem Journey (9:51—19:27). The thematic continuity between these scenes suggests treating them together.

SETTING THE STAGE (LUKE 3:1—9:50)

Luke 3:1—9:50,[1] which covers John's ministry and Jesus's early ministry in Galilee, will occupy comparatively little of our time, as it contains, to my mind, only two pericopae of high import for my thesis, and these only moderately so (in themselves, at least). Still, given my emphasis on a narrative reading, I cannot neglect to give some indication of by what terrain the auditor gets from Luke 1–2 to the later parts of Luke's Gospel.

Luke follows Mark and either Q or Matthew in giving attention to the ministry of John, although he elaborates his John scene (3:1-20) by his

---

1. Despite the strong case of the minority of commentators who on the basis of ancient rhetorical theory take Luke 3:1—4:13 as belonging together with Luke 1–2 as the story of John's and Jesus's respective births, upbringings, and early deeds (see esp. Talbert, *Reading Luke*, and Parsons, *Luke*), I follow most commentators in taking Luke 3:1—9:50 as a unit.

historiographical introduction to the scene (vv. 1–2a), by quoting Isa 40 at greater length (vv. 5–6), and by expanding John's message (vv. 10–15); he also omits the description of John's appearance and ministry (cf. Matt 3:4–6; Mark 1:5–6). Luke's prior introduction of John also represents a significant departure from the other Synoptics regarding John. In Luke's world, John is not only Jesus's forerunner but also the son of the priest Zechariah. As such, his ministry in the dessert, apart from the strictures of Jerusalem and its Temple, may represent something of a rival ritual system, though it is unclear how far the evidence should be pushed here.[2]

After describing John's ministry and imprisonment (3:1–20) and then Jesus's baptism and genealogy (3:21–38), Luke narrates Jesus's temptation in the wilderness (4:1–13), which I address more fully below. Thereafter, Luke takes a significant departure from Mark's order (which he otherwise generally follows) to inaugurate Jesus's public ministry at a synagogue in Nazareth (4:14–30), doing so by having Jesus describe his vocation as the fulfillment of Isaianic prophecy (esp. Isa 61:1 and 58:6), a vocation expressed primarily in terms of liberation for the oppressed (4:18–19) and one that almost immediately earns him the disapproval of his townsfolk (4:28–30), largely because of his self-attribution of Elijah-Elisha typology in a way calculated to enfranchise outsiders at the expense of his own kith and kin (4:24–27).

This inaugurating scene sets forth several important Lukan features, including three worth noting here. First is the description of Jesus's ministry by explicit quotation of Isaiah, which is matched by later explicit (e.g., Acts 8:32–33) and implicit (e.g., Luke 7:22) references to Isaiah for describing Jesus's life and ministry and which follows through on the promise of the Isaianic echoes in the *Nunc Dimittis*. Second, Luke here begins the Elijah-Elisha typology by which he characterizes Jesus at various points in Luke 4–9 (see chapter 1) and which thus continues to elaborate Jesus's prophetic characterization, first under the mantle of Samuel.[3] Third, here begins in earnest the division-lines brought by Jesus, as predicted in Simeon's second oracle.[4]

Much of the rest of Luke 4–9 is in some sense an elaboration of Jesus's Isaianic vocation to release the oppressed—as made explicit in Luke

---

2. See Taylor, "The Jerusalem Temple," 466, 480–81.

3. See Fitzmyer, *Luke*, 1:213–15.

4. John's ministry anticipated these divisions as well (see Luke 3:7–9, 18–20; cf. 7:29–30).

Part 2: The Jerusalem Temple in Luke's Gospel

7:22—as he goes about healing those afflicted with ailments and even raising the dead,[5] teaching (e.g., 4:31–33, 42–44; 5:3, 36–39; 6:20–49; 8:4–18), and performing other miracles (5:4–7; 8:22–25; 9:12–17). In the process he draws large crowds (e.g., 6:17–19), despite his penchant for seeking solitude (4:42–44; 5:16; 9:10–11), and gathers disciples, including the Twelve (6:12–16) and including from among undesirables (5:27–32; 8:1–3). After establishing the nature of his own mission, he sends out the Twelve, giving them power to continue his ministry of liberation (9:1–6). He also earns the ire, and soon the focused enmity (cf. 6:6–11), of various members of the religious elite, particularly over his association with undesirables (5:30–32; 7:33–35, 36–50), his self-attribution of the power to forgive sins as such (5:20–21; 7:48–50), and his shirking of strict Sabbath observance (6:1–5, 6–11).[6] This continues and deepens the lines of division promised by Simeon. This line soon stretches also to include Jesus's own family (as anticipated by Simeon's comment on the sword's piercing Mary's own heart), whose relationship to him becomes marginalized in equalizing preference for all who hear and obey God's word (8:19–21).

This opposition reaches something of a climax in Luke 9:18–22, when Jesus asks his disciples who the crowds (but then also they) say he is; after Peter announces him as the Messiah of God, Jesus warns them to keep quiet and then foretells his own suffering and death at the hands of the religious leaders, including the Jerusalem elite (viz. the elders and chief priests; v. 22).[7] From here, Jesus begins to teach them of the implications of following him (9:23–27) and then leads only three disciples, Peter, John, and James, up to a mountain to witness the divine revelation of his glory—the Transfiguration (9:28–36). After a few intervening episodes, including an infamous discussion among the disciples of their relative status (9:46–48), Jesus, with the day of his "ascension" drawing near, "set[s] his face to Jerusalem" (9:51).

Though unstated, the lines of division are largely rooted in Jesus's subtle challenge to the concentric circles of sacredness that emerge from

---

5. He heals those who are demon-possessed (e.g., 4:33–37; 8:26–39), leprous (e.g., 5:12–16), crippled (5:17–26), and otherwise sick (e.g., 4:38–41; 8:43–48); he also raises the dead (7:11–17; 8:40–42, 49–56). See also 6:17–19; 7:1–10.

6. Kingsbury probably rightly reads these scenes as part of the larger drama over "the crucial question of who rightfully rules God's people Israel: Is it Jesus, Israel's Messiah, or the authorities?" ("The Plot of Luke's Story," 160).

7. Luke is of course here simply apparently following Mark 8:31 (as did Matt 16:21).

the JT itself.[8] Divisions emanating outward from the Holy and Holies and dictating appropriate social and cultic boundaries based on gender, cleanness, and ethnicity are challenged here by Jesus's association with "sinners," women, and other undesirables. Also problematic for those whose symbolic world flows out of the Temple is Jesus's self-attribution of the power to forgive sins—a power generally reserved for God[9] and strongly associated with the sacerdotal activities of the Temple (Lev 4:20–35; 5:10–18, 26; 19:22; Num 15:25–28; 3 Kgdms 8:30 LXX). It is thus no accident that Luke sets up the scene in which Jesus forgives the paralytic (5:17–26)—to great consternation—with a note that Jesus was surrounded by Pharisees and law-teachers *from Jerusalem* (v. 17).[10] Thus Jesus, in Luke's subtle portrait, not only ruffles the feathers of those whose symbolic universe and base of power emanates from Jerusalem but also begins to provide narrative clarification of the narratival shift away from the JT as sacerdotal center: Jesus is beginning to encroach upon the sacred space once reserved for the JT.[11] This presentation takes on much starker dimensions with the theophanic imagery of the Transfiguration, which suggests that God's presence, traditionally associated most closely with the JT, is now tied (instead) to Jesus.[12]

---

8. These concentric circles had the JT, and the Holy of Holies in particular, as their center and flowed (outward) from the assumption—firmly rooted in the OT—that the JT was the unique dwelling place of Israel's God. See Green, "Demise of the Temple," 508–9. Conflict in Luke's Gospel also emerges based around Jesus's apparent shirking of Sabbath requirements, which are less obviously related to the concentric circles of purity emanating from the JT.

9. The problem almost certainly lies in Jesus's apparent claim to absolve sins *as such* (instead of, say, sins committed against oneself, etc.), a claim implied by his use of the passive: "Your sins are forgiven" (5:20; 7:48). See Ellingworth, "Forgiveness of Sins," 241.

10. Cf. Green, *Theology*, 14.

11. Luke may attempt to provide a partial precedent for this sort of encroachment via Jesus's story about David, who enters "the house of God" (τὸν οἶκον τοῦ θεοῦ) and eats the bread meant only for the priests (Luke 6:1–5). The authority of Jesus is made more emphatic in this passage by Luke's omission of the gnomic expression from Mark 2:27: τὸ σάββατον διὰ τὸν ἄνθρωπος ἐγένετο καὶ οὐχ ὁ ἄνθρωπος διὰ τὸ σάββατον.

12. Baltzer long ago observed the linguistic and theological connection between *kabod* and δόξα ("The Meaning of the Temple," 266–70, 275); note the latter's appearance in Luke 9:31, 32 (cf. Acts 7:2, 55). Note also the theophanic imagery of the overshadowing cloud (ἐγένετο νεφέλη καὶ ἐπεσκίαζεν αὐτούς; v. 34), as discussed by Hutcheon, "Temple," 32–33. Still, Luke probably does not include anything like the "Temple Typology" which Evans and Novakovic see as present in Mark's Gospel ("Typology," 990); note especially Luke's omission of Mark 12:6 ("something greater than the Temple is here"). The most we could say is that Luke leaves room for interpretive movement in that direction, without actually making clear to what degree that is his own preferred trajectory.

PART 2: THE JERUSALEM TEMPLE IN LUKE'S GOSPEL

Jesus's Temptation (Luke 4:1–13)

Only brief comment is needed on Luke's well-known rearrangement of the final two of Jesus's infamous temptations. Most scholars agree that Matthew's ordering of the temptations is original, whether original to Q or original because Luke made use of Matthew (ala the Farrer Hypothesis).[13] The question is, Why did Luke make the change?

The majority of commentators seem to be in agreement that the change has little to do with the second temptation (on Luke's order) and everything to do with the third: the point was to make the temptation at the JT last, even if the import of doing so remains unclear. Luke likely makes the change in order to emphasize the final temptation and the fact that it occurs in Jerusalem.[14] Although Conzelmann surely overstated his case regarding the cessation of temptations (and by implication Satanic activity) in proximity to Jesus, still there may be something to Luke's leaving Satan in Jerusalem, where he later re-emerges for the first time in full force by taking possession of Judas (22:3).[15] Luke may be hinting at Jerusalem's role as a habitat for Satan, perhaps also implicating the religious authorities who find their power base there, although the matter is by no means clear. At the very least, then, we may say that Luke changes the order of the temptations for the purposes of highlighting Jerusalem—possibly to polemical end.

Jesus and the Healed Leper (Luke 5:12–16)

One of the early healings Luke narrates comes in Luke 5:12–16, Jesus's healing of a leper by touching him and then commanding him to do several things (discussed below).[16] Several points warrant comment. First, Rowe

---

13. Cf. Marshall, *Luke*, 166–67.

14. So Baltzer ("The Meaning of the Temple," 272), Fitzmyer (*Luke*, 1:165), and Longenecker ("Rome's Victory," 96–97), who take the rearrangement as further evidence of Luke's preoccupation with Jerusalem. Marshall, following J. Dupont, surmises that Luke, from among multiple motives, may have sought to show that "[v]ictory in Jerusalem [at the third temptation] foreshadows the final triumph of Jesus" (*Luke*, 166).

15. Satan re-appears only indirectly in the intervening space (8:12; 10:18; 11:18; 13:16); see Gaventa, "Interpreting the Death of Jesus Apocalyptically," 141–42. Cf. Longenecker, "Rome's Victory," 96n19; Walker, *Jesus and the Holy City*, 69.

16. For a helpful discussion on leprosy (Hansen's disease) vs. the more general and accurate "skin-disease" or "scale disease," see Hartley, *Leviticus*, 187–89. I prefer the traditional, though probably inaccurate, "leprosy" here.

has argued cogently that Luke's second use of the vocative "Lord," found here, should be read in light of and with the same import as its first and immediately prior occurrence in the Third Gospel, Peter's divine vocative in 5:8. The point is not that the leper, as a character, is stating his own recognition of Jesus's divinity but rather that Luke makes use of the native ambiguity of κύριος to attribute to Jesus, on a narrative level, this higher sense of "Lord."[17] I find Rowe compelling on this point, especially in light of 5:12's propinquity to Peter's confession and in light of commonalities Rowe notes between the two scenes.[18] Luke highlights the fact here, then, that it is not only the human Jesus but also the divine Lord who touches and heals this leper.

In light of this,[19] and secondly, it is intriguing that Jesus instructs the man to tell no one but rather to go and 1) show himself to the priest and 2) to offer the things commanded by Moses for his cleansing (see Lev 14), 3) as a witness to them (εἰς μαρτύριον αὐτοῖς). Jesus's command here is arguably the only acknowledgment in Luke's Gospel, after Luke 1–2, of an ongoing sacerdotal role for the JT.[20] As such, it would appear to go against the Gospel's general trend (on my reading) of downplaying the JT's sacerdotal cultic functions post-Luke 2. One should not overlook, however,

---

17. Rowe's reading of κύριε, then, supplies yet another clear example of Lukan subtlety, again by exploiting the double meaning of a word; also, Marguerat, "Luc-Actes," 74–79. See comments on 2:38 above.

18. See Rowe, *Narrative*, 89–92, esp. 90.

19. That Luke has apparently taken the key section of this pericope for my purposes (5:14) almost straight from Mark 1:44 does not negate its significance for my thesis, on the grounds that 1) Luke, after all, makes the choice to retain Mark's wording εἰς μαρτύριον αὐτοῖς despite changing other details in the passage, 2) Luke frames the entire pericope differently by his use of κύριε in v. 12 (following Rowe), and 3) auditors of Luke's Gospel would likely hear this phrase differently in light of other Lukan distinctives (e.g., Luke's use of the μάρτυς word group). Given point 2 above, Luke's meaning need not be constrained by the meaning of the phrase (which I leave for other interpreters) as it appears in Mark.

20. Hamm sees veiled references to Temple worship at several points in Luke's Gospel via connections to the *Tamid* service: in addition to 1:5–25, also 18:9–14 and 24:50–53, as well as Acts 3:1; 6–7; and 10:3, 30 ("Tamid Service," 215–31; "Praying 'Regularly,'" 50–52). I will assess Hamm's proposal below, only noting here that I find his reading doubtful. Even if his proposal has merit, however, it does not necessarily work against—but may at points actually strengthen—my argument, since Luke 18:9–14 is a parable and in 24:50–53 he sees Jesus and his disciples as the ones who are partaking in the *Tamid* service. Luke also references cultic activity in Acts 21, but there Paul's cultic worship is 1) a concession, and 2) ironically interrupted by the very people claiming fidelity to the JT (see Appendix A).

Jesus's rationale for offering the sacrifice: it is to be a testimony to them. Despite the disagreement in number, the obvious antecedent for αὐτοῖς ("to them") is the earlier τῷ ἱερεῖ ("the priest") and so, via *constructio ad sensum*, indicates a testimony to the priestly caste as a whole.[21]

But what is the exact nature of the testimony? Is it simply the witness that the former leper is now clean and thus can offer the sacrifices in order to regain full status as a member of the Jewish people?[22] Standing against this reading is the fact that the language of μαρτύριον is foreign to the relevant instructions of Lev14.[23] Moreover, in Acts especially, yet already at the end of Luke, Luke employs the word group of "witness" to special effect: as the disciples' testimony to others of Jesus's unique mission and identity (Luke 24:48; cf. Acts 1:8, etc).[24] Given this, and in light of the ambiguously divine overtones of the vocative for "Lord" in 5:12, it is likely that members of Luke's ideal audience would have understood "testimony" here to refer to the man's witnessing to the priests of Jesus's ability to heal lepers, which the audience knows is part of Jesus's larger Isaiah-shaped vocation (see 7:22).[25] The audience, then, knows at least something of the (christological)

---

21. The logic is simple enough: the man would show himself to the on-duty priest (singular), but his non-leprous presence via contact with Jesus would serve as a witness to the larger body of priests (plural). Or Luke may simply retain the singular τῷ ἱερεῖ from Lev 13:49, as suggested by Wolter, *Das Lukasevangelium*, 218.

22. This is the reading of, e.g., C. A. Evans, *Luke*, 88. Fitzmyer confesses being slightly perplexed on this point (*Luke*, 1:575); Johnson, too, is uncertain (*Luke*, 92).

23. Cf. Johnson, *Luke*, 92. Moreover, Jesus has already shirked ancient standards of purity simply by touching the man. Note the heightening of prohibitions against skin-diseased persons in some of the writings of the Qumran community. For example, 4Q396, Col 3-4 (=4Q394, Frag 8, Col 2) commands that the skin-diseased must neither enter a holy place nor stay in a house but must remain in isolation and goes on to carp against skin-diseased persons who enter houses and eat holy food after the first-day rites of Lev 14 (specifying only the shaving and washing) but prior to the seventh. Finally, the text says that one contaminated with skin disease may not eat any holy food until the sun sets on the eighth day (4.1). This scroll extends, then, the period of ceremonial impurity, moving it from the completion of the eigth-day rites (per Lev 14) to sunset on the eighth day. This extension of impurity until sunset on the eighth day of purification is common to the legal materials of the Dead Sea Scrolls; see Hempel, "The Laws of the Damascus Document and 4QMMT," 77.

24. My own suspicion is that Luke borrows, with his own modifications of course, this term from Isaiah, and thus his use of this word group, particularly μάρτυς, constitutes part of his pervasive, often subtle, reliance on Isaiah for shaping his narratives, especially Acts. For more on the significance of "witness" within Lukan theology, see Fitzmyer, *Luke*, 1:243.

25. Cf. Marshall, *Luke*, 210; Klein, *Das Lukasevangelium*, 213.

implications to draw from Jesus's power to heal lepers—even if the priests do not.²⁶

"Witness," understood in this way, thus places conditions on Jesus's command for the man to present himself to the priests: He is to fulfill his cultic obligations according to Moses's commands, not for their own sake but rather as a means of witnessing to the more important reality of Jesus's identity and vocation.²⁷ This passage continues, then—although auditors likely would not detect it on the first several hearings of Luke's Gospels (see comments of 17:11-19)—the downplaying of the JT's sacerdotal cultic functions, here secondary and indeed subservient to the need to witness to Jesus. Again, Luke references the Temple cult not as an independently valid institution (within Luke's narrative) but as one intended to bring about proper recognition of Jesus.

There is a further ambiguity the passage admits. What is the precise meaning of αὐτοῖς? Although I have taken it as simply "to them" above, it may of course also carry the advantage-linked sense of either "against them" or, on the positive side, "for their advantage."²⁸ This sense of the pronoun, heard in context, may imply, then, so significant a meaning as to hear the witness of Jesus's vocation and life as either an indictment against the priesthood and their ongoing sacerdotal duties or else an invitation to them to recognize Jesus's identity as Messiah and Lord. Even if Culy, Parsons, and Stigall are right in viewing this as a dative of advantage (which seems likely at least *prima facie*), still Luke leaves room for the informed auditor—who knows that the leaders of the priestly class will play a key role in securing

---

26. Cf. C. A. Evans's (*Luke*, 90-91) approving citation, in light of common ancient belief that leprosy frequently had supernatural origins, of Edwards's comment (*Luke's Story of Jesus*, 39): "[Jesus's] implied argument is that it takes a supernatural person to cure a supernatural disease."

27. *Contra* Garland, *Luke*, 240, who may fail to distinguish between Luke's purposes and the possible motives of the historical Jesus ("Jesus is not concerned about broadcasting his prowess to do miracles"). Likewise, Bovon misreads the passage, in my opinion ("Luke wants neither to portray Jesus as especially observant nor to devalue legal purification vis-à-vis Christian healing"; *Luke*, 1:176), because he overlooks both an important Lukan distinctive (viz., the vocative use of "Lord") and the resonances certain "Markan" aspects of the story gain when heard within Luke's larger corpus (viz., the import of μαρτύριον and the sounding board provided by Luke's later and unique leper scene, Luke 17:11-19).

28. Culy, Parsons, Stigall, opt for dative of advantage (*Luke: A Handbook*, 163). For a reading of the testimony in Mark as a strong prophetic critique of the priests and their cultic practices, see Broadhead, "Mk 1,44." Broadhead also provides a helpful list of other interpretive options regarding the testimony (ibid., 258-60).

Jesus's crucifixion—to see this testimony, because its hearers ultimately reject it, as also a witness against them.

Summary: The Jerusalem Temple in Luke 3:1—9:50

As we have seen, despite hints that Jesus's ministry to the marginalized, his claim to forgive sins, and the theophanic revelation on the mountain begin to encroach upon the symbolic world emanating from the JT, Luke's emphasis on Jerusalem and its Temple in Luke 1–2 finds only modest continuation in this section of his Gospel.[29] This is largely a by-product of Luke's placing Jesus in Galilee, which allows the Lord, after kicking off his ministry there, to turn, dramatically and fatefully, toward Jerusalem itself. Two key exceptions to Luke's general ignoring of Jerusalem and its Temple in this section are his placing the JT temptation last instead of second in the account of Jesus's temptations and Jesus's instructing the healed leper to offer sacrifices in the Temple. The meaning of this latter encounter grows more significant as Luke's Gospel shifts to the journey toward Jerusalem.

THE CONFLICT DEEPENS: ON THE JERUSALEM JOURNEY (LUKE 9:51-19)

Luke 9:51—19:27 follows many of the lines mapped in Luke 3:1—9:50, including continuing to describe Jesus's ministry of liberation along Isaianic lines. A key point of continuity consists also of the ongoing conflict between Jesus and the religious authorities,[30] with "the crowd" floating somewhere in between.[31] Once again the conflict generally plays out obliquely, i.e., not as direct confrontations.[32] The division lines with Israel foretold by Simeon not only continue here, however, but grow even deeper and more irreparable as Jesus fatefully makes his way to Jerusalem, especially after Jesus's

---

29. There is also of course a reference to the Jerusalem elites in Jesus's initial prediction of his death, which specifies the chief priests and elders (along with the scribes) as his persecutors (9:22). As noted above, Luke is here following the language found in Mark's Gospel. Still, it is of some significance from a narrative (and also a redaction-critical) perspective that Luke chooses to retain Mark's text here.

30. Kingsbury rightly notes that Luke often takes the religious authorities stereotypically as a single group (*Conflict*, 105).

31. See Kingsbury, *Conflict*; also, Matera, "Jesus' Journey to Jerusalem," 74–75.

32. With Kingsbury, "Luke's Story," 160.

denouncing of the Pharisees and scribes (11:37–54, esp. 53–54), and they eventually reach fever pitch, after the "Triumphal Entry" with Jesus's ministry in the Temple (19:47–21:38, esp. 19:47).[33] Not only through his actions and ripostes but also by self-disclosure (12:49–53) does Jesus embrace the divisive role foretold by Simeon, and Luke makes explicit the import of the dividing lines brought through Jesus's ministry: those who side with Jesus side with God (9:48; 10:16; 11:23). This recalls John the forerunner's warning against the perilous assertion of blood descent from Abraham as the basis of one's status as a member of God's people (3:8–9). Nothing less than true membership within Israel is at stake, and Jesus himself utters mysterious parables that suggest the final members of God's people may not include the likely suspects (14:15–24).

The conflict, though fundamentally rooted in the authorities' rejection of Jesus, has several specific faces, some of which played into the framing of their conflict with Jesus in Luke 3—9:50, including the authorities' rejection of the repentant "sinners" whom Jesus accepts (15:1–3, 11–32), and their binding up heavy burdens (11:48), especially via strict Sabbath observance (13:10–17).[34] But they are also hypocrites, Luke informs the auditor (11:37–44; 12:1–3), and indeed money-lovers (16:14)—hence, their rejection of Jesus's difficult teachings on the proper use of possessions.[35] Perhaps most shocking of all—and most relevant to my thesis—is the revelation that the religious authorities are the heirs of those who murdered God's prophets of old (11:48), an ominous and telling disclosure indeed given Luke's casting of Jesus in the mantle of the great prophets of old.

While Jerusalem finds frequent mention in this section, references to the Temple are sparse. Jesus does draw auditors there through his instructions to ten lepers (17:11–19)—discussed below—and by telling a Temple-set story of Pharisaical self-justification (Luke 18:9–14). But the latter story portrays not sacerdotal cultic activity but instead prayer (v. 10),[36] and in-

---

33. Kingsbury, *Conflict*, 27.

34. Here the synagogue ruler seems to be lumped together with the religious authorities who oppose Jesus's ministry.

35. Luke later explicitly links their greed and hypocrisy (20:46–47). Matera summarizes the conflict of this section as being over "the presence of the kingdom of God, the need for repentance, the correct use of possessions, and ritual purity" ("Jesus' Journey," 76).

36. Even if there is merit to Hamm's identification of this scene as portraying the *Tamid* service ("Tamid Service," 223–24), it is telling that Luke includes in the scene only mention of the men's prayers—completely omitting references to the activity of the

deed the man who earns Jesus's praise (v. 14) is he who stands at a distance, in contrast to the Pharisee who proceeds boldly forward (v. 13). The men are justified, or not, on the basis not of proper Temple worship but rather of their succeeding or failing to adhere to the ethic of humility Jesus commends here (and elsewhere).

Given the overarching theme of escalating conflict as Jesus makes his way to Jerusalem, the intertextual background of the pivotal initiating verse, 9:51, is significant. Craig A. Evans has argued at some length that the phrase τὸ πρόσωπον ἐστήρισεν (Luke 9:51)[37] most likely echoes the use of τὸ πρόσωπον as the object of στηρίζειν in Jeremiah and Ezekiel, the only books of Scripture in which this combination appears.[38] Evans notes that each such phrase occurs, without exception, "in contexts threatening judgment."[39] Supporting Evans's reading of this echo in Luke 9:51 is the agonistic plot Luke's narrative has drawn to this point, with Jesus the prophet of God facing opposition from the religious leaders, the base of whose exploitative power resides in Jerusalem. This conflict, foretold in Simeon's stark words (2:34–35), erupted in Luke 3—9:50 and will escalate in the Journey section (see below), reaching its climax in Jerusalem (and the Temple) itself, culminating in the wrongful execution of the prophet.

Significantly, this echoed refrain from the prophets Jeremiah and Ezekiel sometimes announces judgment on God's people and even does so with particular reference to Jerusalem.[40] Thus Luke shapes Jesus's march toward Jerusalem for judgment according to prophetic precedent, and through this framing echo, Luke also summons, however vaguely, the portion of

---

priests. Hamm's efforts to fill in the Lukan "vacuum" of the scene (to which he objects) is unnecessary (223).

37. The textual variations cited in NA27 for this phrase do not, even if preferred, frustrate Evans's argument, since the variants still retain the crucial combination of τὸ πρόσωπον as the object of στηρίζειν.

38. C. A. Evans, "'He Set His Face,'" 100. In particular, Evans argues for an echo of Ezek 21:7–11 (LXX). Evans expresses some hesitancy about his case in light of Giblin's claim that Luke writes with "forthright clarity of expression," describing his case as "quite possible if not probable" ("Luke 9:51," 104, 105). Given my own claims in this study *contra* Luke's universal "forthright clarity of expression," especially when employing intertexts from the LXX, I naturally see Evans's hesitancy as unnecessary.

39. C. A. Evans, "Luke 9:51," 100. See Jer 3:12; 14:8; 15:7; Ezek 6:2; 13:17; 21:2, 7; 25:2; 28:21; 29:2; 38:2 LXX.

40. This is the case with Jer 21:10; Ezek 21:2 (parabolically), 7; and 38:2 LXX. It is also used generally of God's people in Jer 3:12, of the women of God's people in Ezek 13:17, and against the idolatry of God's people in Ezek 6:2.

The Jerusalem Temple in Luke 3–19

the prophetic tradition, particularly embodied in Jeremiah and Ezekiel, announcing doom on the holy city.[41] Jesus's approach is nothing less than God's own reckoning with the holy city that had made itself inimical to God's messengers—as Luke's Jesus himself makes clear (11:49-51; 12:57-59; 13:34-35; 19:41-44). I cannot bypass mentioning, moreover, that this reading in turn strengthens my interpretation of Luke 2:38 above as subtle communication of the destructive nature of God's imminent "redemption" of Jerusalem.

Just as earlier Luke appealed to the tradition of Shiloh (likely as interpreted through Jeremiah) as a potential model for Jerusalem's demise, so now Luke addresses the underlying theodical problem by drawing on a different but complementary strand of prophetic tradition. Later in this same section we will see that Luke appeals to yet another prophetic tradition, namely, Jerusalem's reputation as killer of prophets (13:31-35; cf. 11:49-51), in order to explain its eventual judgment. Thus Luke has begun to marshal diverse but not incompatible prophetic traditions—some subtly, some plainly expressed—as the essential pattern to his patchwork explanation for Jerusalem's destruction.

Luke also introduces another element into the agonistic plot he is constructing. Immediately after Jesus sets his face toward Jerusalem (9:51), Jesus attempts to enter a Samaritan village—and is repelled (9:52-53). Luke explains that the Samaritans's reason for rejecting Jesus was that his face was set for Jerusalem (9:53), playing to well-known Jewish-Samaritan enmity at this time. When James and John ask if they should (like Elijah) call down fire to destroy the village, Jesus rebukes them and moves on (9:54-56).[42]

Although it thus appears that the Samaritans are firmly aligned as additional enemies of Jesus, Luke takes pains to rehabilitate them at two later points in this central section of his Gospel: the story of the Good Samaritan (10:30-37)[43] and the healing of the Ten Lepers (17:11-19; see below). Audi-

---

41. In fact, C. A. Evans ("Luke 9:51," 101) cites three passages related to Jerusalem's destruction and either unique to or strongly shaped by Luke in which Luke appears, per Giblin, to echo Ezekiel—strongly suggesting Luke's use of Ezekiel for understanding and framing Jerusalem's demise.

42. Sensitive readers are invited to observe a synkritical comparison between Jesus and Elijah here, to Jesus's advantage: having greater power than Elijah, Jesus also possessed greater restraint.

43. The story of the Good Samaritan, which is often taken to be and probably is a parable, rehabilitates Samaritans not by giving a positive story about a Samaritan that is understood to be "historical" or factual within the world of Luke's narrative, as with the Ten Lepers. Rather, it creates a positive narrative about a Samaritan that introduces

PART 2: THE JERUSALEM TEMPLE IN LUKE'S GOSPEL

tors familiar with his Gospel thus know that the Samaritan village's rejection of him is not representative of Samaritans as a whole. They also know, in fact, that the village rejected Jesus specifically because of his heading toward Jerusalem, which already foregrounds in the audience's mind the issue of a proper cultic site, since Jesus's arrival in (and thus presumably his departure for) Jerusalem would put him there in time for Passover.[44]

Thus, with the ominous chords of Simeon's last prophecy humming in the background, Luke's Jesus marches toward Jerusalem amid a redounding symphony of conflict, division, and judgment.[45]

Suffering and Fig Tree Theodicy (Luke 13:1–9)

Less than halfway into his Gospel's central section but after already establishing many of the significant features of that section, including the escalating conflict between Jesus and the religious leaders (11:37–54; 12:1–3, 49–59) and Jesus's concern for proper use of possessions (12:13–21), Luke has unknown members of the crowd elicit comment from Jesus by referencing Galileans whose blood Pilate mixed with their sacrifices (13:1).[46] This scene immediately follows Jesus's self-proclamation of his divisive role (12:49–53) and his warning that this divisive role means that Israel should rightly judge the times, seeking peace before it is too late (12:54–59)—and so should be understood in light of this earlier scene.[47] Jesus's response to

---

the theological possibility that a Samaritan should inherit life by fulfilling the chief commandment (10:25–29), where a Jew, even a Levite or indeed a priest, had failed.

44. Samaritans opposed pilgrimages to Jerusalem not only out of general enmity but especially also because it was not, in their eyes, the proper worship site; cf. Hamm, "Samaritan Leper," 282.

45. Another agonistic line Luke maps, although less strongly than the division between Jesus and the religious leaders (with "the people/crowd" often in view), is the conflict between Jesus and Satan, an inevitable result of Jesus's ministry of liberation (10:17–20; 11:14–26; 13:16). Given these lines of conflict, it is little surprise that the religious leaders' eventual assault on Jesus occurs with Satanic collaboration (22:1–6, 53).

46. Numerous are the times that Luke has members of the crowd, disciples, and religious authorities prompt Jesus in this way—11:27–28 (woman in crowd), 11:45 (lawyer), 12:41 (Peter), 14:15 (unknown person), etc.

47. Caird helpfully links the two pericopae, which he sees as spelling out the need for "national reformation" if Israel is to avoid destruction by Roman hands (*St. Luke*, 168–69). Nolland notes a connection between 13:1–9 and the warning to reconcile with one's accuser in 12:58 and takes 13:1–9 as the conclusion to the section comprised of 12:1—13:9 (*Luke*, 2:716–19).

the unknown members of the crowd is that these Galileans were no worse sinners than any other Galileans of their day (13:2–3a). Then he turns the tables on these unknown inquirers, commanding them to repent lest they suffer a similar fate (13:3b). Jesus goes on to tell the story of the eighteen people who died when the Tower of Siloam fell and reaffirms the same point: his hearers ("all of you," second person plural) must repent or likewise perish (13:4–5). Beyond the emphasis on repentance (a Lukan leitmotif) and the attendant rejection of strict retribution theology, the precise meaning of this passage is difficult to determine. Many commentators—rightly, in my view—see at least a hint here of Jerusalem's dire status as an imminent recipient of divine wrath,[48] a view very likely given the multiple references to Jerusalem in the passage,[49] the immediately preceding warning about reading the signs of the times (12:54–59), and Jesus's lament over Jerusalem shortly thereafter (13:31–35).

The parable that immediately follows points in this direction as well[50]: A fig tree (συκῆ) planted in a vineyard (πεφυτευμένην ἐν τῷ ἀμπελῶνι) failed to yield fruit for three years, and so the owner commanded the vine-dresser (ἀμπελουργός) to cut it down; but the vine-dresser interceded on behalf of the fig tree, asking for one more year in which to dig around and fertilize the fig tree (σκάψω περὶ αὐτὴν καὶ βάλω κόπρια), after which, should it still fail to produce, it would indeed be cut down (13:6–9). As many have noted, this parable has a beginning and middle but ends before concluding, and so remains open[51]—an openness that dovetails with its invitation to repentance.[52]

This parable is unique to Luke, although it strongly resembles a story in Ahikar.[53] It also recalls the Parable of the Tenants found in all three Synoptics (Mark 12:1–12; Matt 21:33–46; Luke 20:9–18). Each of these parables in turn echoes the poignant song depicting Judah as a vineyard that produced thorns instead of grapes in Isa 5:1–7a. Isaiah 5 goes on to

---

48. E.g., Caird, *St. Luke*, 168–69; Danker, *Jesus and the New Age*, 259.

49. Note the oblique (and muted?) reference to past sacerdotal worship in the JT by mention of the sacrifices.

50. On the puzzling relationship between this parable and 13:1–5, see Martens, "'Produce Fruit Worthy of Repentance,'" 169–70.

51. See Snodgrass, *Stories with Intent*, 259.

52. It is in this sense closely akin to the Parable of the Two Lost Sons (Luke 15:11–32).

53. Green emphasizes the element of clemency in Luke 13 as a key difference from the parallel in Ahikar 8:35 (*Luke*, 515); also, Martens, "'Produce Fruit Worthy of Repentance,'" 171.

Part 2: The Jerusalem Temple in Luke's Gospel

specify the "thorns" of God's people as their unjust, oppressive dealings with one another and their general backwardness of perspective—which God will ultimately right (vv. 7b–30).[54] The indictment of God's people, including specifically the residents of Jerusalem (Isa 5:3), for their injustice and wrong-headed rebelliousness strongly matches the overarching dynamics of Luke's Gospel, especially 9:51—19:27 (see above).

Several verbal parallels point to Isa 5:1–7 in Luke 13:6–9 as well.[55] Isaiah 5:2 mentions a tower (πύργος) in the midst of the vineyard. Although no such tower appears in Luke's parable, the occurrence of the same word in Luke 13:4 (the "Tower of Siloam") as the lead-up to the parable may have suggested Isa 5 to Luke, and may signal his ideal audience there as well. Both parables feature a vineyard (ἄμπελος), although, while the vineyard stands for Judah in Isa 5, a mere fig tree within the larger vineyard appears to fill this role in Luke 13 (see below). In both Luke 13 and Isa 5, God plants (φυτεύω), although, again, it is a vineyard in Isa 5 and a fig tree in Luke 13 God plants. Finally, in Isa 5:6 God refuses, because of the vineyard's fruitlessness, to cultivate ("dig," σκάπτω) it, whereas the vine-dresser aims to do this as part of the last-ditch effort to save the fig tree from its own fruitlessness (Luke 13:8). Though potentially viewed as evidence that Luke does not intend a strong connection to Isa 5 here, the changes Luke has made to Isa 5's song are, rather, instructive.

Before elaborating the instructive nature of Luke's changes, there are a number of odd omissions that require comment. Luke curiously omits here several key words from Isa 5 that occur in the Parable of the Tenants in Mark (and also Matthew). The omission of πύργος from the parable may be such an omission, although I view it instead as obviated by its appearance in Luke 13:4. Still, this prevents Luke from following Mark (and Matthew) in describing God's also *building* a tower in the vineyard (ᾠκοδόμησεν πύργον) as in Isa 5:2 (Mark 12:1; Matt 21:33). Note also Luke's failure to mention God's setting around (περιτίθημι) the vineyard a hedge/fence (φραγμός), drawn straight from Isa 5:2 and appearing in both Mark 12:1 and Matt 21:33. Finally, Luke leaves out God's initially digging a winepress in his vineyard (προλήνιον ὤρυξα in Isa 5:2 vs. ὤρυξεν ὑπολήνιον in Mark 12:1 and ὤρυξεν ἐν αὐτῷ ληνὸν in Matt 21:33).

---

54. This passage has strong resonances with Luke's own favored theme of divine reversal (e.g., Isa 5:15 and the Magnificat), and the overtones of economic injustice of course strike a Lukan chord as well.

55. Cautiously endorsing Isa 5:1–7 as the background for this passage are Pao and Schnabel, "Luke," 333.

It is curious and probably significant that Luke also omits from his version of the Parable of the Tenants (Luke 20:9–19) each of the above omissions from his Parable of the Fig Trees. Where Mark and Matthew have in quick succession God's building a tower, hedging a fence, and digging a winepress, Luke's Tenants Parable has, in the layout of the Synopsis, only blank space. The omission is all the more striking given that it is the second largest omission Luke makes to Mark's text in this passage (although he makes numerous modifications, mostly sylistic).[56] The likely solution to the riddle is that Luke intentionally omits these words and concepts, apparently taken directly from Isaiah by Mark, in order to de-emphasize a connection between his Parable of the Tenants and Isa 5. Although Luke may have had any number of reasons for muting a connection between the Parable of the Tenants and the song of Isaiah 5, one noticeable effect of this decision is the amplification of the connection between his Parable of the Fig Tree in Luke 13 and Isa 5: by removing interference from his later parable, Luke effectively increases the odds that his audience would hear Isa 5 here.

Moreover, the omission of those features of Isa 5 that appear in Mark's and Matthew's Parable of the Tenants is explainable on Luke's emphasis here not on the entire vineyard but rather on the fig tree: Luke is telling the story of a fig tree within the vineyard, and so to mention the fence and grape-press would be simply beside the point, since these are features of the vineyard as a whole. Given his mention of cultivation via digging (σκάπτω, Luke 13:8; cf. Isa 5:6) and the larger pervasive echoes of Isaiah in Luke's writings, there is strong evidence that Luke recalls Isa 5 here and does so in a way that members of his ideal audience would likely have detected (as have, e.g., the editors of NA27).[57]

But what is the import of Luke's alluding to Isa 5 here? One thing this allusion does is to prepare the audience, along with the hints of Luke 1–2 and 13:1–5, for the harsh pronouncement against Jerusalem in Luke 13:31–35, for it conjures Isaiah's vivid portrait of God's coming judgment on his people, with Jerusalem in particular focus. The context of the parable,

---

56. The largest omission is Luke's leaving off Mark 12:11, which is ten words long, versus the nine words Luke omits from Mark 12:1.

57. Danker sees Isa 5 as a background text here but argues for Mic 7:1 as the key intertext, based on Luke's apparent citation of Mic 7:6 in 12:53 (*Jesus and the New Age*, 260). Though Luke does likely allude to Mic 7:6 just earlier—a fact that helps connect 13:1–9 with the preceding pericope—Isa 5 has far stronger thematic and verbal parallels to 13:6–9 than does Mic 7:1 and so provides the dominant LXX background.

Part 2: The Jerusalem Temple in Luke's Gospel

namely the hints and then clear pronouncement of Jerusalem's demise in 13:1–5 and 13:31–35, respectively, lead to a likely allegorical association of the fig tree with Jerusalem or probably with Israel in general (since Galilee also features prominently in 13:1–5 and since his audience would know that the Flavian assault would bring destruction on the entire region, not just Jerusalem).[58] It is also possible to side with Kenneth Bailey in seeing the reference to the fig tree as an indictment of the Judean leadership and not the entire nation.[59] Though appealing, however, this reading does not seem adequately to prepare for the harsh tones of 13:31–35 directed toward all of Jerusalem, already foreshadowed in the verses leading up to this parable (13:1–5). An Israel-fig tree connection is strengthened by the shared language between this parable and John's earlier warning against

---

58. Contra Wolter, *Das Lukasevangelium*, 477. Modern interpreters, haunted no doubt by the spirit of Jülicher, often strongly resist allegorical readings of Jesus's parables. Yet here the connection to Isa 5, which is clearly allegorical, suggests just such a reading. See C. A. Evans's assessment that "it is probable that Luke's contemporaries would have understood" a reference to Israel with the fig tree, citing Jer 8:13; Mic 7:1 (*Luke*, 206); also, Tiede, *Luke*, 247; Kinman, "Lucan Eschatology," 675, and references in 670–71, 675n25; and Snodgrass: "From OT and Jewish texts on fig trees, the symbolism of the fig tree for Israel is obvious" (*Stories with Intent*, 263). Supporting this allegorization further is the apparent equation of Israel with the fig tree in the parallel parable in the Ethiopic version of the *Apocalypse of Peter* (chap. 2; see Bauckham, "The Two Fig Tree Parables"), although Bauckham argues that this parable comes not from Luke but from "independent gospel tradition" (ibid., 283); *Apoc. Pet.* also explicitly equates God with the owner. Fitzmyer also allows for an "allegorical thrust" in the parable: "It should be recalled that a fig tree often stood in the OT as a symbol of Judah or Israel" (*Luke*, 2:1005, 1008). (Nolland, however, contests this claim [*Luke*, 2:718].) Moreover, the allegorical readings of patristic and medieval interpreters—Jülicher's boogeyman—generally went far afield from the allegorical elements I am highlighting here (see Snodgrass, *Stories with Intent*, 260; but cf. Cyril of Alexandria, *Commentary on Luke*, Homily 96).

59. Bailey, *Poet and Peasant*, 2:82. Bailey argues for this by noting the allusion to Isa 5:1–7 here and noting its specific application to the leadership in Luke 20:9–16. He addresses the apparent disjuncture this creates between 13:1–5 and 13:6–9 by claiming they are "closely related" "units of tradition" pairing a call for the people to repent (vv. 1–5) with a statement of the leadership's "need [for] forgiveness" (vv. 6–9) (*Poet and Peasant*, 2:87). Blomberg agrees with Bailey's taking the fig tree as allegorical of only Israel's leadership but notes that "the principle of judgment on those who do not repent obviously applies universally (Lk 13:3, 5)" (*Interpreting the Parables*, 269). Likewise, Green muses: "Does the narrator hope that his audience will hear Isa 5:1–7 in the background of this parable? If so, an identification of Israel with the vineyard is likely, with the further identification of the fig tree as Israel's barren leadership also conceivable" (*Luke*, 515n126). Among the potential pay-offs of identifying the fig tree as a reference specifically to the leadership is the mention of spreading manure (v. 8) as "insult humor" (Bailey, *Poet and Peasant*, 2:84).

self-assurance on the basis of ethnic lineage (Luke 3:7-9).⁶⁰ From a theodical angle, Luke may be inviting his audience to consider that just as God previously visited his people with destruction for their immorality (and note the emphasis on economic injustice both in Isa 5 and in the central section of Luke's Gospel), so God has done so again; this would constitute a clear appeal to retribution theology.

In this way, the parable supplies a theologically satisfying answer to the dominant theodical issue of the day, again by appealing to prophetic tradition, but it does so with an additional wrinkle. Unlike in Isa 5, where God rejects the people, here God's intention to reject them (again taking the fig tree as a reference to God's people) is rebuffed by the vine-dresser, an undisclosed intercessor, who gains for (this segment of) God's people a brief reprieve. The presence of an intercessor indicates that God's eventual judgment on the people was not only just, as in Isa 5, but was in fact delayed through mercy. Although there is a strong modern allergy to allegory regarding Jesus's parables, the connection to Isa 5 suggests an allegorical reading, and Luke's presentation of Jesus as would-be intercessor for Jerusalem in 13:34 (and also 19:41-44) suggests the vine-dresser may represent Jesus himself.⁶¹ This would not be the last time Luke presents Jesus in an intercessory role (see Luke 22:31-32).⁶² Given the not infrequent intercessory function of Israel's prophets, especially Moses,⁶³ that Luke so poignantly

---

60. The shared words are ποιέω, καρπός, and ἐκκόπτω (cf. Green, *Luke*, 515n125); both passages also refer to trees, though with differing vocabulary (δένδρον, συκῆ), and both emphasize repentance.

61. See Klein, *Das Lukasevangelium*, 476. Snodgrass, who advises that allegorical readings, even when valid, must only be taken so far, shows tentative willingness to equate the vine-dresser with Jesus (Snodgrass, *Stories with Intent*, 263). More willing to see the vinedresser as a cipher for Jesus (though only from the perspective of the disciples) is Jeremias, *Parables of Jesus*, 170-71. Though perhaps weakening my case, Cyril of Alexandria, among ancient commentators, allowed the vinedresser as allegorically representative of Jesus (*Commentary on Luke*, Homily 96, cited in *Ancient Christian Commentary*, 224). Note the subsequent appearances of Jesus, via allegory, as a character within the Lukan parables (e.g., as the king-to-be in 19:11-27; as the son in 20:9-19). Nolland seems to ponder the possible allegorical identification: "Is it over-interpretation to identify Jesus's ministry with the special nurture offered to the tree in its final year?" (*Luke*, 2:719). Fitzmyer's hesitancy on this point (*Luke*, 2:1005) is understandable but not definitive. Firmly dissenting is Hultgren, *The Parables of Jesus*, 245. Note that Luke, on many readings, allegorizes the Parable of the Persistent Widow (18:1-8) such that God corresponds (via the logic of "the lesser to the greater") to the parable's judge.

62. Referenced by Jeremias, *The Parables of Jesus*, 171.

63. Prophets as intercessors: Moses (Exod 32:11-14, 30-34; 34:9; Num 14:13-19; Ps

casts Jesus as a prophet, indeed as the prophet "like Moses," throughout Luke and Acts further supports such an identification, as does the fact that Jesus's tenor when addressing Jerusalem's fate as the Gospel proceeds are decidedly pathos-laden: the compassionate vine-dresser of Luke 13:6–9 becomes the doleful Messiah of Luke 13:34–35; 19:41–44; and 23:28–31.[64] The theodical import of the passage is clear: Not only does God judge Israel (especially Jerusalem) for its unrighteousness justly and according to prophetic precedent (Isa 5), but God would have, except for the intercessor, judged the city long before. Thus God proves not only just and faithful but even merciful—though the window for repentance is limited and is, within the narrative timeline of Luke's gospel, quickly closing.[65]

Alas, Jerusalem's Demise (Luke 13:31–35)

Here, following numerous hints and insinuations, and roughly halfway into his Gospel, Luke finally announces in the clear words of Jesus the imminence of Jerusalem's demise. This ekphrastic scene comes shortly after the Parable of the Fig Tree and so (as argued above) colors interpretation of that passage—and, via the hermeneutical circle, vice versa. Intervening between the two are a scene of conflict with a synagogue ruler over Jesus's healing a Satan-bound "daughter of Abraham" on the Sabbath (13:10–17), two parables on the kingdom of God (vv. 18–21), a geographical notice highlighting the movement toward Jerusalem (v. 22), and a question and response about who will be saved, with the rejection of many who would seem to be first in line (vv. 23–30).

Luke 13:31–35, which parallels Matt 23:37–39 with considerable accuracy even in terms of word order,[66] offers much grist for rumination, but central for my study are v. 33, which establishes a connection between Jesus

---

105:23; Jer 15:1); Samuel (1 Kgdms 12:17–18; Jer 15:1); Jeremiah (e.g., Jer 7:16).

64. Jesus's grief over Jerusalem is muted only in 21:20–24. Many of course rightly note a shift in tone from this parable, in which judgment is suspended, to Jesus's subsequent announcements of Jerusalem's fate, in which judgment is more certain (e.g., Snodgrass, *Stories with Intent*, 264). No hard line of separation need be enforced, however, given the natural progression from warning to pronouncement, which corresponds to this parable's appearing prior to Jesus's pronouncements in Luke's Gospel.

65. See Klein, *Das Lukasevangelium*, 476.

66. On this see Weinert, "Abandoned House," 72, although I disagree with his overall reading of this pericope in Luke.

and Jerusalem, and especially the enigmatic v. 35a. I will consider these shortly.

The appearance in v. 31 of "some Pharisees" who tell Jesus to flee because Herod wants to kill him is a typically Lukan "interruption," which appears "to change the subject" but which actually provides opportunity to elaborate the theme of judgment discussed in 13:22–30.[67] Despite the ominous nature of the report,[68] Jesus dismissively refers to Herod as a fox (v. 32), but then he cryptically acknowledges his own fate: he must continue his work of exorcising and healing "today and tomorrow" until he "finishes" his work on the third day (v. 32)—very likely implying his death[69]—because it is impossible for a prophet to die outside Jerusalem (v. 33). This clearly recalls Jesus's harsh description of Jerusalem as murderer of God's prophets (Luke 11:49–51) and unmistakably affirms Jesus as a prophet who is marked by divine necessity (v. 33) for a prophet's death.

The reminder of Jerusalem's status as prophet-killer leads to Jesus's mournful words about Jerusalem's unwillingness to be gathered to him (v. 34). Jesus's description of Jerusalem's impenitence here, and his furthering the charges against it ("who stone those who are sent to it"),[70] recalls the fruitlessness of the fig tree in 13:6–9, and Jesus the intercessor now appears to despair of the city's fate.[71]

---

67. See Green, *Luke*, 534–35, who also notes how the temporal reference of v. 31 ("at that very hour") ties the two scenes together, as does the geographical notice of Jesus's approach to Jerusalem in v. 22; also, Nolland, *Luke*, 2:738.

68. Darr observes that, because Herod has already killed John the Baptist, his desiring to see Jesus in Luke 9:9 is decidedly "ominous" (*Herod the Fox*, 170). Not only is the report of 13:31 plausible, then, but so is the threat that is reported!

69. Luke's use of τελειοῦμαι here (cf., e.g., Jer 11:22 LXX) likely has a double-meaning: Jesus will not only *complete* his mission in Jerusalem but will do so by *dying* (in agreement with Fisk, "See My Tears," 153). For this point, and more, including potential scriptural echoes in Luke 13:32–33 (some tenuous), see Derrett, "The Lucan Christ and Jerusalem," 36–43. Despite a number of interesting connections, I am not yet convinced that Luke intends his audience to hear Luke 13:31–35 against Deut 16:16—17:17, as Derrett contends.

70. See Green, *Luke*, 538. Attempting to clarify Jesus's mysterious statement that it is impossible for prophets to die outside of Jerusalem—against the clear scriptural evidence to the contrary—Green takes "Jerusalem" as synecdoche for all of Israel here (*Luke*, 538). If correct (and I remain on the fence), this would strengthen my reading of Anna's reference to Jerusalem in 2:38 as a double entendre both utilizing synecdoche (or metonymy) and intending the obvious referent—the city itself.

71. Luke may also allude to the execution of the prophet Zechariah by stoning (2 Chron 24:17–22); see Fisk, "See My Tears," 158.

Part 2: The Jerusalem Temple in Luke's Gospel

This brings us (rather quickly) to v. 35, the first sentence of which (ἰδοὺ ἀφίεται ὑμῖν ὁ οἶκος ὑμῶν) is crucial. This short and enigmatic sentence raises several questions for commentators: What, first of all, do the constituent pieces of the verse mean—what is the meaning of οἶκος, and what is the import of ἀφίεται ὑμῖν? What light, moreover, is brought by Matt 23:39, which is identical to Luke 13:35a, with the perhaps telling addition of ἔρημος at the sentence's close?[72] And what light do the intertextual echoes of this short verse—if any—shed on these basic questions?

I will tackle the second question first: What do we make of Luke's non-inclusion of ἔρημος? The question is of course complicated by the nebulous status of text-critical questions (at least for some) regarding Matthew and Luke. If we follow most scholars in assuming Matthew and Luke's mutual borrowing from Q and further follow those who have so boldly reconstructed this hypothesized document, then ἔρημος is a Matthean addition, and Luke has simply recorded what he found written in his (now-immaterial) source.[73] In this case, it is Matthew's addition, rather than Luke's non-inclusion, that is significant.[74]

On the Farrer(-Goodacre) Hypothesis, however, Luke knew and used the text of Matthew, and so he actively omitted ἔρημος, presumably to significant effect. If Luke did use Matthew and thus omitted ἔρημος (assuming, as we must, that he did not do so by accident or whimsy), then there are any number of conjectures one might make. Perhaps Luke simply intended to tone down Matthew's expression while retaining his basic meaning. Or perhaps Luke intended something entirely different from Matthew—and here we have a whole new range of options. Given the condemnatory words about Jerusalem Luke attributes to Jesus in passages connected to and both preceding (11:49–51) and following (19:41–45) this one, as well as the tones of judgment in the scene (13:22–30) that immediately precedes and that Luke himself links (cf. 13:31) to this one, whatever else he may mean, Luke surely means that "the house" (somehow linked to Jerusalem, but for a fuller discussion of its meaning, see below) is forsaken, left, given up—i.e.,

---

72. The manuscripts of Luke's Gospel that do, according to NA27, include ἔρημος are likely later attempts to harmonize with Matthew. Cf. Fitzmyer, *Luke*, 2:1036.

73. See Q 13:35 in Robinson et al., eds., *The Sayings Gospel Q*, 701–3.

74. Playing Luke off against Matthew here, Weinert claims that Luke's non-inclusion of ἔρημος shows that he "has no particular wish to stress the desolate state of Jerusalem's abandoned house" ("Abandoned House," 73), but this is by no means the case on traditional source-critical grounds (which Weinert assumes) and is not necessarily so even if Luke knew Matthew, as I explore below.

something along the lines of desolation.[75] Moreover, the omission of the harsh ἔρημος may accomplish several other things: 1) leaving more room for the possibility of Jerusalem's eventual renewal (cf. 21:24), and 2) not interrupting the progression within his Gospel from the deserving possibility of Jerusalem's destruction (13:6-9),[76] to the likelihood of such (here), and on to the near-certainty (19:41-45) and, finally, inevitability (21:20; 23:28-31) of its devastation.

More relevant to my thesis are two points. First, by omitting ἔρημος or, alternately, by not including it (apart from any putative knowledge of Matthew or Q), Luke allows for polysemic possibilities for ἀφίεται: Luke retains/connotes the meaning of desolation but also leaves room to highlight the (passively referenced) action by which that desolate end comes about—i.e., God's leaving.[77] This abandonment aspect of ἀφίεται provides an important interpretive framework for the rending of the Temple veil in Luke 23:45 and for Luke's de-emphasis on the Temple as a sacerdotal cultic site, and in fact it helps to connect the two (as discussed in chapter 5). While some take the verb as "future present,"[78] it is perhaps circumspect to leave room also for a present progressive sense: the abandonment has begun and is in process—as Luke has indicated beginning with the births of Jesus and to a lesser degree John.[79] Second, the non-inclusion of ἔρημος mutes potential echoes of Jer 22:5 (εἰς ἐρήμωσιν ἔσται ὁ οἶκος οὗτος)—a fact insufficiently appreciated.[80] These points, which are the most signifi-

---

75. Weinert's interpretation of ἀφίημι in 13:8 as "a temporary respite" misses the point: this so-called "respite" stands under certain destruction if it does not prove a fruit-bearing reprieve ("Abandoned House," 73n16).

76. I have interpreted this parable as a reference to greater-Judea, but that certainly includes Jerusalem as well.

77. Thus the passive here, as often in Luke and Acts, is a reference to divine action.

78. E.g., Fisk, "See My Tears," 163. Johnson leaves room for either sense, although he does not observe that Luke may employ both senses (*Luke*, 219), thus fleshing out the (likely) parallel meaning of οἶκος as both a reference to the people—who are being left to their own devices (present progressive)—and to the Temple—which is being abandoned (progressive) and will be made positively desolate (future).

79. *Contra* Nolland, who strangely assumes the present tense "suggests a fate already sealed," despite the wide syntactical possibilities of the Greek present tense (*Luke*, 2:742).

80. Cf. Weinert, "Abandoned House," 76; also, the editors of NA27. Bock, *Proclamation from Prophecy and Pattern*, 117: "There is the declaration that her (Jerusalem's) house is now *desolate*, following the pattern of Jeremiah (Jer. 12.7; 22.5)" (emphasis added). Likewise, Marshall claims v. 35a "alludes to" Jer 12:7 and 22:5 (*Luke*, 576); Nolland: "Jer 22:1-8 provides the closest background here" (*Luke*, 2:742); also, Pao and Eckhart, "Luke," 336. This tendency to identify Jer 12 and especially 22 as the primary background

Part 2: The Jerusalem Temple in Luke's Gospel

cant implications for my thesis of Luke's ἀφίεται without a trailing ἔρημος, fortunately do not hinge on a particular source-critical decision.

Regarding the meaning of οἶκος, Francis Weinert has argued at length that οἶκος should not be taken "primarily" as a reference to the Temple but rather to "Israel's Judean leadership, and those who fall under their leadership." He does this in part by appealing to Jer 22:1–9 as "the most probable OT background for Luke 13:35a,"[81] and intertextuality is indeed crucial for determining the meaning of οἶκος here. Generally, I find myself in company with those who hold that Luke 13:35a echoes a number of Scriptures, especially prophetic warnings.[82] As noted just above, Weinert's proposal of Jer 22:1–9 is unlikely as a primary background, especially since the single best basis for linking the passages verbally (ἔρημος) is precisely the word that Luke leaves out.[83] Is Weinert correct, then, in identifying οἶκος as a reference to the Judean leadership?

Because of the proximity to the Parable of the Fig Tree (Luke 13:6–9), as well as the conceptual connection between the warning there and Jesus's lament here, members of Luke's audience may have heard in οἶκος at least

---

for Luke 13:35a, to the exclusion of Jer 33 (LXX), is somewhat puzzling. Both Jer 22 and 33 (LXX) employ the verb form of (the dubiously Lukan) ἔρημος (22:5; 33:9), along with numerous uses of οἶκος. Thus Jer 22, despite its preferential treatment by many scholars, enjoys no better verbal parallels with Luke 13:35a than does Jer 33. While preferential treatment of Jer 12:7 might be justified based on its use of ἀφίημι along with οἶκος, in Jer 12:7, it is not the οἶκος but the "inheritance" that is "abandoned" (ἀφῆκα). Moreover, and most decisively, the narrative dynamics of Jer 33 (LXX) match the narrative dynamics of Luke's Gospel far better than do those of either Jer 12 or Jer 22; see further discussion below.

81. Weinert, "Abandoned House," 76. Weinert's first two arguments for his interpretation of οἶκος are unconvincing: 1) that Luke conceives of Jerusalem's "house" in "personal" rather than "spatial" terms, and 2) that Luke rarely employs οἶκος for the JT (true enough) and, when he does, associates it with God—maintaining this only by tenuous logic particularly regarding Luke 11:51 (Weinert, "Abandoned House," 75).

82. E.g., Green, *Luke*, 539.

83. But this is true not only because of Luke's non-inclusion of ἔρημος. Weinert's case for Jer 22 seems to rest largely on the conclusions reached in Marshall's NIGTC commentary. Weinert's own logic for preferring Jer 22:1–9 over other options, especially other prophetic options, is fuzzy (see "Abandoned House," 75). He leaps from the claim that Luke generally characterizes the leaders of Israel as opponents to Jesus, with the people as more friendly (which is basically correct), to Jer 22:1–9 as the appropriate background because Jer 22 calls for heeding of the prophet by the kingly household, the people, and all the royal court: where, then, is the opposition? Thus this passage does not in fact appear to match the agonistic dynamic which Weinert (rightly) sees at play in Luke's Gospel.

some reference to Isa 5:7: ὁ γὰρ ἀμπελὼν κυρίου σαβαωθ οἶκος τοῦ Ἰσραηλ ἐστίν καὶ ἄνθρωπος τοῦ Ἰουδα νεόφυτον ἠγαπημένον. If this is the case, οἶκος likely entails a reference to the residents of Judea as a whole, with Jerusalem particularly in focus (cf. Isa 5:3). Use of οἶκος in this way as a reference to a geographically or ethnically specified group is common in the LXX (e.g., Isa 7:13, 17; 8:14, 17, 18; 14:1; etc).

But we need not conclude that this passage plays off of a single intertext. Jeremiah 33 (LXX) also has strong resonances, partly because it presents Jeremiah the prophet's issuing a trenchant warning to Jerusalem[84] and because it, like this section of Luke's Gospel, highlights the possibility of averting disaster through repentance (33:2-3, 17-19)[85] and particularly because the heightened conflict of that passage (largely absent in Jer 22:1-9) and the intra-Judean divisions caused there by the prophet (cf. Jer 33:8, 10-12, 16-19 LXX) match the dynamics at play in Luke's Gospel.[86] Indeed, Jer 33 (LXX) presents a conflict between the priests and false prophets who oppose the prophet Jeremiah on the one side, and, on the other side, the rulers (οἱ ἄρχοντες) who ultimately acquit him—with the people (ὁ λαός) caught in the middle (cf. esp. vv. 7-9, 11, 16). The opposition of the priests combined with the nebulous position of the people in Jer 33 thus strongly resembles Luke's characterization of the priests and people throughout this section and into his Passion Narrative,[87] and the pro-prophet stance of the

---

84. As Fisk, "See My Tears," notes "For Jesus to utter *any* lament over the city of Jerusalem would thus be to invite comparisons with the Weeping Prophet [Jeremiah]" (162), although, in discussing Luke 13:35a, Fisk focuses on potential echoes of Jer 22, to the exclusion of Jer 33 (LXX). Virtually all of the evidence which Fisk adduces to support a connection to Jer 22 apply also to Jer 33 (LXX).

85. Just as the characters in Jer 33:19 (LXX) look back on God's relenting in punishment because of the people's repentance, so Jesus in Luke 13:31-35 seems to look back on Jer 33, hoping against hope for repentance.

86. The incredulity of the priests, false prophets, and people in Jer 33:8-9 (LXX) that God would have instructed Jeremiah to utter words against the holy city—an incredulity likely based on their assured belief that Jerusalem and its Temple were God's unique dwelling place and thus enjoyed God's protection—of course also matches the now theodically-challenging beliefs of many of Luke's contemporaries, including perhaps members of his audience.

87. Luke adds to the charges by the religious leaders found in Mark the accusation that Jesus misleads the people/nation (Τοῦτον εὕραμεν διαστρέφοντα τὸ ἔθνος; 23:2), thus going against his tendency to exonerate the people vis-à-vis the religious leaders (compared to Mark) by having ὁ λαός eventually join the chief priests and leaders (23:13) in calling for Jesus's death (23:18, 23-25)—perhaps in order to show the leaders to be guilty of the very crime with which they charge Jesus (misleading the nation). He omits

Part 2: The Jerusalem Temple in Luke's Gospel

rulers is perhaps recalled in Luke's reference to Herod, who, despite his reported threat here, will ultimately acquit Jesus (23:6–12), as Luke's ideal audience knows.[88] Given these strong similarities between the overarching features of Jer 33 (LXX) and Luke 13:31–35, the fact that Jer 33:1–19 frequently employs οἶκος (eleven times), and in every case but one (v. 10) refers to the JT, indicates that Luke intends, and his ideal audience would have heard, a reference to the Temple here.

Moreover, the background probability of a reference to the JT here, even apart from Luke's alluding to Jer 33 (LXX), is quite high: not only does any use of οἶκος in combination with Jerusalem almost automatically conjure an image of the JT for auditors with ears attuned to the LXX,[89] but Luke's frequent interest in Jerusalem and the Temple, especially as the destination of Jesus's journey, also bolsters this reading. Here, then, Luke is again striking a polysemic note: οἶκος refers both to the residents of Judea, perhaps specifically Jerusalem, and to the Temple itself.[90]

In fact, Luke has good reasons for connecting the two.[91] Although Weinert rejects οἶκος as a reference to the Temple in large part because

---

the charge that Jesus putatively threatened the Temple itself (Mark 14:58) in order to reserve it for the trial of Stephen (Acts 6:13–14)—precisely the point in Luke's writings at which he levels his strongest, baldest critique of the Temple (see my Appendix).

88. A potential obstacle for my reading here is Luke's occasional references to οἱ ἄρχοντες as included among Jesus's opponents. Note, however, that I am not contending that Luke intends Jer 33 (LXX) to resound throughout his entire presentation of Jesus's conflict with the Judean leadership, that this use of ἄρχων inheres only beginning in Luke's Passion Narrative (23:13, 35; 24:20; but cf. 14:1) and perhaps with reference to another Scripture (viz., Ps 2—see Acts 4:25–26), and that, with regards to Luke 13:31–35, any reference to a ruler here must be first and foremost to Herod, with the ambivalent Pharisees as the next likeliest candidate (esp. in light of 14:1). Moreover, the ruling authorities behave ambivalently toward God's prophets in Jer 33:20–24 (LXX).

89. See Walker, *Jesus and the Holy City*, 61.

90. Compare Bar 2:26—a single verse—which employs οἶκος three times, first in reference to the JT and then in reference to the people of Israel and Judah; it also attributes the Temple's demise to the wickedness of the inhabitants. Included on the list of those who take the "house left desolate" line as a reference to Jerusalem and the JT is Allison, "Matt. 23:39 = Luke 13:35b," 76 (although Allison, in this early article, refers to the putative Q saying divorced from its context in Luke), despite his emphasis on Jer 12 and 22, to the exclusion of Jer 33 (LXX). Fisk ("See My Tears," 159–64) takes it as a reference to the Temple specifically, though noting that this also of course means the desolation of Jerusalem itself (164). Fitzmyer notes that "[w]hether 'house' is understood as a reference to the Jerusalem Temple or in a broader sense of God's people resident there . . . the message of judgment is ominously the same" (*Luke*, 2:1035).

91. Note, besides, that Jeremiah also bound together the fate of the Temple with the

Luke describes it not as the "house of the Lord" (as is common in the OT) but as ὁ οἶκος ὑμῶν, Luke's use of ἀφίεται ὑμῖν suggests that Luke specifically *wishes* to highlight God's abandonment of this οἶκος. While Luke will narrate God's abandonment of the JT most strikingly with the tearing of the Temple veil (Luke 23:45), Luke has been indicating this abandonment in subtle ways throughout his Gospel, especially via the downplaying of the Temple's sacerdotal cultic function beginning with Luke 1–2. It is completely appropriate, then, that Luke should reference the Temple as ὁ οἶκος ὑμῶν here, since God is in the process of leaving the JT to Jerusalem's impenitent inhabitants,[92] and, given this, it is appropriate that we should hear also in his phrase (ὁ οἶκος ὑμῶν) a reference to the people of Jerusalem/Judea—for they are, in Luke's eyes, in the process of being left on their own. Simply put, when God abandons the Temple, God also leaves the people who control that institution—not for better but for worse—to their own devices.[93]

Luke's probable recalling of Jer 33 (LXX) here also connects this passage to Luke's (more subtle) warnings in Luke 1–2, for Luke thus again appeals to a Scripture that recalls the fateful downfall of God's one-time holy site, Shiloh. In Jer 33:6 (LXX) the prophet warns that "this house" (in

---

lives of the (immoral) residents of Jerusalem (Jer 33:6, 9 LXX).

92. So also Klein, *Das Lukasevangelium*, 494. Cf. Garland's comment: "If Jesus does refer to the temple [and Garland remains on the fence], then he no longer regards it as God's house, but already as a den of robbers (cf. 19:46)" (*Luke*, 560); also, Walker, *Jesus and the Holy City*, 62: "Normally one might expect a reference to '*his* house' (*i.e.* God's house) rather than '*your* house,' but this is precisely the point at issue: it is no longer 'God's house.'" Commenting on 13:35a, Nolland highlights God's abandonment of Jerusalem, connecting 13:35a to Luke 21 (*Luke*, 2:742–43).

93. This still admits a good deal of potential confusion regarding the precise moment at which God abandons the Temple. The rending of the veil is the most climactic, most significant, and probably culminating moment of God's abandoning the Temple for Luke, despite the fact that God's people continue to frequent and even to worship within the Temple thereafter (Luke 24; Acts 1–5). This latter worship is after all not qualitatively different from the kind of worship offered in Christian homes in Acts or indeed different from the kind of worship offered in synagogues, and the Temple's somewhat central placement in the early third of Acts is explainable in light of Jerusalem's role as launching pad for the Christian mission. The same narrative de-emphasis on the Temple's sacerdotal functions observed in Luke's Gospel, however, occurs in Acts 3, when Peter and John go to the Temple at the afternoon *Tamid* offering but then their healing of a man interrupts the offering by causing a minor riot (see Acts 3:11), and also in Paul's trip to Jerusalem in Acts 21–22. These later scenes are probably best understood as echoes of the narratival shift away from the Temple as sacerdotal cultic site in Luke's Gospel and thus also as reminders of God's rejection of the JT.

PART 2: THE JERUSALEM TEMPLE IN LUKE'S GOSPEL

context, clearly the JT) will be made like Shiloh, and the Shiloh warning is repeated in v. 9. Jeremiah 33 (LXX) thus serves as an important hub for Luke's treatment of the Temple: it connects the Shiloh thread of Luke 1–2, which establishes the scriptural precedent for God's abandoning a cultic center, with the rejection-of-prophets rationale, which argues for God's (reasonably) punishing his people, especially Jerusalem, for rejecting both the prophets and their message of justice (thus Luke 11:49–51 and the Fig Tree Parable)—all while also incorporating the theme of conflict within Israel. Thus Luke 13:31–35, especially through its recalling of Jer 33 (LXX), connects the seemingly disparate strands that Luke has put forward to this point and, by weaving them together, establishes the basic thread-pattern of Luke's theodical vision regarding Jerusalem and its Temple.

The final sentence of the pericope, Luke 13:35b, serves to anticipate Jesus's arrival in the city at the "Triumphal Entry" (Luke 19:28–40)[94] and connects this lament to the lament there (Luke 19:41–44), in which the status of Jerusalem has grown more dire still.

The Leper Healed, Redux (Luke 17:11–19)

Toward the end of Jesus's infamous journey toward Jerusalem (and highlighting in 17:11 the journey's movement, or rather lack thereof[95]) comes the story of Jesus's encounter with ten lepers at the border between Samaria and Galilee. Unlike Luke 5:12–16, this scene is unique to Luke's Gospel, and unlike the leper of Luke 5, these ten stand at a distance, crying out for help (vv. 12–13). In v. 14, Jesus commands them to go and show themselves to the priests in language highly reminiscent of that used to issue the equivalent command to the leprous man in Luke 5, drawing auditors' ears to the earlier scene.[96] As they go, they are cleansed (ἐκαθαρίσθησαν) and one of

---

94. See Fitzmyer, *Luke*, 2:1035.

95. Hamm helpfully observes, "For the reader who has been attending to the progress of the journey, this note [17:11] comes as both a surprise and as a trigger of memory. The surprise is that, at least geographically, either the journey has made no progress at all or it has made the curious progress of circling back to Galilee" ("Samaritan Leper," 282). In addition to setting the stage for the motley nature of the group of lepers this geographical notice also serves to recall the earlier rejection of Jesus by the Samaritan village (9:52–55), suggesting again the issues of Jewish-Samaritan hatred and of the question of a proper cultic site. Nolland notes the strong echo of 9:51 in 17:11 (*Luke*, 2:845).

96. ἀπελθὼν δεῖξον σεαυτὸν τῷ ἱερεῖ (Luke 5:14) vs. πορευθέντες ἐπιδείξατε ἑαυτοὺς τοῖς ἱερεῦσιν (Luke 17:14). See Johnson, *Luke*, 260.

them, seeing he has been healed (ἰάθη), returns to Jesus and falls at this feet praising God (vv. 14–16a). Only then does the text famously reveal this man to be a Samaritan (v. 16b). Jesus then inquires (vv. 17–19), "Were not ten made clean? But the other nine, where are they? Was none of them found to return and give praise to God except this foreigner?" (NRSV), and the scene closes with Jesus's commanding the man to rise and go, assuring him that his faith has healed/saved him (v. 19).

Although the primary emphasis of the passage centers on the status of the man as a Samaritan foreigner who responds properly to the healing he receives, unlike the other lepers—some or all of whom are implied to be Jews—most crucial for this present study are the questions of vv. 17–19. These queries unmistakably imply that, despite their following Jesus's earlier command, these nine should have returned to Jesus to give glory to God.[97] Although Jesus does not thereby necessarily preclude their later presenting the purification offerings prescribed by Lev 14, he clearly relegates the purification rites to secondary status, implying that proper response to God's healing leads one not to the cultus of the JT but to the source of that healing, Jesus himself. Note also that 1) when Jesus commands the Samaritan to go (v. 19), he does not repeat the command to go to the priests but rather states that the man's faith has saved him, implying that any need to go to the priests has in fact been obviated, and 2) Luke describes the man's return to Jesus in language that is explicitly evocative of worship: he falls at his feet (cf. Acts 10:24), thanking him (εὐχαριστῶν αὐτῷ).[98]

Moreover, the eventual revelation that the man is a Samaritan problematizes Jesus's earlier commandment to the ten to present themselves "to the priests" (v. 14)—i.e., it is narratively significant that Luke reveals the man's ethnicity only after the command to go to the priests has been issued and shirked.[99] The audience, now aware of the conundrum, is invited to ask: To which priests exactly were the ten—who turn out to be this motley crew including both Jews and Samaritans—to present themselves, the priests in Jerusalem or near Mt. Gerizim (or both)?[100] This ambiguity, combined both

---

97. See Green, *Luke*, 626.

98. See Hamm, "Samaritan Leper," 284. Nolland, despite in my opinion muddying his discussion with fruitless speculation regarding the potential impact of hypothetical sources on the final shape of the pericope, nonetheless rightly observes "the theophanic nature of the encounter with Jesus" (*Luke*, 2:847).

99. *Contra* Marshall, who claims that the mention of plural priests in v. 14 anticipates the later disclosed diversity of the group (*Luke*, 651).

100. Because of the fragmentary and late nature of the sources, it is difficult to get a

Part 2: The Jerusalem Temple in Luke's Gospel

with Jesus's later praising the one who returned at the expense of the nine and with the worship language employed in the man's falling at Jesus's feet and giving thanks, strongly suggests that Jesus solves with his person and ministry the problem of the rival Samaritan-Jewish priesthoods: Jesus himself is the proper locus for God's saving activity. Thus, Green rightly notes that Luke here "presents Jesus in the role of the temple—as one in whom the powerful and merciful presence of God is realized and before whom the God of the temple (whether in Jerusalem or Mount Gerizim) can be worshiped."[101]

Luke began the Journey section by narrating Jesus's rejection by a Samaritan village on account of his heading toward Jerusalem, which the otherwise odd geographical note in 17:11 recalls.[102] Despite Jesus's potentially derogatory description of the healed man as ὁ ἀλλογενὴς οὗτος, it is a theological necessity within Luke's world that the Samaritans, at least in part, become a reconciled part of God's people.[103] By implying that Jesus may fulfill the cultic function boasted, prized, and bitterly contested by

---

firm handle on Samaritan institutions at this time and thus is difficult even to confirm positively that Samaritan priests existed in either Jesus's or Luke's day (for a rather skeptical take on ancient Samaritan cultic institutions, see Hjelm, *The Samaritans and Early Judaism*, 235–36). Despite the destruction of the Samaritan temple on Mt. Gerizim more than one hundred years prior, commentators (e.g., Green, *Luke*) take the existence of Samaritan priests at this time for granted, and in light of the apparent existence of such priests in the second century (e.g., Justin Martyr may have witnessed the offering of the Samaritan Passover on Mt. Gerizim—see Pummer, *Early Christian Authors*, 23), it is reasonable to assume the priesthood continued, with whatever normal interruptions, vagaries, and vicissitudes, from John Hyrcanus's destruction of the Temple through the days of Jesus and the early church.

Jervell solves the problem in an entirely unsatisfactory, and hardly Lukan, manner, claiming that "Luke considers the Samaritans as belonging to the Jewish cult. . . . With Luke's understanding of the law and the cult, it is inconceivable that he could have directed the Samaritan to a specifically Samaritan cult" (*Luke and the People of God*, 121). Jervell has muddled things by overlooking the dynamics of the story itself: *within* the story, the Samaritan goes to no cultic site, since Jesus's healing, and the praise and worship which it evokes, obviates the need to go to *any* temple—(narratival) facts that certainly must be taken to have considerable bearing on "Luke's understanding of the law and the cult."

101. Green, *Luke*, 626. Hamm, who denies that Jesus replaces the temple in Luke-Acts, acknowledges that Luke is on a "trajectory" toward the Fourth Gospel's replacing the Temple with Jesus ("Samaritan Leper," 287).

102. See Hamm, "Samaritan Leper," 282.

103. See of course Acts 1:8. Also, Ravens, *Luke and the Restoration of Israel*, 98–106; and Jervell, *Luke and the People of God*, 123–27.

rival Jewish and Samaritan holy sites, Luke thus powerfully hints at a solution to the Jewish-Samaritan hatred he highlighted at the beginning of this section of his Gospel (9:52–56): in Jesus the enmity is removed. Indeed, auditors of Acts, hearing his Gospel again, would know that this is precisely how things were to play out in the Lukan world (Acts 8). Luke thus adds another weapon to his theological arsenal for interpreting the destruction of the JT: its existence, obviated by the person of Jesus, was in great need of obviation, since it stood as an otherwise insuperable barrier between Jews and Samaritans.

Summary

Following, but sharpening, the Galilee-to-Jerusalem geographical shift found in Mark and Matthew, Luke's Jesus embarks on his fateful journey to Jerusalem with a poignant expression ("he set his face," 9:51) that likely recalls God's judgment upon God's people in the prophets of old, especially Ezekiel. This sets the stage for the escalating conflict throughout that journey, reminding those with ears to hear of Simeon's prophecy over the infant Jesus (2:34–35).

This rising conflict in turn sets the stage for revelations about Jerusalem's fate. Both through its location immediately after warnings to repent that also hint of danger in Jerusalem and through its appropriation of imagery and language from Isa 5, Jesus's Fig Tree Parable (13:6–9) threatens destruction against the holy city. Jesus makes the threat explicit shortly thereafter (13:31–35), warning that God will abandon Temple, city, and residents alike—an abandonment already indicated narratively by Luke's diminution of the JT's sacerdotal cultic functioning in Luke 1–2. Jesus's warning likely alludes, among several echoed passages, to Jer 33 (LXX), which recalls Shiloh, the one-time holy place, and portrays the prophet Jeremiah amidst conflict that corresponds generally to the agonistic environment within which Jesus's own ministry operates in Luke's Gospel. Luke thereby establishes a connection between the Shiloh and rejection-of-the-prophets rationales for Jerusalem's destruction.

The scene with the ten lepers (17:11–19) furthers Luke's criticism of the JT by drawing into focus the issue of cultic conflict between Samaritans and Jews—a problem raised at the inception of the Jerusalem Journey. In this latter scene, Jesus in himself solves the problem of a proper cultic site by serving as the locus for healing and worship. This theme dovetails with, and provides clarification of, the Lukan narratival diminution of the JT as a cultic site. It also helps to frame for members of Luke's ideal audience an earlier scene in which Jesus heals a leper (Luke 5:12–16). There Jesus instructed the healed man to go, show himself to the priest, and to offer sacrifices "as a testimony to them" (εἰς μαρτύριον αὐτοῖς). This scene thus stood in some contrast with Luke's overall muting of sacerdotal activities of the JT post Luke 1–2. Hints within that early scene aid Luke's ideal audience in interpreting the scene as coherent with these Lukan emphases (esp. the qualifying mention that the man is to go to the priests in order to provide a witness to or against them), and those hints receive firm punctuation here as Luke depicts Jesus, rather than the Temple (and pointedly so), as the proper locus of God's healing and salvific activity.

5

The Jerusalem Temple in Luke 19–24

JESUS, THE KINGDOM, AND THE JERUSALEM TEMPLE (19:11-48)

Although Luke 19:11–48 consists of four distinguishable scenes, they are tightly bound together in theme, in meaning, and in narrative time, and so I will treat them together. While I have above followed the majority opinion in setting the end of the Journey section at 19:27, this need not imply an unbridgeable chasm between Luke's Kingship Parable (19:11–27)[1] and the subsequent scenes.[2] Several indicators, in fact, link the scenes together. Not only do numerous verbal links connect the scenes (i.e., notes of advancement toward Jerusalem at v. 11 and v. 28, repetition of ἔμπροσθεν at the close of the parable in v. 27 and the subsequent geographical reference in v. 28, as well as the backward looking καὶ εἰπὼν ταῦτα at the start of v.

---

1. I am following Johnson's terminology for the parable ("Kingship Parable," 139–59). As Denaux rightly notes, the traditional moniker, "The Parable of the Pounds," comes from Matthean influence and does not properly account for Lukan modifications or context (*Parable of the King-Judge*, 35–36).

2. Some treat Luke 19:28–44 as the capstone or denouement of the Journey section; see Denaux, "The Delineation of the Lukan Travel Narrative." Even if a single "map" of this section of the Third Gospel were possible, it is certainly unnecessary. Even Denaux is willing to downplay the significance of defining the precise bounds of the travel section's close: "The problem of the end of the travel narrative is secondary in comparison with that of its very existence" (*Studies in the Gospel of Luke*, 39).

Part 2: The Jerusalem Temple in Luke's Gospel

28),[3] but so does Luke's emphasis on the contested nature of the kingship within the parable and the uniquely Lukan emphasis on kingship in the Entry scene (see below). Thus separating the parable from its subsequent co-text obscures, rather than clarifies, the meaning of each,[4] and so I have chosen to treat the parable here along with the usually partitioned-off 19:28–48.

In recent decades, interpreters have noted that, despite the *parousia*-minded interpretations of the past, within the Lukan world, the occasion of Luke's Kingship Parable is in fact the belief of some that the kingdom would appear co-temporally with Jesus's arrival in Jerusalem (v. 11).[5] Luke Johnson, pointing to the kingship language of the subsequent Entry as well as in Luke 22:28–30 and elsewhere, takes the parable as confirming, not refuting, this expectation.[6] Allowing for an allegorical meaning yet without insisting on a thoroughgoing correspondence between points in the parable and in Luke's narrative world, Johnson reads the nobleman as Jesus, the opponents as the religious leaders, and the servants as the apostles who receive Jesus's kingdom (22:28–29).[7] I confess that I find Johnson's reading more persuasive than others',[8] though even his reading leaves numerous difficulties. Among these are the slaughtering of the king's opponents (not

---

3. See Denaux, "Parable of the King-Judge," 43–44, also 55–57. I remain unconvinced, however, that the parable ends at v. 28, as Denaux contends.

4. As Denaux, "Parable of the King-Judge," 43, notes.

5. "The standard view, that the parable seeks to explain the delay of the Parousia, does no justice at all to the link between the expectation of immediacy and the arrival of the historical Jesus" (Nolland, *Luke*, 3:913). See the helpful discussion and summary of previous scholarship on this point in Denaux, "Parable of the King-Judge," 46–49; also, Johnson, "Kingship Parable," 139–41, 143–53. Green, *Luke*, on the other hand, takes the parable as shifting the question from *when* the kingdom will arrive to "the issue of *faithfulness in anticipation*" (674–75). This would not be the first time Luke's Jesus attempted to use a parable to reorient a wrong-headed question (see Luke 10), and so Green has a point, although Johnson's view remains compelling, especially in light of the strong kingly resonances which Luke places in the Entry scene and in Luke 22.

6. See especially Johnson, "Kingship Parable," 150–53.

7. Johnson, "Kingship Parable," 157–59.

8. Weinert, reading the nobleman's opponents as Galileans who continued to oppose Jesus's activity, rejects most allegorical aspects of the story while building his case largely around a stringently allegorical reading of select details within the parable (e.g., the personal nature of the attack and the distanced nature of the opposition); his emphasis on developing authority—which matches Jesus's agonistic relationship to Israel's religious authorities leading up to the crucifixion—is more helpful, I think ("Parable of the Throne Claimant," 510–11).

readily recognizable in Luke's narrative), the generally cruel, ferocious, and exploitative nature of the king,[9] and, relatedly, the complete hegemony of the eventual king versus the less obviously exercised sovereignty of Jesus within the Lukan world (e.g., the continued persecution of Jesus's followers by the persecutors of Jesus in the early chapters of Acts). It is also important not to overlook the fact that there is more to Luke's Kingship Parable than mere confirmation: it clearly also nuances, even subverts, the expectations of Jesus's audience regarding the kingdom. Verse 11 implies that these expectations—elusive though they otherwise may be—center on the timing and location of the kingdom's arrival, yet Johnson's reading speaks mainly to the issue of the kingdom's timing and sheds little light on the issue of the kingdom's relationship to Jerusalem.

Those who, like Johnson, reject readings of the parable that front the delay of the *parousia* as the chief instigating force behind it rightly draw our attention away from Luke's (purported) audience and to the parable's function within the gospel narrative itself, especially as a response to expectations of some of those surrounding Jesus. Yet the precise make-up of this audience is by no means clear, which is all the more surprising given Luke's usually careful attention to specifying Jesus's audience during the Journey section.[10] Though some take this as implying that Jesus speaks to all likely

---

9. Green seems to object to an allegorical reading like Johnson's largely on the basis of the king's cruel vindictiveness in v. 27, as well as potential charges of anti-Semitism this might entail (*Luke*, 676). Regarding the portrait of Jesus, Green certainly has a point; as is often noted (though still frequently underappreciated), allegorical association need not entail a full identification between characters, and Green may be on the right trail, given Jesus's humbly "kingly" entry in the next scene, in suggesting a "parodic or ironic" portrait of Jesus's kingship here (ibid., 676). Parsons notes that this parable makes use of a well-known *topos*, the cruel tyrant (*Luke*, 280–81), which likely suggests an intentional contrast between—rather than identification of—Jesus and the parable's king. On the issue of the cruelty of the tyrant, see Schultz, "Jesus as Archelaus," 111–12. Schultz highlights the geographical significance of Luke's placing this parable when Jesus is near Jericho, since Archelaus (whom the tyrant seems to mimic) built a palace there after receiving the kingship (Josephus, *Ant.* 17.340).

One possibility is that Luke vividly describes the tyrant's cruelty in order to play up the Archelaus connection, specifically because of Archelaus's well-known slaughtering of the three thousand Passover pilgrims (Josephus, *Ant.* 17.213–18, 237, 240–43, 313)—thus tingeing his tale with hints of violence in Jerusalem. In this case, the point would be both ironic and prophetic: ironic because Jesus the king would himself meet slaughter as a Passover pilgrim, and prophetic because it warns of eventual violence in Jerusalem for those who reject the would-be king.

10. As perceptively noted by Johnson, "Kingship Parable," 145.

Part 2: The Jerusalem Temple in Luke's Gospel

audience members—i.e., disciples, crowd, and opponents[11]—the text suggests a connection between Jesus' approach to the city (διὰ τὸ ἐγγὺς εἶναι Ἰερουσαλὴμ αὐτὸν; v. 11) and the audience's anticipation of the kingdom's arrival, thus precluding Jesus' opponents from the group. The ambiguity of audience within Luke's gospel, then, may point us—cautiously indeed—toward seeking also a meaning that would speak primarily to Luke's audience. This hint is further strengthened by the allegorical parallaxes between the parable and the events of Luke's narrative (noted above).[12]

As noted in chapter 2, many strands of Second Temple (and pre-Bar Kokhban) Judaism strongly associated Jerusalem with God's eschatological purposes[13]—a belief to which Luke alludes (ironically, I have argued) in 2:38. Luke has an observable tendency to link Jesus's messianic and kingly statuses,[14] and so members of Luke's audience might be expected either to hear in Jesus's approach to Jerusalem echoes of Jerusalem-centric eschatological hopes or to attribute such beliefs to the "expectant ones" mentioned in v. 11. In this case, Luke may be playing off of, and even to some degree playing up, this expectation. While there is indeed a connection between the kingdom's arrival and Jesus's going to Jerusalem (as Luke seems to indicate), the audience knows that Jesus will be ill-treated and murdered in Jerusalem, and so the parabolic rejection of those who oppose the future king—i.e., those whose center of power is Jerusalem—places the city's role in the eschatological drama in a tenuous position.[15] It is perhaps not go-

---

11. So Johnson, "Kingship Parable," 145; and, endorsing Johnson but with equivocation on the "crowd," Denaux, "Parable of the King-Judge," 49.

12. It seems to me (as it has others) these parallaxes—i.e., points at which the parable does not readily cohere with the events and characters they represent from Luke's narrative—offer reasonable grounds at least for surmising that Luke may have in some sense forced this parable into his narrative or else forced it into its current form, framed as it is by, and orienting largely around, the editorial v. 11.

13. See Denaux, "Parable of the King-Judge," 50.

14. Note Luke's uniquely connecting Jesus's messianic and kingly identities in 23:2; Johnson, "Kingship Parable," 152.

15. My reading of the import of this parable for Jerusalem has some similarities to the conclusion of Sanders that "[the] parable of the Pounds ... makes it clear *why* Jerusalem has been rejected as the place of the appearance of the kingdom of God," though largely superficially so ("The Parable of the Pounds," 660–68). I think Jerusalem is rejected as site of the kingdom only in one sense, and not in another: the kingdom is conferred to Jesus and first makes its earthly home in Jerusalem, but the kingdom cannot be made coterminous with Jerusalem in part because of the rulers' rejection of Jesus. Moreover (and quite significantly), Sanders, in his essay, overlooks Luke's penchant for separating the rulers from the people and thus is (gravely) mistaken in taking the king's opponents

ing too far, then, to claim that (on this view) Luke, by framing the parable against the question of Jerusalem and the kingdom of God (v. 11), serves to "loosen ... the link between the Kingdom of God and Jerusalem, while strengthening that between God's Kingdom and Jesus' kingship."[16] Just how much this framing serves to "loosen" the connection between Jerusalem and the kingdom remains open to question, and Luke here, as elsewhere (viz. Acts 1:6–8), seems to offer little more than vague insinuation. It may be significant in this regard to note Luke's subsequent ironic description of Jesus's kingship, from the humility of the so-called "Triumphal" Entry to king Jesus's poor treatment during his "trial" (23:2, 38).[17] In this case, the surprising nature of Jesus's kingship matches the surprising nature of the kingdom: as with the king, so with the kingdom. The kingdom's advent may be surprising not only because of its timing and nature (cf. 22:24–27) but also because of its location and eschatological scope.

This brief interlude, while hardly unraveling the twisted and multiple threads of the Kingship Parable, at least lays groundwork for what follows.

Thus Luke's Jesus, having drawn near to (19:11) and then undertaken the ascent toward Jerusalem (19:28), meets with the fanfare of his disciples while he descends the Mount of Olives (v. 37), and thus, as the Jerusalem Journey reaches its climax, Jesus enters the Temple (v. 45, 47; cf. 20:1).

---

in the parable as a reference to the entire Jewish people (ibid., 667–68). More helpful, if only partially correct, is Sanders's assertion that "Jerusalem is the key; the point is geographical, not temporal" (ibid., 666); the point here is likely *both* geographical and temporal, but Sanders rightly emphasizes Luke's geographical emphasis.

16. Denaux, "Parable of the King-Judge," 50. Here, then, I see this parable potentially operating in a manner similar to Johnson's description of the Parable of the Good Samaritan: it appears "to subvert the implicit understanding of" those whose expectations spur the parable ("Kingship Parable," 147). He is subverting not only their expectation of the kingdom's imminent appearance (and this may be a problem of both time and manner) but also what is the basis for that incorrect assumption, their belief in Jerusalem as the inevitable hub of that kingdom. Unfortunately—in my view—Johnson does not, in his early essay on this parable, consider "subversion" as a possible purpose of the Kingship Parable. In this regard, it may be instructive to view Jesus's response to what some of those around him thought (δοκεῖν) here along with the disciples' mistaken surmises (δοκεῖ) relative to the kingdom in 22:24–27.

17. Johnson detects this tension, resolving it by taking the parable not as a refutation but a confirmation of the belief in 19:11 ("Kingship Parable," 150–51). I agree with Johnson that Luke, especially in the chapters that follows, presents Jesus as king, though I think this serves as an ironic refutation, or at least a subversion, of the expectation of 19:11: yes, Jesus is king, but this does not mean for Jerusalem what some thought it would mean, least of all because the leaders of Jerusalem are precisely those who reject the rightful king!

Part 2: The Jerusalem Temple in Luke's Gospel

The Entry scene offers several Lukan distinctives commentators generally take as significant for its interpretation. One such distinctive is Luke's emphasis on Jesus as king, especially through a number of scriptural references: allusions to Gen 49:11 and Zech 9:9 (LXX) via the description of Jesus and the colt (vv. 28–36),[18] and the quoting of Ps 117:26 (LXX) and highlighting its overtones of royal entry through (likely) insertion of ὁ βασιλεὺς and omission of the palm branches (cf. Mark 11:8), which point to the Feast of Tabernacles and thus away from the one-time royal context of the psalm.[19] The Kingship Parable, then, gives way to Jesus's humble yet kingly entrance. Just as the now and future king of the parable faces both support and opposition, so Jesus also (and once again) encounters favor mixed with hostility—and note Luke's insertion of the Pharisees's rebuke (vv. 39–40), unparalleled in Mark. Jesus—as prophet, Messiah, savior, and throughout Lord—has encountered opposition since the beginning of his ministry and, despite the overall favorable reception, finds hints of that opposition now when, heralded as king, his journey to Jerusalem reaches its climax.

This scene gives way immediately to a uniquely Lukan vignette: Jesus's second lament over Jerusalem (vv. 41–44), juxtaposed between Jesus's "kingly" arrival and his entering the Temple.[20] Broadly speaking, the inserted, uniquely Lukan scene indicates the Third Evangelist's considerable

---

18. See Green, *Luke*, 683–85.

19. See Green, *Luke*, 686–87; also, Kinman, "Parousia," 285–89. Luke also retains several of the royal hints found in Mark—e.g., the people's setting their garments before Jesus in v. 36 (cf. the treatment of Jehu in 4 Kgdms 9:13). The textual status of ὁ βασιλεὺς in v. 38 is itself open to dispute, though the evidence seems to favor Lukan authorship. On the cultic and royal background of the psalm, see the references in Kinman, "Jesus' Royal Entry," 246.

If Ps 117 (LXX) was indeed sung inside the Temple pre-70 CE (so Zeitlin, "The Hallel," 25), then its appearance here as Jesus makes his way toward the Temple may offer (tenuous) support for my claim that Luke's Gospel presents Jesus's ministry as entailing the abrogation of the JT as cultic center.

20. Some may view Luke's omission here of Mark's intercalated fig tree scene (Mark 11:12–14, 20–25) as significant for determining the place of Jerusalem and its Temple in Luke's Gospel. I see the omission instead as primarily incidental. To leave the fig tree intercalation would interrupt both Jesus's arrival to "cleanse" the Temple as the climax of the Journey section and Jesus's ongoing presence in the Temple as he instructs and debates there throughout Luke 20 and 21 (see below). Removing the otherwise awkward intercalation (for Luke's purposes), then, Luke relocates and re-purposes it in Luke 13— where Mark's tones of judgment due to barrenness are fully present, even if there hope for repentance, however small, still remains. Luke inserts his own tones of judgment here via the dolorous 19:41–44.

interest in Jerusalem's fate. Here Luke clearly recalls Jesus's earlier lament over Jerusalem (13:31-35, esp. v. 35b), even while upping the ante: Jerusalem's disaster, somewhat obliquely referenced there, is now spelled out in vivid color—its enemy will surround it and assail it from all directions so that its children will be crushed, and even its stones demolished (vv. 43-44). The cause of this devastation is the city's failure to come to terms of peace (v. 42) because it does not recognize "the time of its visitation" (τὸν καιρὸν τῆς ἐπισκοπῆς σου; v. 44).

Jesus's use of the language of "visitation" clearly references his long-awaited arrival in Jerusalem (so carefully crafted by Luke) and also has rich resonances in the LXX. Frequently in the LXX, ἐπισκοπή, and to a lesser degree the related verbal form ἐπισκέπτομαι, indicate God's visiting or attending to human beings, sometimes benevolently but often for judgment.[21] In both Isaiah and Jeremiah, these words make reference to God's judgment on Jerusalem (Isa 29:6; Jer 6:15; 51:13 LXX). In Ezek 7:22, ἐπισκοπή seems to refer to the Temple itself, which the residents of Jerusalem have profaned.[22] The ambiguity of Luke's construction here aids in the creation of its meaning; σου is surely an objective genitive,[23] leaving open the subject of τῆς ἐπισκοπῆς (thus "the time of [blank]'s visiting you"). The Septuagintal background points strongly to God as the actor behind ἐπισκοπή, while Luke's narrative itself makes clear that this phrase applies also to Jesus's

---

21. See Gen 50:24, 25; Exod 3:16; 13:19; Job 7:18; 10:12; 24:12; 29:4; 31:14; 34:9; Ruth 1:4; 1 Kgdms 2:21; Isa 10:3; 23:17; 24:22-23; 29:6; Jer 6:15; 10:15; 30:2; 51:13; Ezek 34:11; Zeph 2:7; Zech 10:3 (LXX). Cf. C. A. Evans, *Luke*, 290; Marshall, *Luke*, 719. Pokorný suggests Luke's Jesus's use of ἦλθεν/-ον sometimes (e.g., Luke 19:10) recalls God's visiting (ἐπισκέπτομαι) the lost sheep of Israel, as in Ezek 34:11-12, 16 (*Theologie*, 138).

22. Ezek 7:22: καὶ ἀποστρέψω τὸ πρόσωπόν μου ἀπ' αὐτῶν, καὶ μιανοῦσιν τὴν ἐπισκοπήν μου καὶ εἰσελεύσονται εἰς αὐτὰ ἀφυλάκτως καὶ βεβηλώσουσιν αὐτά. If Luke was aware of Ezek 7 (very likely) and understood ἐπισκοπή there to refer to the JT itself (plausible, even likely), then his ambiguous construction here (τὸν καιρὸν τῆς ἐπισκοπῆς σου) might open further avenues of meaning: namely, that Jesus's arrival here (ἐπισκοπή) entails not only judgment (the common connotation which ἐπισκοπή carries in the LXX) but also the arrival of the true Temple itself (ala Ezek 7:22). Unsurprisingly, I find this possibility intriguing, given its coherence with (and also heightening of) my overall reading of Jerusalem and its Temple in Luke's Gospel, but the minority report of Ezek 7:22—which Luke may or may not have had in view here—can hardly bear so weighty a claim: subtle though I believe Luke's message occasionally to be, I must admit that, were he in fact *this* subtle (or obscure), his hints almost certainly elude the detective possibilities of modern interpreters—hence, we have arrived at what Hays's calls the "vanishing point" with this potential echo.

23. Cf. Culy, Parsons, Stigall, *Luke*, 613.

Part 2: The Jerusalem Temple in Luke's Gospel

arrival at the JT (with Jerusalem in view). These colliding factors strongly suggests that this "visitation" refers not only to the arrival of the prophet who weeps for Jerusalem but also to the very arrival of God—and so Jesus's arrival at the Temple is rendered, by Lukan ambiguity, theophanic.[24]

The scene that follows, Jesus's so-called "cleansing" of the Temple, is marked by a number of further Lukan distinctives. Jesus enters the temple and drives out "those who were selling" with an amalgamated citation of Isa 56:7 and Jer 7:11 (19:45–46), then he commences to teach in the Temple daily, so that the chief priests and scribes attempt to drive him out, though the people's favoring Jesus prevents their plan from gaining traction (vv. 47–48). Thus Luke's scene, especially vv. 45–46 (the "cleansing" proper) is considerably shorter than the parallel text in Mark 11:15–19 (cf. Matt 21:12–13). Also unlike Mark, Luke makes the Temple scene the climax of Jesus's journey, emphasizing its culminating force partly by removal of Mark's cursing of the fig tree.[25]

Luke's abbreviated "cleansing" scene kicks off a prolonged teaching ministry by Jesus in the JT (Καὶ ἦν διδάσκων τὸ καθ᾽ ἡμέραν ἐν τῷ ἱερῷ; v. 47). In the chapters that follow, Luke emphasizes Jesus's location in the Temple with some frequency (20:1; 21:1–2, 5–6, 37a), and neither Luke's Jesus nor Luke's narrative shifts from the Temple environs until the notice of Jesus's daily commute between the JT and the Mount of Olives in 21:37. Thus James Dawsey is surely right in noting the unhelpful disjunction many commentators (and translations) place between not only vv. 45–46 and vv.

---

24. See C. A. Evans, *Luke*, 290–91; Rowe, *Christology*, 165–66, 200–201; Sanders, "A Hermeneutic Fabric," 151. Kinman rightly notes that "Luke alone among the Evangelists . . . makes explicit the connection between the entry and God's judgment on the city" ("Parousia," 280). There may be merit to Kinman's argument that the Entry, as narrated by Luke, is an insult and affront to Jesus the king, especially because of the Pharisees's wrong-headed response and the failure of the city's elite to come out and welcome him properly. In this case, however, the subsequent lament (vv. 41–44) is not in response solely to that affront, as Kinman claims ("Parousia," 290), but also sums up the consistent rejection of Jesus throughout Luke's Gospel by Israel's religious leaders, even while foreshadowing the sharpening nature of that rejection after Jesus's entering the JT.

25. By removing Mark's fig-tree cursing scene (Mark 11:12–14), Luke has Jesus's entering the JT occur not on the day following the "Triumphal Entry" (cf. Mark 11:12) but rather in immediate succession from Jesus's entry and lament: Luke's Jesus journeys to Jerusalem in order, firstly, to take possession of the Temple.

Kinman, "Lucan Eschatology," suggests that Luke 19:41–44 replaces Mark's "Cursing of the Fig Tree," perhaps largely because the latter might seem to imply "the complete end of God's dealings with Israel" (678).

47–48 but also between 19:45–48 and the chapter(s) that follows.[26] These considerations have of course led many scholars to speak of Jesus's "taking possession of, or residence in, the Temple" in Luke's Gospel.[27]

The crucial questions that remain are, What is the point of the initial cleansing (vv. 45–46), and how does it relate to Jesus's subsequent teaching in the Temple? In answering these questions, there are several important bits of evidence to consider. First of all, this is the first time Jesus appears in the JT since his precocious appearance there in Luke 2:41–52. Also, Jesus's subsequent teaching in the Temple (Luke 19:47—21:38) occurs within and as part of a sustained and heightened conflict between Jesus and Jerusalem's religious authorities,[28] with Jesus enjoying the people's favor (cf. 19:48; 20:1, 6, 9, 19, 45; 21:38) as he instructs them and denigrates the religious authorities. Finally, Luke makes several omissions to Mark's account: he considerably shortens the ordeal of Jesus's forcibly removing the wares handlers and curiously omits πᾶσιν τοῖς ἔθνεσιν from Jesus's citation of Isa 56:7.

That Jesus teaches the people in the JT, with the religious leaders ever scheming, ever working, to break his influence over the people, suggests that the point of Jesus's behavior centers on questions of the JT's proper function and of the identity of Israel's proper leader(s).[29] Just as Jesus amazed the teachers in the Temple as a child (2:47), so now he confounds them as adult (20:7, 20–26, 27–38, esp. 40, 41–44). Thus Luke makes clear that Jesus, and none of the religious authorities, is the proper teacher within God's house. Jesus has consistently challenged his audience regarding proper use of possessions, and Luke has long-since characterized the Pharisees as lovers of

---

26. I have attempted to recognize the hermeneutical connection between 19:45–49 and what follows in Luke's narrative by locating them within the same (present) chapter. See Dawsey, "Confrontation," 155. Dawsey argues that Jesus's cleansing of the JT in Luke is not a sort of "one-off" in which he drives out the money-changers and sellers of goods; rather, it is a prolonged "cleansing" that includes as an essential element Jesus's teaching within the Temple and continues until Luke 21:38. While Dawsey is certainly right to note Luke's emphasis on Jesus's ongoing presence in the JT and thus the connection between Jesus's initial activities in the Temple and his subsequent teaching, "taking possession of" the Temple describes this behavior at least as aptly as Dawsey's preferred "cleansing."

27. Following Conzelmann's lead in this are, e.g., Kingsbury, *Conflict*, 106; Fitzmyer, *Luke*, 2:1260, 1265; Marshall, *Luke*, 722 (somewhat non-committally).

28. Green, *Luke*, for example, labels the section 20:1—21:4 as "Conflict with the Jerusalem Leadership."

29. Cf. Green, *Luke*, 731: "At stake is the question of legitimate authority: Does Jesus bear the divine imprimatur or does the Jerusalem leadership?"

money (16:14). Within Jesus's Temple-instructing, Luke will remind his audience that the criticism of greed and unscrupulousness applies also to the scribes (20:45–47; cf. 11:43). In light of this, Luke's shortening of Mark's Temple cleansing—removing any mention of people buying in the Temple, the tables of money changers, the seats of those selling animals, or those trying to carry implement through the JT (Mark 11:15–16)—may indicate that he intends his audience to hear in Jesus's simply "driving out those who were selling" (ἐκβάλλειν τοὺς πωλοῦντας) primarily a reference to the well-known greed (within Luke's narrative world) of the religious leaders—i.e., those who controlled the Temple.[30] In this case, Jesus's actions in v. 45 represent a judgment both on their greed and on their leadership. The logic of Luke's thought seems to run: Instead of using the Temple as a source of personal prestige and wealth acquisition (v. 46b),[31] these religious leaders should have set it aside as a house of prayer (v. 46a)[32]; because they failed to do so, they have lost control of the Temple, in the narrative and perhaps proleptically as well.

Luke's reference to Isa 56:7 gives the clearest explication of Luke's theology of the Temple after Jesus's arrival: it is to be a house of prayer—as it will be for the early Christians in Acts. The coming of Jesus means the arrival of the kingdom, and so the eschatological promise[33] of Isa 56:7 now applies: the JT now has a new role, as a house of prayer. Granted, Luke will subsequently add to this role the apparently complementary function of serving also as a place for instruction by those who stand in proper relationship to God's purposes—first Jesus (Luke 19:47—21:38) and then his commissioned apostles (Acts 3:11–26; 5:20–26; cf. Luke 22:28–30).[34] When Luke's Jesus calls the JT a "house of prayer," designated as such by God, he indicates both what the Temple now is and what it is not: that it is now

---

30. "His purpose is to purge his Father's house (2:49) of all unsuited service of mammon. Recall his words in 16:13d, 'You cannot serve both God and mammon'" (Fitzmyer, *Luke*, 2:1266).

31. Cf. Green, *Luke*, 731.

32. The meaning of Jesus's action in casting out those who were selling undoubtedly relates to the prophetic texts Luke has Jesus cite, not only from context but also by means of the participle of manner, λέγων (v. 46).

33. Given the resonances with Isa 56 (esp. vv. 4–5) that Luke places within the story of the Ethiopian eunuch in Acts 8, it is safe to conclude, I think, that Luke read Isa 56 eschatologically.

34. The JT also remains a place for praise and worship (cf. Luke 24:53), although it can hardly be said to be unique in this regard (e.g., Acts 4:23–31).

properly a house of prayer casts doubts on its ongoing sacerdotal functioning. Luke's omission of πᾶσιν τοῖς ἔθνεσιν here does not indicate that Luke does not after all read the passage eschatologically; rather, Luke is simply pointing to the new (reduced) role the Temple fulfills within the eschaton,[35] hinting at but not yet disclosing the import this has for the nations—which would mean, for Luke's Jesus, a premature disclosure, ruining the surprise of Acts (for the disciples),[36] and would mean, for Luke, failing to narrate things in proper sequence (καθεξῆς).[37] This is true especially since the Temple will serve as a house of prayer (as Acts plays out) exclusively for Jews.[38]

The reference to Jer 7 recalls the prophet's harsh criticism of Judah for its avarice and injustice (vv. 6, 9a)—strengthening the likelihood that Luke's audience would have heard in Jesus's driving out those who were selling (Luke 19:45) a reference to the authorities' greed and unscrupulousness. Although Luke clearly inherited this material from Mark, one feature of Jer 7 gains startling poignancy in light of Luke's overall treatment of Jerusalem: immediately after accusing the nation of treating God's house as "a den of robbers," Jer 7 likens Jerusalem's imminent rejection to God's abandonment of Shiloh (v. 12, and again in v. 14). While Luke certainly does not play up the connection here, his earlier references to Jerusalem-Shiloh typology would increase in "volume" via the reference to Jer 7 here.[39]

To sum up my discussion of vv. 45–48, then, Luke abbreviates Jesus's Temple "cleansing," referring only to "those who were selling," probably in order to (re-) emphasize the leaders' greedy, avaricious, and status-seeking behavior—which is, after all, a key source of their conflict with Jesus in Luke's Gospel—and quotes Isa 56:7, which, taken eschatologically, states for Luke's audience the proper role of the Temple in light of the kingdom's arrival. As hinted throughout his Gospel, the JT is no longer a sacerdotal

---

35. Cf. Fitzmyer, *Luke*, 2:1266: "[Jesus's] act implies the transformation of the Temple and its role in reconstituted Israel . . . Reconstituted Israel will have no need of the Temple for its God, 'who dwells not in house made by (human) hands' (Acts 7:48)."

36. I find the well-known segregating of Luke's Jesus from Gentile contact instructive in this regard.

37. Simeon's early prophecy of the universality of salvation is just that—a prophecy. Luke's Jesus, too, obliquely references that hope here—since Luke, as noted earlier, clearly read Isa 56 eschatologically.

38. The charge that Paul has brought Gentiles into the Temple is precisely what precipitates the riot in Acts 21:28.

39. I consider this to be so in light of the high probability that those who understood the reference to Jer 7:11 here would also recall the passage's poignant (and several) pairing(s) of Jerusalem with Shiloh.

Part 2: The Jerusalem Temple in Luke's Gospel

cultic center but is, within Lukan theology, now properly a place of prayer. It serves also as a place of instruction, though only those who stand in proper relationship to the God of the Temple, Jesus's "Father" (cf. 2:49), may do so. This scene serves as a bridge between Jesus's journey to Jerusalem and the heightened conflict that characterizes his teaching in the Temple upon arriving.[40]

It is appropriate here to reconsider Klaus Baltzer's provocative reading of Luke 19. Decades ago, Hans Conzelmann observed that, unlike Mark, "[Luke] does not connect the Entry with the city at all—according to Luke Jesus never enters it [Jerusalem] before the Last Supper . . . [instead] he connects it [the Entry] with the Temple."[41] Working from this observation, Baltzer argues that Luke has modified Mark's Triumphal Entry specifically in order to allude to Ezekiel's vision of God's presence re-entering the JT. In this regard, Baltzer directs attention to 1) the departure of the Lord's glory from the Temple in Ezek 8–11,[42] noting the clear reference to the Mount of Olives in 11:23, 2) the re-entry of the Lord's glory into the temple in Ezek 43, and 3a) Luke's several added references (compared to Mark) to Jesus's glory at the Transfiguration (9:31, 32), which go along with Luke's unique reference there to Jesus's imminent "exodus" at Jerusalem (9:31), 3b) as well as the potential connection between the cloud at the Transfiguration and the frequent linking of that phenomenon with God's presence in the OT. He claims further (4) that Jesus's ejection of the ware-dealers from the JT in Luke 19:45–46 is in fulfillment of the removal of abominations emphasized in Ezek 43:8–9.[43]

As a whole, Baltzer's thesis is plausible—and certainly also provocative—although, like so many questions of intertextuality, it is impossible to substantiate (or, alternately, to disprove). Certainly Luke places comparatively greater emphasis on Jesus's glory at the Transfiguration (versus both Mark and Matthew) and also establishes a connection between that scene and the entry scene in Luke 19 (cf. 9:31). Also supporting Baltzer's reading is the initial framing of Jesus's journey to Jerusalem (9:51) with reference to

---

40. See Kurz, *Reading Luke-Acts*, 54.

41. Conzelmann, *The Theology of St. Luke*, 75.

42. LXX: καὶ ἐξῆλθεν δόξα κυρίου ἀπὸ τοῦ οἴκου (Ezek 10:18); καὶ ἀνέβη ἡ δόξα κυρίου ἐκ μέσης τῆς πόλεως καί ἔστη ἐπὶ τοῦ ὄρους, ὅ ἦν ἀπέναντι τῆς πόλεως (Ezek 11:23).

43. Baltzer, "The Meaning of the Temple," 267, 274–76. Baltzer also draws attention to Luke's singular use of νεφέλη, versus the plural use in Matthew and Mark, in Luke 21:27.

Jeremiah and especially Ezekiel. This earlier reference to Ezekiel, when Jesus begins his judgment-bearing march to Jerusalem, would pair naturally with a subsequent allusion to Ezekiel when Jesus enters the JT. The earlier reference might provide clarity on another level as well: both Jeremiah and Ezekiel depict God (as well as sometimes the respective prophets themselves) as the one who "sets his face" for judgment (Jer 3:21; Ezek 14:8; 15:7). Although Evans resists reading Jesus's setting his face (Luke 9:51) with theophanic overtones,[44] such overtones are readily accessible and gain poignancy in light of Luke's other insinuations of Jesus's divinity,[45] including the possible theophanic echoes here in Luke 19. Thus Baltzer's thesis of a theophanic reference within Jesus's taking possession of the Temple in Luke 19:28–48 has gained plausibility with age, though ample room for doubt remains.

The up-shot of this discussion is that Baltzer's thesis, in combination with the Septuagintal echoes to Luke's use of τὸν καιρὸν τῆς ἐπισκοπῆς in 19:44, points to the likelihood of theophanic resonances within Luke 19:41–48—Jesus's final approach toward and entry into the Temple. These resonances suggest a deeper meaning to Luke's portrayal of Jesus as not merely "cleansing" the Temple but also as also his taking up residence there: Is the audience not invited to hear in Jesus's actions a strong hint that God's very presence, God's glory, has come to the Temple in the person of Jesus? These theophanic resonances also help to substantiate my reading (following others') that Luke indicates throughout his Gospel that Jesus's arrival means the interruption of the JT's cultic functions. For when Jesus's journey finally reaches its *telos*, Jesus arrives not simply in Jerusalem but specifically in the Temple itself, announces it as a house of prayer in fulfillment of the eschatological expectations of Isa 56:7, and maintains a teaching ministry there, challenging and opposing the traditional (priestly) power brokers of the Temple.

---

44. Evans, "Luke 9:51," 98.

45. Also included would be Peter's calling/confession (Luke 5:1–11), the scene with the ten lepers (17:11–19), Luke's ambiguous use of "Lord" throughout his Gospel (ala Rowe, *Christology*), the Septuagintal echoes of τὸν καιρὸν τῆς ἐπισκοπῆς σου in 19:44 (discussed above), and possibly the theophanic echoes detected by Hutcheon ("'God Is with Us'"). Note Luke's use of ἐπισκιάζω in his Gospel: in 1:35, God's power *overshadows* Mary at the divine conception of Jesus, while the theophanic cloud *covers* Jesus, the disciples, and the ancient prophets at the Transfiguration (9:34); moreover, Jesus's ministry represents God's *visiting* (ἐπισκέπτομαι) his people (1:68, 78; 7:16).

Part 2: The Jerusalem Temple in Luke's Gospel

JESUS IN JERUSALEM: BUILD-UP, PASSION, WAITING (LUKE 20-24)

It is in Jerusalem and its Temple that the conflict prophesied by Simeon (2:33–35), foreshadowed by John (3:1–20), begun with Jesus's ministry in Galilee and exacerbated during Jesus's Journey, reaches its climax. Jesus, having taken possession of the JT, now engages in what will prove to be mortal combat with the Jerusalem authorities. After a controversy in the JT regarding Jesus's power (20:1–8), Jesus tells the Parable of the Tenants (20:9–18), and the scribes and chief priests, knowing he told the parable against them, seek to lay hands on Jesus, restrained only the people's favorable view of him (20:19). After hypocrites (20:20–26) and Sadducees (20:27–40) fail to trap Jesus and after Jesus stumps the leaders with a riddle (20:41–44), he warns his disciples, in the hearing of the people, against the scribes' greed and hypocrisy (20:45–47), contrasting them unfavorably with an honest, indigent widow (21:1–4). All of this is part of Jesus's daily teaching the people in the JT, with clear popular support (21:37–38). Bested, the Jerusalem authorities no longer engage in the challenge-and-riposte games that characterize the earlier portions of the Gospel; rather, their murderous intentions materialize (22:2), with Satanic aid (22:3), in a plot to arrest Jesus (22:4–6)—and so begins the Passion Narrative of Luke's Gospel (Luke 22–23), followed by the Post-Resurrection scenes (Luke 24).

Scholars usually treat Luke 22–23 as a distinct section within Luke's Gospel, but I here group it with the rest of Luke 20–24, doing so on geographical grounds and without implying a rejection of the strong case for its distinctiveness as a section. As Elizabeth Struthers Malbon (with others) has noted, literary texts, like any terrain, admit of multiple, complementary maps—and here my map, fittingly, orients to Luke's geographical emphases.[46]

Many fine volumes treat Luke's Passion narrative,[47] and precious few of their insights will see adequate daylight here. Among the distinctive features of Luke's portrayal of Jesus's passion are his emphasis on the Jerusalem authorities' culpability in Jesus's death[48] and his tempering of the anguished isolation that characterizes much of Mark's account. Luke takes numerous

---

46. Malbon, *Mark's Jesus*, 24–27.

47. Chief among them, in my mind, is the multi-gospel treatment of Brown, *Death of the Messiah*.

48. On this, and for more on my own (usually mainstream) views regarding Luke's Passion Narrative generally, see my article "The Rhetoric of Luke's Passion," 355–76.

other departures from Mark's account, and below I treat two that hold significance for my study.

The Fate of Jerusalem, the Temple, Jesus's Disciples (Luke 21:5–38)

Intervening between Jesus's praise of the widow (21:1–4) and the events that precipitate his crucifixion (22:1–6) is a scene in which Jesus announces the fate of Jerusalem, the Temple, and his disciples (21:5–38). Although this scene has obvious bearing on my study, not only has much of its import been properly unpacked by previous commentators but also those conclusions are generally well-known and well-accepted. Thus I will give it comparatively modest attention here.

Luke indicates that the discourse takes place within the Temple grounds themselves (vs. the private setting of Mark 13:3–4), since the scene begins with a question from a disciple about the JT's beautiful (and apparently readily viewable) appearance (21:5–6) and ends with the notice that Jesus taught daily in the JT, withdrawing to the Mount of Olives at night (21:37).[49] Thus Jesus's words regarding the Temple here should be heard as part of his overall teaching within the Temple (going back to 19:47–48), as well as part of his spiraling conflict with Jerusalem's religious leaders.[50]

Jesus's speech consists of a summary of things to come (vv. 8–11) followed by an elaborated, chronological description: persecution of the disciples (vv. 12–19), then Jerusalem's destruction, leading to "the times of the Gentiles" (vv. 20–24), followed by further eschatological signs (vv. 25–28), capped with parabolic warnings about watchfulness (vv. 29–36).[51] Luke therefore draws a rather firm temporal and causal boundary between Jerusalem's destruction and the eschatological portents that follow, in comparison to Mark 13, although Luke still seems to present Jerusalem's devastation as an eschatological event.[52] Luke also makes clear that the conflict

---

49. See Kurz, *Reading Luke-Acts*, 57; C. A. Evans, *Luke*, 311; Green, *Luke*, 743; Bachmann, *Jerusalem und der Tempel*, 274–75; Tannehill, *Narrative Unity*, 1:162.

50. As Green helpfully notes: "[T]he antagonism between Jesus and the Jewish leadership associated with the temple inevitably raises the question of the temple itself" (*Luke*, 733).

51. In this breakdown, I largely follow Green, *Luke*, 731–32.

52. See ibid., 731, 735: "Jesus' explicit denial that the end time would come immediately after the fall of Jerusalem (v 9b)—effectively driving a temporal and, thus, hermeneutical, wedge between these two events—is an important interpretive move on his part." Also, Marshall, *Luke*, 770; C. A. Evans, *Luke*, 307, 310; Fitzmyer, *Luke*, 2:1329.

Part 2: The Jerusalem Temple in Luke's Gospel

lines that have entangled Jesus will now pass on to his disciples (vv. 12–19). That the description of Jerusalem's devastation comes immediately following the prophecy of persecution of his disciples strongly suggests a causal link between the two, and the details of that description, as well as Luke's larger framing of the fall, strengthen the connection. As Green notes, Luke depicts Jerusalem's fall with "a virtual collage of scriptural texts that draws the anticipated destruction of Jerusalem and the temple into an interpretive relationship with the fall of the city at the time of the Exile."[53] So its devastation is a result of divine judgment, and the earlier warnings about its rejection of the prophets (especially Jesus himself) sound here with its devastation following its rejection of Jesus's followers. Its rejection coincides with "the times of the Gentiles," which may reference both Gentile hegemony over Judea/Jerusalem and the extension of God's salvation to the Gentiles.[54]

Requiring consideration—however briefly—is the import of the apparent temporal marker in v. 24: Jerusalem will be trampled under the feet of the Gentiles "until the times of the Gentiles are fulfilled (ἄχρι οὗ πληρωθῶσιν καιροὶ ἐθνῶν)." While this certainly appears to leave open the possibility of Jerusalem's (physical) restoration—i.e., when "the times of the Gentiles" has ended—Luke neither dwells on the point nor takes up the theme of restoration again (or in earnest) but instead strikes other eschatological emphases, including the Son of Man's return (vv. 25–28). The other clear reference to the hope of restoration in Luke's writings comes in Acts 1:6–8, and there Luke also clearly shifts away from the expectation of Jerusalem's political and physical restoration—to the mission to which Jesus calls his followers.[55] While Luke thus leaves open the possibility of Jerusalem's restoration (here and in Acts 1:6–8), he also makes it clear that this possibility is entirely secondary to other aspects of the eschatological drama.[56] This suggests that regarding the possibility of Jerusalem's restora-

---

53. Green, *Luke*, 738–39. Among the scriptural hues Luke chooses to omit is mention of the "desolating sacrilege" (Mark 13:14), perhaps out of historiographical concern. His description of Jerusalem's being surrounded by (Roman) armies more accurately depicts the actual demise of Jerusalem during the first revolt; thus the "desolating sacrilege," which recalls Antiochus Epiphanes's setting up an idol inside the Temple, probably struck Luke's historiographically-oriented mind as something of a canard regarding the Roman destruction of Jerusalem.

54. See Green, *Luke*, 739.

55. Cf. the helpful discussion in ibid., 739.

56. Thus I agree with Tannehill that Luke leaves open the possibility of Jerusalem's

tion Luke is (a) agnostic (i.e., may consider it neither impossible nor certain), even while he is (b) interested in redirecting his audience's attention away from this hope toward more productive avenues of eschatological expectation.

Finally, and tentatively, Jesus' remark in v. 28 that, when the (later) eschatological portents occur, "you" should lift up "your" heads "because your redemption (ἡ ἀπολύτρωσις ὑμῶν) is near." Although the make-up of Jesus's audience for the speech as a whole is not entirely clear and although some indications point towards the amorphous crowd of people,[57] the "you" here clearly points, as with the second person address of vv. 12–19, specifically to followers of Jesus.[58] The appearance of ἀπολύτρωσις here is noteworthy since it otherwise occurs nowhere in Luke's oeuvre and is also absent from the parallel accounts of Mark and Matthew. Given its observability/audibility, then, it may recall Luke's use of the almost equally rare λύτρωσις in 1:68 and especially in 2:38.[59] Both strike the chord of nationalistic hopes for Israel's political redemption, yet here they find their antiphonal response in a passage that vividly highlights Jerusalem's imminent demise. For anyone who missed the irony of (H)Anna(h)'s "waiting for the redemption (λύτρωσιν) of Jerusalem" in 2:38, the reappearance of ἀπολύτρωσις here may serve to spur them to deeper understanding: not Jerusalem but rather the faithful followers of Jesus are those who, when eschatological crises hit, will find true (ἀπο)λύτρωσιν.[60]

---

physical restoration but disagree with his claim that Jerusalem's restoration is "an essential part of the revelation of God's salvation to all flesh (see 1:68; 2:38; 3:6)." It is not essential if for no other reason than that Luke knows it does not in fact happen (from a recent post-70 CE perspective). Tannehill's (incorrect) claim that "[a]dmission that all hope for Jerusalem and for a large portion of Israel is lost would represent either loss of faith in the power of God or modification and limitation of the grand vision of God's purpose with which the story begins" (*Narrative Unity*, 1:163) thus precisely articulates two heads of the trenchant theodical challenge Luke faces.

57. So Kurz, *Reading Luke-Acts*, 56–57.

58. If the audience for the speech is the crowd of people as a whole, then Jesus is singling out a particular demographic within the crowd (his disciples) even while using language that seeks to draw the crowd as a whole into the sub-group—even as, perhaps, Luke makes use of "you" language here also in an attempt to draw his audience closer to Jesus's inner circle.

59. The word occurs nowhere else in Luke and Acts.

60. Noting the irony of the connection but failing to apply it to exegesis of 2:38 is Green, *Luke*, 741.

Part 2: The Jerusalem Temple in Luke's Gospel

Daughters of Jerusalem (Luke 23:27–31)

Luke's unique and puzzling "Daughters of Jerusalem" scene appears well into his Passion Narrative, coming just after Pilate's reluctant condemnation of Jesus (23:13–25) and the notice that Simon carried Jesus's cross (v. 26). Here the amorphous mass of people (πολὺ πλῆθος τοῦ λαοῦ καὶ γυναικῶν[61]) seemingly repent of their earlier involvement in securing Jesus's execution (23:13, 18, 21)—or, if Luke invites us to read between the lines, the Jewish people are simply divided regarding Jesus, in line with Simeon's prophecy.[62] Nevertheless, the mass of people, viewed as a coherent character, here resume their more commonly sympathetic posture in Luke's Gospel (v. 27).[63]

Jesus's warning to the women, who stand here as often in the LXX as representative of the city's residents as a whole,[64] redounds with riddles and allusions. The mention of women who "were beating themselves" (ἐκόπτοντο; v. 27) seems to recall Zech 12:10–14,[65] although the significance of such an echo is indeterminate. Here Luke may be simply drawing on imagery from Zech 12, without intending to evoke a deeper meaning from the reference[66]—a possibility rendered more likely if v. 29 draws on the imagery, but not meaning, of Isa 54:1[67] and if v. 31 draws on the imag-

---

61. Unfortunately, I do not have space to examine the significance of Luke's singling out the women here, despite its being a worthy and fascinating question. McKnight is probably not far off the trail in noting the "surprising lead given to the women" and their bravery in commiserating with a criminal, in contrast to the disciples' cowardice (*Jesus and His Death*, 141–42).

62. See Green, *Luke*, 811–12.

63. See the discussion in Green, *Luke*, 809; also, Brown, *Death of the Messiah*, 2:918–19.

64. See Brown, *Death of the Messiah*, 2:920–21; also, Green, *Luke*, 815, and the passages he cites.

65. In the minority and in agreement with Green, *Luke*, 815.

66. Green likewise seems unsure how much meaning to read into this echo, citing it only as providing "imagery" for Luke (*Luke*, 815)—and this may be as deep a significance as we may safely extract. Brown notes that "[t]he atmosphere here is not far from that of Jer 9:16–19" (*Death of the Messiah*, 2:921).

67. Brown argues against Luke's drawing on Isa 54 here precisely because, despite some similarities (and note also the presence of mountains in Isa 54:10), Luke's meaning appears to differ from that of Isaiah (*Death of the Messiah*, 2:923). But, in light of Luke's profound reliance on Isaiah elsewhere in Luke and Acts, Brown may undervalue the background probability that Luke should be drawing on Isaiah here. It is also possible that Luke, taking Isa 54:1 in isolation from its context, reads it as a straight macarism

ery, but not meaning, of Ezek 17:24.[68] Luke 23:30 is a clear citation of Hos 10:8, but again the allusion's deeper or contextual meaning is difficult to discern. Worse, the very meaning of Jesus's statement about green and dry wood in v. 31 is notoriously opaque.[69]

Whatever the precise import of each detail of Jesus's complicated warning to the women (and to the city they represent) in vv. 28–31, the warning clearly serves to recall and re-punctuate both Jesus's status as a prophet and Jerusalem's treatment of the prophets as a key source of its demise (cf. 11:49–51; 13:33–34),[70] as well as the city's punishment for failing to understand the meaning of the events unfolding with Jesus's ministry there (19:41–44)—a meaning that of course extends, in Luke's mind, beyond even Jesus's prophetic status.[71] Thus, "the fate of Jerusalem and its inhabitants has been sealed by what the adversaries of Jesus are now doing"; the die is cast.[72]

The Rending of the Veil (Luke 23:45)

Following Jesus's pronouncement to the "daughters of Jerusalem," Luke (very) roughly follows Mark in narrating Jesus's crucifixion, adding a short scene (23:39–43) and possibly a line from Jesus (23:34a) and making several omissions, including of the passersby's mockery regarding Jesus's alleged statement about destroying the Temple and raising it in three days (Mark 15:29–30; cf. Luke 23:35).[73] Luke rejoins Mark in noting the darkening of

---

for the childless, though, to be certain, only in light of the context in which he interprets it here—i.e., the city's impending doom. This would not be the first time an NT author cited a prophecy from Scripture out of what modern auditors consider to be its proper context.

68. See Brown, *Death of the Messiah*, 2:925.

69. Brown is relatively optimistic, however, taking the subject of the protasis as the Jerusalem leaders and the subject of the passive apodosis as God—thus, paraphrasing Brown, "[I]f *the Jerusalem leaders and people* do this when the wood is green, what will God do to them when it is dry?" (*Death of the Messiah*, 2:925–27).

70. τὰ τέκνα ὑμῶν of 23:28 echoes τὰ τέκνα σου of 13:34.

71. Cf. Green, *Luke*, 814; Brown, *Death of the Messiah*, 2:921–22.

72. Brown, *Death of the Messiah*, 2:927.

73. This omission makes sense given that Luke has already omitted the corresponding accusation from Jesus's trial(s); as noted earlier, Luke reserves this charge for Stephen's trial in Acts 6–7. Luke may also wish to downplay any impression of Jesus's (and thus the early church's) being socially or politically dangerous—a frequently-noted Lukan emphasis.

Part 2: The Jerusalem Temple in Luke's Gospel

the sun from the sixth to ninth hours (Mark 15:33; Luke 23:44, though equivocating on the precise beginning time of the darkness and specifying the cause of the darkness as an eclipse) but then immediately reports also the dramatic tearing of the Temple veil (ἐσχίσθη δὲ τὸ καταπέτασμα τοῦ ναοῦ μέσον; Luke 23:45). Luke's well-known re-ordering (darkness-*veil*-cry-death, 23:45–46, vs. darkness-[cry-response]-cry-death-*veil* in Mark 15:37–38), as well as his omission of Mark's description that the veil was torn in two from top to bottom (εἰς δύο ἀπ' ἄνωθεν ἕως κάτω; 15:38), has given interpreters much grist for commentating and debating.[74] Interpretations of the ultimate meaning of the veil's rending center often on whether Luke's rearrangement works to connect the rending of the veil to the darkening of the sun in v. 44 (e.g., Matera) or to Jesus's last cry and death in v. 46 (e.g., Sylva), and also on how Luke's overall treatment of the JT informs this episode—with most post-1980 discussions taking a largely Weinert-ian line (i.e., assuming in Luke a "positive attitude" toward the Temple).[75] As I have endeavored to show, Weinert's attitude-centric positive assessment is problematic not only because it neglects significant pieces of evidence from Luke's writings but also, more fundamentally, because it frames the question as a matter of Luke's personal biases rather than allowing that Luke may be a theologian in a meaningful sense and thus may be responding to deeper (esp. theodical) questions.

---

74. Matera claims that Luke moves the rending of the veil prior to Jesus's death in order 1) "to avoid the impression that the death of Jesus is the end of the temple and its cult" and 2) "to align the torn curtain with the sun's failure and the three hours of darkness" ("The Death of Jesus," 475). Matera reaches these conclusions largely based on his assessment—here informed significantly by Weinert, if the footnotes are any indication—that "Luke's attitude toward the temple . . . is much more positive [than Mark's]" (ibid., 474). Chance emphasizes Luke's bringing the darkness, the rending, and Jesus's death into close proximity, taking them as "the satanic character of the Jewish leaders in Jerusalem," "the destruction of Jerusalem," and the Jewish leader's rejection of Jesus, respectively, basing his claims largely on Luke's pattern of connecting Jesus's rejection with the Temple's destruction (*Jerusalem*, 118–21); thus the rending symbolizes the destruction of Jerusalem and the Temple. Sylva argues that Luke repositions the tearing of the veil in order to establish a connection with Jesus's cry to God and thus to show "Jesus' communion with the God of the temple" ("Temple Curtain," 250). See also Green, "Demise of the Temple," 495–515, whom I discuss below. See the many interpretive options laid out in Nolland, *Luke*, 3:1157.

75. This is certainly true of Matera, "Death of Jesus"; and, to some degree, Green, "Demise of Temple," 498; Sylva, "Temple Curtain"; and Brown, *Death of the Messiah*, 2:1103.

Although I cannot hope exhaustively to discuss, and certainly not to solve, the riddles at play here, I will attempt to offer an interpretation that is, at the minimum, plausible. The first thing to note, after perusing the secondary literature on this question, is the broad range of interpretations on offer: most are conflicting; several are flatly contradictory. One way out of the cul-de-sac may be to pay less attention—at least initially—to Luke's re-ordering of the veil-rending and more attention to Luke's overall presentation of the JT. While Joel Green, for one, might object to this maneuver as a downplaying of "local co-text,"[76] even he acknowledges, when analyzing this passage, the need to appeal to the larger Lukan framing.[77] Not only do the diverse interpretations of the passage, most of which focus on Luke's re-ordering, thus point in this direction, but so do other considerations. One such consideration is Luke's concern for a well-ordered narrative. While there may be interpretive significance to Luke's re-ordering the veil-rending, he also likely moved it in order to pair it with the darkening of the sun in v. 44. As is widely noted, portents surrounding the death of important people were common in the ancient world,[78] and grouping the portents together helps, in typical Lukan fashion, to stream-line the narrative (which had already begun to balloon through the addition of the "Daughters of Jerusalem" and penitent criminal scenes).[79] Whatever theological function may have been served by placing the veil-rending prior to Jesus's death, this move certainly served the organizational and stylistic function of bringing the portents together. Luke's re-ordering may also have served the historiographical function of adding verisimilitude to Mark's account by

---

76. See Green, *Luke*, 13.

77. Green, "Demise of the Temple," 507–15.

78. Suetonius, for example, reports death portents for each of the twelve Caesars whose lives he narrates. Cf. Danker, *Jesus and the New Age*, 379.

79. With regard to Luke's "stream-lining" narratives, it is well-known that Luke, when adapting a scene from Mark, often offers a comparatively abbreviated rendition—e.g., Luke 6:1–5 (ninety to ninety-two words) vs. Mark 2:23–28 (109 words); Luke 6:17–19 (sixty-two words) vs. Mark 3:7–12 (101–2 words); Luke 8:5–8 vs. Mark 4:3–9; etc. Luke of course on occasion does the opposite, expanding the scene, as in Luke 7:36–50 (cf. Mark 14:3–9), where Luke not only expands but also repositions.

Luke's desire to group the darkening of the sun and the rending of the veil is even more likely if both are divine testimony regarding Jesus (positively) and his opponents (negatively), as argued by McConnell: "[A]n accompanying occurrence . . . reinforces the testimony through the eclipse; simultaneously the veil of the temple is divided down the middle" (*The Topos of Divine Testimony*, 278–79). McConnell likens Luke 23:45–46 to the darkness reported at Caesar's death in Plutarch's account (also taken as divine testimony).

Part 2: The Jerusalem Temple in Luke's Gospel

preventing the potential for (mis)interpreting the centurion's exclamation as a result of the rending of a veil which, taking the narrative historically, he most likely could not see.[80]

If the points above open space for a consideration of the veil-rending in Luke that does not hinge on Luke's ordering of events, what light is brought by Luke's larger presentation of the JT in his Gospel? For one thing, Luke's presentation of the JT is by no means as "positive" as some have claimed, and so the traditional reading that the rending of the veil stands here, as in Mark and other early Jewish and Christian interpretations,[81] as symbolic of Jerusalem's eventual destruction cannot be summarily ruled out.[82] It is crucial, however, to take Luke on his own terms (and not those of Mark or other early Christians), and so we must go enter more deeply into the world of Lukan thought in pursuit of this question.

Toward this end, note Luke's use (following Mark) of ναός in 23:45. To be sure, there is a geographical/spatial logic behind Luke's use here: he often appears to employ ἱερόν for the Temple grounds/mound at large and ναός for the inner sanctuary (cf. Luke 1:9, 21, 22), as would be fitting here.[83] Even so, the re-appearance of ναός, after so long an absence, recalls its otherwise unique appearance in Luke's opening scene, in which Zechariah's priestly administration of the *Tamid* in the JT is interrupted by the announcement

---

80. While the question of whether the centurion could/did see and respond to the rending of the veil—or whatever else—in Mark's Gospel does not concern me here (I gladly leave that vexed question to others), it is certainly likely that Luke, who as many believe, positions himself as a writer within the broad category of ancient history, would have objected on the grounds of verisimilitude to the suggestion that a centurion standing beside the cross could have seen the rending of whichever Temple veil. Thus Luke has a historiographical motive for moving the rending of the veil—if only to eliminate this possible misunderstanding. Not only would the centurion not have presumably had a line of sight from which to see the rending of the Temple's veil—even the outer veil—but the darkness would have made seeing impossible anyway. Making a strong recent case for καταπέτασμα as a reference to the inner veil is Gurtner, "LXX Syntax," 344–53.

81. See the evidence (and further secondary sources) cited by Chance, *Jerusalem*, 119–20.

82. No less an interpreter than Brown reads Luke's veil-rending as an indication of divine wrath, "a forewarning that the continuing rejection of Jesus will bring the destruction of the holy place" (*Death of the Messiah*, 2:1104, 1106). Brown indicates that this reading does not exhaust the meaning of the veil-rending in Luke, however (see *ibid.*, 2:1106).

83. Gaston takes (proto-) Luke's near omission of the Temple itself (ναός) in favor of the temple area (ἱερόν) as a clear indication of Luke's de-emphasis on the cultic function of the Temple (*No Stone*, 275).

of John's imminent birth. As noted above, the JT, which in terms of setting dominates Luke 1–2, enjoys a sacerdotal cultic function until Simeon's interruption of Jesus's dedication in Luke 2—an interruption that both reorients the scene in which it occurs and marks a shift away from the JT as a sacerdotal cultic center in Luke's gospel.[84] Here ναός, with its explicitly sacerdotal cultic overtones (in Luke's world and otherwise), reappears—and yet reappears only so that its curtain may be torn. That it is torn at the time of Jesus's death recalls the earlier hints that Jesus's life and ministry mean the end of the JT as sacerdotal cultic center—first in the Zechariah and Simeon scenes of Luke 1–2, then in the leper stories of Luke 5 and 17, and finally in Jesus's own designation of the JT as a "house of prayer" in Luke 19.[85] This interpretation of the rending of the veil[86] finds support in Luke 13:35a, which, on my reading, warns of God's abandoning the JT. The present progressive sense of ἀφίεται there points to the already-initiated but not-yet-completed nature of God's abandonment of the Temple—a process that, begun with Jesus's birth, reaches its consummation with his death. While this abandonment does not mean that the JT ceases to hold

---

84. As I have noted, the interruption of the *Tamid* offering in 1:9–22 prefigures the later interruption by Simeon. Even so, I persist in labeling the Simeon interruption as the major hinge on which Luke's presentation of the JT's functions turns because it is there that the shift first becomes clear, in my view; as such, the Simeon scene is more instructive and important for interpreting the Zechariah scene than vice-versa.

85. Luke continues this omission of the JT's cultic function—while noting its utility by the early Christians as a place of prayer—in Acts, though adding a polemical line by using ναός to refer (in its only two occurrences in Acts) to foreign idols (17:24; 19:24) and punctuating the end of the JT's cultic function by the calamitous interruption of Paul's attempt to fulfill his (reluctantly assumed) cultic vows in Acts 21—when the doors of the Temple are literally but also symbolically and ominously closed. Talbert and others have of course argued for a parallel between Jesus's arrest, trial, and execution and Paul's arrest and near-execution in Acts 21–22.

86. Among other commentators, my reading is perhaps closest to that of Green, "Demise of the Temple," although we arrive at our conclusions on different grounds and although he prefers to speak of the end of the temple as a "cultural center" rather than "sacerdotal cultic site"; still, our counterpart phrases are, I think, largely synonymous—and the difference is perhaps largely accounted for by his "socio-cultural" emphasis versus my theodical (and thus theological) focus. The key difference between our readings is my claim that God here abandons the Temple, against his interpretation of the rending as symbolic of God's now extending "the good news to those outside the social boundaries determined by the temple itself" (506)—which nevertheless seems to me to imply God's abandoning the JT as God's unique cultic institution. In agreement with my interpretation of Luke's veil-rending as God's abandonment of the Temple is Longenecker, "Rome's Victory," 98.

Part 2: The Jerusalem Temple in Luke's Gospel

any significance or utility in salvation history (it is still, after all, a house of prayer and worship), it does, on my reading, indicate the Temple's rejection as the uniquely chosen dwelling place of Israel's God.[87]

With this framing, we may now (re-)narrow our focus to (re-)examine the reason for Luke's re-ordering of events here. Doing so, we find that the above interpretation dovetails well with Dennis Hamm's insightful reading of Luke 23:44–47. Hamm notes that by moving the rending of the veil to its current location, Luke draws attention to its occurrence at the ninth hour[88]—precisely when the *Tamid* service was being offered in the temple itself.[89] If, as seems likely, Luke's ideal audience had the requisite cultural knowledge regarding the twice-daily sacrifice to make this association, then Luke's emphasizing that the tearing of the veil occurred simultaneously with the *Tamid* offering supports my reading of Luke 23:45. After all, it requires no great imaginative leap to recognize that the rending of the veil, occurring when it does, represents an interruption (however temporary) of the priestly worship in the temple[90]—and thus imitates, and recalls, Simeon's disruptive appearance in Luke 2:21–28 and, to a lesser degree, Luke's narration of Jesus's activity in the Temple (2:41–52) and Gabriel's *cultus* interrupting appearance to Zechariah (esp. 1:21–23). In addition to this, the symbolic importance of God's rending the veil while the service is in process—though of course potentially working in multiple directions—clearly suggests the abrogation of such priestly activity.[91] This reading, in

---

87. Sylva, who questions the reading of Luke 13:35a as God's abandoning the Temple, claims that, even if correct, on this view such abandonment cannot apply to the time period narrated in either Luke or Acts, since the apostles (Luke 24:53; Acts 2:46; 3:1) and Paul (Acts 21:2) both participate in worship there ("Temple Curtain," 249n25). Sylva overlooks the fact, however, that this worship is never, in Luke's narration, specifically sacerdotal, except in Paul's concessive worship of Acts 21—which is (significantly) interrupted by the very people who claim zeal for defending the worship of the Temple! That the Temple continues to have a function, both as a house of prayer/worship and (along with Jerusalem more generally) as the launching point for the worldwide mission of Jesus's disciples, does not mean that God has *not* abandoned it as the uniquely chosen and sanctioned cultic site nor that God has not forsaken its priestly administrators.

88. Thus, in Luke's arrangement of things, only a brief genitive absolute clause (τοῦ ἡλίου ἐκλιπόντος) now separates the tearing of the veil from the temporal notice.

89. See Hamm, "Tamid Service," 224–25.

90. This is true whether the καταπέτασμα refers to the inner veil partitioning off the Holy of Holies (thus visible only to the attending priests) or to the veil before the Sanctuary (thus visible to all the assembled Israelite worshipers). For an argument that καταπέτασμα refers to the inner veil, see Gurtner, "LXX Syntax," esp. 345–47.

91. Perhaps also pointing in this direction is Dawsey's suggestion that Luke moves

conjunction with Luke's use of ναός, also helps to establish a connection between this event and the Zechariah scene, since the latter also depicts the *Tamid* service.[92]

Thus, local co-text and the larger context of Lukan thought suggest that Luke 23:44-46 may represent not only God's interruption of the *Tamid* service in the Temple but also God's finally realized abandonment of the Temple—and thus its end, in the Lukan world, as the proper cultic site of Israel's God. This double-sided act—God's self-removal from the JT and its corresponding end as proper cultic site—clears the way for Act's emphasis on the universality of God's salvation (again, first sounded by Simeon; Luke 2:29-32).[93] Though Luke has hinted at the obstructive role of the JT, and its power brokers, in the spread of salvation in Luke 17:11-19 and Luke 19:41-45, the point will find clear expression in Acts.[94]

Before moving on, it is apropos to note that this reading of the rending of the veil in Luke 23:45 works in two directions from a theodical perspective. First, as Bruce Longenecker has noted, God's abandonment of the Temple at Luke 23:45 means that Israel's and Jesus's (and Luke's) God does not suffer a loss of honor with Rome's subsequent military conquest of the temple; in fact, God's abandonment is the very thing, from the perspective of Lukan theology, that opens the JT to attack.[95] Thus the frequent and widely broadcast Flavian boasting of Jerusalem's destruction does not, Luke informs the auditor, have any bearing on God's power and should not be mistaken as a referendum on God's honor. Secondly, on the other side of the theodical problem facing Luke, the potential accusation that God was unjust in abandoning the JT is answered: God abandoned it only after repeated warnings (Luke 11:49-51; 13:1-9, 31-35; 19:41-45; 23:28-31) and

---

the rending of the veil prior to Jesus's death because Jesus's ministry in the JT (which Luke elaborates from the shortened "cleansing" scene in Mark) must conclude—with the veil's rending—before he can give up his spirit ("Confrontation," 158). Cf. Danker's comment that Luke indicates that "[t]he people of God were authorized by the events at the crucifixion of Jesus to get along without traditional liturgical and bureaucratic structures ... without reference to standardized cultic practice" (*Jesus and the New Age*, 380).

92. See Hamm, "Tamid Service," 220-21.

93. On this, see the helpful discussion in Green, "Demise of the Temple," 504-14.

94. This theme finds expression especially in the Temple authorities' hostility to the nascent Christian movement (Acts 3-7) and then later their violent reaction to Paul's presence in the Temple (Acts 21-22), and probably also in the opposition of some Christian Pharisees (if Luke associates them with the JT) to inclusion of the Gentiles apart from their being circumcised and made to follow the Law of Moses (Acts 15).

95. Longenecker, "Rome's Victory," 98.

Part 2: The Jerusalem Temple in Luke's Gospel

in just (even merciful) response to its power brokers' rejection of God's prophets and, finally, their rejection even of the great prophet, Messiah, Lord, and Son of God (cf. Luke 21:9–19).

Jesus's Final Commission, and Waiting in Jerusalem (Luke 24:44–53)

The final pericope for consideration in this chapter is also the final scene of Luke's Gospel, Luke 24:44–53. Following Jesus's several post-resurrection appearances, he opens the disciples' minds to understand the Scriptures (24:44–47), commissions them as witnesses beginning in Jerusalem (vv. 47–48), promises to send power and the Father's promise from on high (v. 49), and then ascends to heaven (v. 51). Then the disciples, after worshiping him, return to Jerusalem with great joy, καὶ διὰ παντὸς ἐν τῷ ἱερῷ εὐλογοῦντες τὸν θεόν (vv. 52–53). As is well-known, this ending to Luke's Gospel has strong similarities, in theme and plot detail, to the beginning of Acts.

In need of consideration here are the Septuagintal echoes that many detect in Jesus's final blessing to the disciples (vv. 50–52). Many see in Luke's description of Jesus here a strong, intentional resemblance to priestly actions, as detailed in, e.g., Lev 9:22–24, and above all, in Sir 50:20–23. The similarities with Sir 50:20–23 are indeed somewhat striking, including Simon's/Jesus's 1) raising the hand and 2) blessing the people (twice in Sirach, once in Luke but twice mentioned), 3) the people's worshiping God (Sirach) or Jesus (Luke), 4) with grateful hearts (Sirach) or great joy (Luke).

Table 6: Priestly Blessings

Sir 50:20-23	Luke 24:50b-52
τότε καταβὰς ἐπῆρεν χεῖρας αὐτοῦ ἐπὶ πᾶσαν ἐκκλησίαν υἱῶν Ισραηλ δοῦναι εὐλογίαν κυρίου ἐκ χειλέων αὐτοῦ καὶ ἐν ὀνόματι αὐτοῦ καυχήσασθαι· καὶ ἐδευτέρωσαν ἐν προσκυνήσει ἐπιδέξασθαι τὴν εὐλογίαν παρὰ ὑψίστου.	καὶ ἐπάρας τὰς χεῖρας αὐτοῦ εὐλόγησεν αὐτούς. καὶ ἐγένετο ἐν τῷ εὐλογεῖν αὐτὸν αὐτοὺς διέστη ἀπ' αὐτῶν καὶ ἀνεφέρετο εἰς τὸν οὐρανόν.
Καὶ νῦν εὐλογήσατε τῷ θεῷ πάντων τῷ μεγάλα ποιοῦντι πάντῃ, τὸν ὑψοῦντα ἡμέρας ἡμῶν ἐκ μήτρας καὶ ποιοῦντα μεθ' ἡμῶν κατὰ τὸ ἔλεος αὐτοῦ.	Καὶ αὐτοὶ προσκυνήσαντες αὐτὸν ὑπέστρεψαν εἰς Ἰερουσαλὴμ
δῴη ἡμῖν εὐφροσύνην καρδίας καὶ γενέσθαι εἰρήνην ἐν ἡμέραις ἡμῶν ἐν Ισραηλ κατὰ τὰς ἡμέρας τοῦ αἰῶνος·	μετὰ χαρᾶς μεγάλης.

In view of such evidence for Luke's reliance on Sir 50, many believe,[96] though some doubt.[97] Joel Green, for one, rejects the possibility that Luke portrays Jesus in this way precisely because "Luke otherwise demonstrates no interest in portraying Jesus in priestly garb."[98] Instead, Luke presents Jesus on the "leave-taking" model of Jacob (Gen 49) and Moses (Deut 33), "with the echoes of Sirach [merely] emphasizing the stature of Jesus."[99]

Green's (and others') rejection of a priestly emphasis here may be too hasty, however.[100] For one, Luke's description of the blessing has little

---

96. See esp. van Stempvoort, "The Interpretation of the Ascension," 34–37; and Lohfink, *Die Himmelfahrt Jesu*, 167–69. Also, Hamm, "Praying 'Regularly,'" 50; Maile, "The Ascension in Luke-Acts," 42.

97. Included with Green on the list of those who doubt a connection is Litwak, *Echoes*, 148–49, who sees a stronger connection with Lev 9:22.

98. Green, *Luke*, 861.

99. Ibid., 861; Green points to "Abraham" with the Gen 49 reference but surely means Jacob. Green finds support in Nolland, *Luke*, 3:1227.

100. Green's dismissal of Mikeal Parsons's analysis ("Narrative Closure and Openness," esp. 205–6), for one, is misguided. He accuses Parsons, among other things, of circular reasoning regarding Luke's putative priestly presentation of Jesus here (*Luke*, 861). What Parsons actually claims, however, is 1) that a priestly presentation of Jesus here, which numerous commentators observe, would provide a strong and fitting example of Luke's use of circularity to provide closure, and 2) that the dismissal of a priestly reading here on the basis that Luke elsewhere does not present Jesus as a priest overlooks Luke's possible use of this literary device. There is a certain circularity to Parsons's reading of

analog in the proposed Jacob and Moses parallels, beyond the very general similarity that great personages bless their successors, whom they are leaving behind. Unlike those blessings, which elaborate lengthy and involved futures for each of the sons/tribes of Jacob, Luke's account not only fails to specify any content regarding the blessing but also does not specify that the blessing was to the Twelve (minus one)—which would have served as a nice, if imperfect, analog to the blessing of Jacob's sons. The parallels to Sir 50:20–23 are all the more striking given the very general nature of the parallels with Gen 49 or Deut 33.[101] Secondly, the parallels are decidedly priestly—the raising of the hand in blessing, the blessing itself, and the worship in response to the blessing,[102] followed by mention of the worshipers' gladness/joy. Thirdly, while Green is correct in noting that Luke does not elsewhere portray Jesus in priestly garb, Green's reading of Luke 17:11–19, which largely agrees with my own reading, can easily point in this direction at least. Moreover, despite his usually admirable attention to narrative flow and context, Green fails to consider that, within Luke's narrative world, Luke 24 consists of rather rarefied air: with the brief exception of Acts 1:4–9, here alone in Luke's writings do we have a post-resurrection, pre-ascension Jesus. This would be an ideal moment, then, for Luke to punctuate a new aspect of Jesus's identity—especially an aspect of his identity that only reaches full fruition after his resurrection.

The question, then, is not whether this image for Jesus is presented elsewhere in Luke's writings but is, rather, 1) whether a presentation of the post-resurrection, pre-ascension Jesus as priest coheres with Luke's overall characterization and presentation of Jesus and 2) whether it coheres with his treatment of the Temple. Regarding point one, the question of Luke's characterization of Jesus, Luke certainly has no problem importing and attributing a diversity of identities and roles to Jesus—Messiah, Lord, Son of Man, prophet, and so forth—so an attribution of priestly qualities here,

---

course, but it is not the circularity of logically bankrupt tautology but rather the inescapable circularity of the "hermeneutical circle" since there are other grounds—viz., the verbal echoes outlined above—for reading Jesus as priestly here than simply to posit that such a reading shows that Luke provides closure via circularity.

101. Leviticus 9:22–24 also commends itself in this regard (καὶ ἐξάρας Ααρων τὰς χεῖρας ἐπὶ τὸν λαὸν εὐλόγησεν αὐτούς . . . καὶ ἐξελθόντες εὐλόγησαν πάντα τὸν λαόν, καὶ ὤφθη ἡ δόξα κυρίου παντὶ τῷ λαῷ . . . καὶ εἶδεν πᾶς ὁ λαὸς καὶ ἐξέστη καὶ ἔπεσαν ἐπὶ πρόσωπον), though it lacks mention of the people's joy/gladness. This passage may well lie behind both Luke 24 and Sir 50.

102. If v. 52's προσκυνήσαντες αὐτὸν is judged to be non-Lukan or "non-original," then the case for reliance on Sir 50 (or Lev 9) is weakened but not undone.

while by no means implied by the other images by which he characterized Jesus, is at least broadly coherent within his polyvalent portrait of Jesus. Furthermore, there may in fact be hints in this direction in several scenes: the boy Jesus's service in the Temple (Luke 2:41–52), as well as Jesus's taking possession of the Temple (Luke 19:45—21:38), the leper stories of 5:12–16 and 17:11–19 (see *loc.*), and also Luke's de-emphasis on the Temple's sacerdotal cultic function with the arrivals of John and especially Jesus. This final point gets also at the question of whether Jesus's having a priestly role would cohere with Luke's treatment of the JT: it indeed makes sense and all the more so if Luke here presents Jesus as priest "*outside* of the temple, and, indeed, outside of Jerusalem."[103] To argue in this latter direction would be inescapably circular, however, and so it serves not to establish the case for a priestly Jesus in Luke 24:50–51 but only to strike down Green's (representative) objections to such.

In light of the similarities noted above, then, I find it likely that Luke here indeed draws on Sir 50:20–22, or else he draws on a very similar description of a priest (perhaps Lev 9)—in either case intending a priestly portrayal of Jesus here. This portrayal helps make sense of Luke's de-emphasis on the JT's sacerdotal cultic role throughout his Gospel: Jesus's arrival means the end of the JT's cultic functions precisely because Jesus, among the many other roles he fills, comes also as priest, though in Lukan theology he apparently attains full priestly status only with his death.[104] The audience is left only to surmise the further fact that, because of his unique relationship to God and indeed because of Jesus's own (admittedly fuzzy) divine status in Luke, Jesus's priestly service is not bound by physical locale—although there are hints also in this direction, especially in Jesus's treatment of the lepers in 5:12–16 and 17:11–19, and this dovetails with the decentralizing theme of Stephen's speech in Acts 7 (see my comments on Acts 7 in the appendix). Moreover, this reading works well within the

---

103. Green, *Luke*, 860.

104. If true, this introduces a potential timing problem, with Luke's moving the rending of the veil prior to Jesus's death while his priestly status appears only post-resurrection. The problem is hardly insurmountable, however. Luke is of course not always vigorously strict in his schematization of time, even when schematizing salvation history—thus, e.g., he depicts Gentile converts (such as the Ethiopian official) prior to the official mission to the Gentiles in Acts 10, and Luke's shift away from the Temple as a cultic site (argued for in this chapter) begins with the Zechariah scene in Luke 1 and yet gains full steam with Jesus's presentation in the Temple in Luke 2.

PART 2: THE JERUSALEM TEMPLE IN LUKE'S GOSPEL

architectonics of Luke's Gospel: in this final scene, Jesus completes the unfinished priestly blessing with which Luke began his Gospel.

Even so and in keeping with his multivalent characterization of Jesus throughout his Gospel, Luke presents Jesus here as more than a priest: "then they worshiped him" (using προσκυνέω; v. 52).[105] In other passages, Luke drops hints and suggestions of characters' worshiping Jesus (e.g., 17:16), but here for the first time is the worship unmistakable. Thus the priestly blessing leads the faithful to worship not God, as in Sir 50, but Jesus.[106]

SUMMARY

The conflict between Jesus and the religious leaders reaches its crescendo as Jesus arrives at and takes possession of the Temple. Luke frames this arrival with his puzzling Kingship Parable, which comes in response to questions of the kingdom's imminence and location as Jesus approaches Jerusalem. In Luke's hands, Jesus's arrival itself may recall and reverse Ezekiel's vision of God's departure from the Temple.

The subsequent series of conflict scenes occurs within the Temple itself and collectively demonstrates the Temple's new (reduced) role—no longer as a sacerdotal cultic site but rather a place of prayer and instruction. Jesus's interruption of the Temple's sacerdotal functions and his transmuting it into a place of prayer and instruction enacts Luke's earlier muting of the JT's role as sacerdotal cultic site.

This transmuting reaches full realization only with the culmination of the conflict that has characterized Jesus's ministry. As Jesus hangs on the cross, ready to expire, the veil of the ναός is torn—interrupting the afternoon *Tamid* offering, effecting and symbolizing God's abandonment of God's one-time "house." This moment thus encapsulates and weaves

---

105. See Marshall, *Luke*, 910.

106. The claim that Luke's description of the disciples' worshiping in the Temple (τῷ ἱερῷ) διὰ παντὸς in v. 53 alludes to the *Tamid* service (so Hamm, "Praying 'Regularly'"; cf. Bachmann, *Jerusalem und der Tempel*, 344–45) is hardly compelling. Although this phrase could refer to Israel's daily priestly service (as in Lev 28:10, 15, 23, 24, 31; 29:6, 11, 16, 19, 22, 25, 28, 31, 34, 38), it was hardly a technical cultic term in the LXX (2 Kgdms 9:7, 10, 13; 4 Kgdms 4:9; 25:29, 30; 1 Chron 16:11; 2 Chron 9:7) and is certainly not one in the Lukan corpus (e.g., Acts 2:25; 10:2; 24:16). See also, Rom 11:10; 2 Thess 3:16; cf. Heb 2:15 vs. 9:6; 13:15. If Luke intends a reference to the *Tamid* service, then it is subtle indeed and hardly brings the Jerusalem cult and its sacerdotal details back to center stage and might in fact point to a priestly role for the disciples (given the priestly echoes of vv. 50–52)—but an allusion to the *Tamid* remains, in my opinion, rather unlikely.

together the various Lukan threads accounting for the demise of Jerusalem and its Temple: the Shiloh-esque rejection and abandonment of the house controlled by those who persist in immorality and who persecute God's prophets (and indeed God's Prophet), and thus the abrogation of its unique role as proper cultic site.

Luke ends his Gospel not here, however, but rather with teasing hints of a priestly Jesus, completing the blessing that Zechariah was prevented from offering (as Luke began his Gospel). Thus Luke offers a tantalizing but faint counterpoint to the numerous scenes in which he mutes the priestly workings of the Temple. In doing so, he brings his Gospel full-circle.

6

Conclusion

JERUSALEM AND THE TEMPLE IN LUKE'S GOSPEL—A GARMENT OF MANY STRANDS

In the foregoing analysis of Luke's Gospel (chapters 3–5), I have attempted to demonstrate that Luke presents a coherent, if multivalent, portrait of Jerusalem and its Temple.¹ I have identified four major aspects to this portrait. First, Luke interprets Jerusalem and its Temple in terms of the abandoned οἶκος of Shiloh (Luke 1–2; 13:35a; echoed faintly in 19:46), thus giving a powerful scriptural warrant—one long-since employed by Jeremiah—for God's rejecting his own holy place. Second, within Luke's Gospel narrative, the proper function of the JT is to point characters (and also auditors) to recognition of Jesus. Luke sculpts his narrative with a progressively realized eclipsing of the JT's sacerdotal operations with Gabriel's annunciation of John's birth (1:9–22) and especially by Jesus's birth (2:22–40, 41–52), ministry (5:12–16; 17:11–19; 19:45–48), and finally death (23:45), with hints of a post-resurrection Jesus as priest (24:50–53). These narrative hints receive some degree of narratival clarification as Jesus's ministry slowly encroaches

---

1. Regarding Luke's polyvalent picture, compare Holmås's claim that "when it comes to the theological justification for the criticism of the temple, Luke gives us a composite picture," one comprised of 1) a criticism of "Jerusalem's blindness and unbelief in response to God's eschatological act of salvation" and 2) a criticism for its exclusivity—criticisms Holmås believes are ultimately linked ("'My House Shall Be Called,'" 398).

CONCLUSION

upon the sacred space reserved for the JT—through extending forgiveness of sins, crossing boundaries of purity and gender, and embodying God's holy presence. Third, Luke presents Jesus as a prophet whose person, mission, and message entails a fateful collision with the city that Luke characterizes as murderer of the prophets (11:49–51; 13:31–35; 19:41–44; 23:27–31). Fourth, Luke appeals to a spectrum of (mostly prophetic) Scriptures that depict God's judging his people for their wickedness (Isa 5 in Luke 13:6–9; Ezek and Jer in Luke 9:51; possibly Isa 63:4 in Luke 2:38), and in this regard Luke especially emphasizes the wickedness of the Jerusalem authorities.

Throughout, Luke employs Scripture, and despite his frequently subtle echoes, his use of Scripture elaborates and clarifies the position of Jerusalem and the Temple in his narrative world and theology. Luke does this in several ways, including his often inviting auditors to hear echoes as having typological import. Thus, for example, Luke 1–2 presents both Jesus and John after the pattern of Samuel. Although Luke goes on to characterize the Messiah and his forerunner after other great figures as well, the initial Samuel framing of Luke's gospel helps also to establish a typological connection between the Jerusalem religious authorities of Jesus's day and the rejected house of Eli and also between Jerusalem and Shiloh.

Luke also makes use of irony and the double-meaning of words to communicate his complex theological position regarding Jerusalem and the Temple. The first and perhaps most poignant instance of this is his description of Anna in 2:38 (καὶ ἐλάλει περὶ αὐτοῦ πᾶσιν τοῖς προσδεχομένοις λύτρωσιν Ἰερουσαλήμ). To adopt the straightforward meaning of this sentence is simply an avenue that is not open for Luke's ideal audience, who know both that Jesus, after characterizing Jerusalem as murderer of the prophets, would himself be wrongly executed by its authorities and that those expecting Jerusalem's redemption in the sense of restoration at the time of Jesus's birth held this hope vainly indeed. I have argued for Lukan double-meaning also regarding οἶκος from the pivotal phrase of 13:35a (ἰδοὺ ἀφίεται ὑμῖν ὁ οἶκος ὑμῶν).

I have attempted to root my case in both the immediate context (or co-text) and location of a given passage, as well as its larger Lukan context. Given the latter concern, I have attempted to lay out what I see as the major (relevant) dynamics of Luke's narrative, including especially the agonistic dynamic that is foretold by Simeon and that transpires, with crescendo-ing force, across the entirety of Luke's Gospel (and throughout Acts).

Part 2: The Jerusalem Temple in Luke's Gospel

If even partially successful, my study has demonstrated that Luke's treatment of Jerusalem and the Temple goes far beyond mere personal preference or bias—as though Luke had a simple personal disposition toward these sacred institutions that has somehow bled through into his writings in a facilely identifiable way. Far from it! Rather, Luke proves (again) to be a genuine theologian wrestling with Scripture and with tradition in his attempt to answer for his audience (and perhaps also for himself) the pressing questions of his day. These are, as I have explored, above all questions of theodicy: How could God let his city that bears his name be destroyed, his house be defiled? Does this show that the God of Israel—now also the God of Jesus, Paul, and those members of this strange sect ("Christians")—to be effete in the face of Roman might? Or perhaps worse: Does this show God to be faithless? Luke does not necessarily or often front these theodical questions in his Gospel—and we would hardly expect him to, given that he is narrating events 40-plus years prior to that crisis—but he does frequently concern himself with Jerusalem's fate and does also explicitly raise issues of theodicy, as in Luke 13:1–9.[2] If Luke as a theologian suffers from subtlety of expression to go along with his depth of vision, keenness of insight, and passion of inquiry, we can only say that he finds himself in good company.[3] Comparing Luke to Paul's letters, "whose mode of argumentation has a more recognizably didactic and persuasive look," Joel Green notes that "the Third Gospel presents its message in the form of a narrative" and its "mode of persuasion is perhaps more subtle, but no less theological."[4] Thus Luke sometimes teases his audience with unstable meanings (2:38; 13:35a), asymptotic hints (19:11; Acts 1:6–7), translucent tales (13:6–9; 19:11–27), and tickling reverberations (throughout).

As the preceding paragraphs suggest, many of the relevant themes and hints for my thesis find their origin in Luke 1–2 and especially in Luke 2:22–52—which establish the Shiloh-Jerusalem connection, which first

---

2. Also revealing Luke's interest in theodicy are the Parable of the Persistent Widow, with its odd and potentially subversive portrait of God as Judge (18:1–8), and the Parable of the Friend at Midnight (11:5–8); see chapter 2.

3. Surely this charge could be leveled against any number of great theologians from the past, from Origen to the Cappadocian fathers to Kierkegaard to Barth and Balthasar. This is not to obscure, of course, the fundamental differences between Luke's narratively constructed theology and the more formal theological methods of later theologians.

4. Green, *Theology*, 3. Admittedly, my analysis of Luke's Gospel has not been able exhaustively to explore how Luke "engages in the theological task and the strategies by which he engages his audience in transformative discourse" (Green, *Theology*, 132–33).

Conclusion

clearly establish Jesus as a prophet (like Samuel), which most decisively begin the Lukan shift from Temple as sacerdotal center to place of prayer and instruction, and which allude to the eventual conflict between Jesus and some within Israel. Each of the four major threads I have uncovered, then, as well as Luke's use of irony and double-meaning regarding Jerusalem and the Temple, find their foundation here. This fact, combined with the emphasis on narrative beginnings by previous scholars, has directed me to give this early portion of Luke's Gospel comparatively greater attention. From the standpoint of ancient theodicy, Luke leans heavily on (non-stringent forms of) retribution theology to address—or perhaps to head off—questions regarding God's faithfulness. Could a faithful God allow the holy city and Temple to suffer so terribly? Luke answers with a resounding, if doleful, "yes." For Israel's God, Luke informs us, has done similarly in the past, both in the complete rejection of Shiloh and in the previous rejection of Jerusalem, and, furthermore, God did so only in response to persistent national impenitence, including the immorality of the leaders and the rejection of God's prophets, finally of the prophet who was in fact more than a prophet, Jesus himself. Luke addresses questions of God's power less directly (as already noted by Longenecker), largely bypassing them by showing God's abandonment of the JT during the ministry and especially the crucifixion of Jesus—hence, the destruction of Jerusalem in no way reflects negatively upon God's power or honor. While Luke seldom, in my view, directly contrasts God's power against Roman might—thereby tackling head-on the insinuations of Flavian propaganda regarding Israel's God—he does seem to marginalize Roman might through Jesus's reference to the end of the "times of the nations" (Luke 21:24). Certainly, moreover, he highlights God's power, as animated in Jesus, especially vis-à-vis Satanic power (10:18–19; 13:16). In Luke's master portrait, then, despite abandoning Jerusalem and its Temple to the devices of their wicked human masters, God is neither lacking in power nor deficient in faithfulness but amply displays God's abiding faithfulness in the ministry of Jesus and later through the ongoing mission of Jesus's disciples.

Appendix
Jerusalem and the Temple in Acts

AN OVERVIEW

The task here is simply to map, with brushstrokes all-too-broad, the landscape of Acts on the question of Jerusalem and its Temple. Most significant for this question is Acts 1–7, although a later episode provides clarification and emphasis to the lines that occur at the beginning of Luke's second volume.

NEW DEVELOPMENTS: JERUSALEM AND THE TEMPLE IN ACTS 1–7

Acts 1 picks up where Luke 24 leaves off narratively, yet it soon moves theologically beyond anything made explicit in Luke's Gospel. The disciples' query in 1:6 about whether the Lord Jesus would now "restore the kingdom to Israel" places the limelight on contemporary Jewish eschatological hopes, much as did Luke 1–2 (viz., via the descriptions of Simeon and Anna).[1] Jesus' response in vv. 7–8 serves to qualify and thus also partially to rebuff these expectations: alluding to Isa 49:6 (precisely a passage and part of Scripture in which such hopes find expression) Jesus characterizes the programme to follow in terms of a centrifugal mission (going out from Jerusalem), thereby making somewhat tenuous expectations of a complementarily centripetal mission (to Jerusalem).[2]

---

1. See Bauckham, *Jewish World*, 328–46.
2. Cf. Parsons, "The Place of Jerusalem," 168. Also, Bauckham, *Jewish World*, 327,

APPENDIX

As Acts plays out, the hint proves to be well-taken: Jerusalem will indeed serve as a launching pad (the centrifugal function) for the Christian mission, but whatever initial promise the gathering of Diaspora Israel at Pentecost (Acts 2) has for a centripetal movement to Jerusalem,³ the city does not quite live up to its billing as the eschatological gathering site for hordes of Gentiles (as in Isa 2:2–3; 60:3, 10; 61:5).⁴ Much the contrary, the city and its leaders continue their behavior from Luke's Gospel; they persist in resisting God's plan and in persecuting those who are truly faithful (Acts 4:1–22; 5:17–42; 6:12—8:1). Thus they fail both to acknowledge their wickedness in crucifying God's Messiah and Holy One (5:28) and to perceive the unfolding fulfillment of Israel's eschatological expectations.⁵

All of this comes to a head, as Luke narrates it, with Stephen's trial.⁶ Here the persecution (earlier cooled just shy of boiling point by Gamaliel's timely intervention [5:33–39]) finally bubbles over into murder by mob

---

345–46; Spencer, *Journeying through Acts*, 36; Pokorný, *Theologie*, 45–46. Others maintain that because Jesus does not explicitly reject a centripetal mission, he does not in fact criticize this expectation (e.g., Keener, *Acts*, 1:683, 687n341), but even so, the narrative of Acts itself frustrates expectations of Jerusalem as a gathering point for the nations. The muting of a centripetally-moving mission here may have interpretive significance for the centripetal half of the Lukan and Isaianic pair in Luke 2: Simeon (centrifugal) and Anna (centripetal).

3. I remain on the fence regarding claims that in Acts 2 Luke narrates the descent of the eschatological temple (on this, see above all Beale, "The Descent of the Eschatological Temple—Part 1"; Beale, "The Descent of the Eschatological Temple—Part 2)." Such a claim would be coherent with my reading of Luke's Gospel and would in some ways be anticipated by those portions of Luke's Gospel that, on my reading, state God's abandonment of the JT and imply the abrogation of the Temple's cultic functions with the ministry of Jesus (thus proleptically indicating the reality brought to fruition at Pentecost: that Jesus, via his Spirit, completely abolishes any need for a physical temple by creating the new, eschatological temple). Luke may, on the other hand, describe Pentecost along the lines of Sinai (as Beale claims) but intend to leave open-ended the import of the scene, not specifically limiting himself to a vision of the Church as the eschatological temple.

4. The picture is of course rather complex, even within Isa 40–66. In Isa 60, for example, the Gentiles who come to Zion generally do so in order to receive punishment.

5. For example, Luke portrays the healing of the lame man in Acts 3:1–10 in terms evocative of Isa 35:6—both passages envision the lame (χωλός—Acts 3:2) leaping (ἅλλομαι—Acts 3:8) for joy—yet the authorities, in their questioning of Peter and John, completely miss the point.

6. For a discussion of the charges against Stephen (judged to be reflective of Luke's and Luke's auditors' engagement with Diaspora Jewish synagogues), see Arai, "Zum 'Tempelwort' Jesu."

action. It also instigates, so the narrative implies, the subsequent persecution of the church by Saul (8:1–3).

Stephen's speech is not only pivotal narratively, however, but it also brings full expression to Luke's theology of the Jerusalem Temple. Coming at the end (and bringing to culmination) Luke's picture of a Jerusalem leadership that at every turn opposes and intimidates the servants of God, Stephen's speech gives verbal expression to the realities already hinted at by Luke's narrative. In Stephen's speech, Luke leads the listener (as in the narrative Stephen leads his own audience) to see that God's activity and saving purposes have often extended beyond the bounds of God's specially chosen geographical bounds—first with Abraham (vv. 2–8), then with Joseph (vv. 9–16), and also with Moses (vv. 17–44). As the speech nears its climax, Stephen quotes two prophecies, first from Amos 5:25–27 (Acts 7:42–43), upbraiding Israel for its idolatry, and then from Isaiah 66:1 (Acts 7:49–50). The Isaiah quote is, in context, quite shocking. For Stephen prefaces it with the assertion that God does not dwell in "things made by human hands" (χειροποίητος; v. 48). By then quoting Isaiah 66:1 ("What kind of house will you build for me. . .?") Stephen clearly applies to the JT this word reserved in the LXX for idols![7] In doing so, not only does Luke give a clear instigating cause for the subsequent mob violence against Stephen but he also goes beyond the theology of the JT expressed in his Gospel. Moving beyond earlier statements that Jerusalem would be rejected for its immorality and the general opposition of its leaders to God's purposes and servants and moving beyond hints of a shift away from Jerusalem's sacred position as the unique cultic center for Israel's God, Luke here announces that the attempt to limit God's presence to the Jerusalem emple is, in fact, nothing less than idolatry. This provides yet another—and one last—powerful warrant justifying God's abandonment of the city and its Temple, a final weapon in Luke's theodical arsenal.

Other than this significant step beyond the theology of Jerusalem and the Temple presented in Luke's Gospel, Acts continues, sometimes by amplification, the theological lines mapped across the earlier Lukan narrative. Hints of Shiloh are (to my knowledge) absent, but Jerusalem is again the city that boasts the dangerous occupation of persecuting God's servants.

---

7. To the point: χειροποίητος occurs nine times in the LXX (Lev 26:1, 30; Isa 2:18; 10:11; 16:12; 19:1; 21:9; 31:7; 46:6); the only passage in which the reference to idolatry is potentially uncertain is Lev 26:30. Heightening the sting of Stephen's accusation, Isaiah regularly uses the term to refer to the vain images of foreign nations (two exceptions, 2:18 and 31:7, refer to Israel's own idols).

APPENDIX

Thus, also, it opposes the nascent church that now (finally) embodies the wealth ethic (2:43–47; 4:32–37) that Jesus preached[8] and for which he indicted Israel's leadership. Moreover, God's Spirit has been poured out upon the Church, making more explicit Luke's earlier hints that Jesus' presence means the end of the JT as unique cultic site. Indeed, although the JT serves frequently as the setting for the Church's activities in Acts 1–7, its cultic and especially sacerdotal functions are consistently muted.[9] It is now, Luke seems to indicate, nothing beyond a place for prayer and instruction—and thereby no more significant a locale than the houses[10] and synagogues that serve similar functions at many points in the narrative of Acts.

But does not, we might ask, the fact that Jerusalem, and especially the Temple, serves as the setting for the rise of the Church indicate that Luke gives it some significance beyond what I have indicated above? Indeed I believe it does—and here we return again to contemporary Jewish eschatological expectations. In my thinking, Luke has two trenchant reasons for setting Jerusalem and its Temple as the locus for these eschatological events. For one, he presumably believes this is in fact where and how the Church began—in Jerusalem, at Pentecost. A theological concern supplies his second reason, however: by locating the Church's eschatologically significant origins in Jerusalem, Luke endeavors to demonstrate that the hopes for Israel's restoration foretold by the Scriptures were indeed fulfilled, even if not exactly as anticipated. Especially left ambiguous was, again, the expectation that Jerusalem would serve as the gathering point for the nations (the centripetal movement to Jerusalem). Luke was almost certainly aware of this expectation and perhaps attempted to finesse it by emphasizing the centrifugal counterpart to this expectation, as well as by demonstrating the Jerusalem leadership's persistent opposition to God—a major plot element

---

8. The violation of this wealth ethic is a better explanation for God's harsh treatment of Ananias and Sapphira, it seems to me, than the claim that Luke presents them as violating the Lord's "temple presence" (*contra* Le Donne, "The Improper Temple Offering").

9. In Acts 2, for example, a cultic rationale—the Pentecost pilgrimage—serves as part of the backdrop to the episode, although everything specifically sacerdotal is excluded from Luke's narration. Likewise, in Acts 3:1 Peter and John indeed go to the Temple "at the hour of prayer," or the time of the second *tamid* offering, yet the offering receives no attention in the text; rather, Luke uses the prayer time as a backdrop to the (for him) more significant story of the apostles' healing the man, along the lines predicted by Isaiah. Moreover, the *tamid* offering, though not narrated, is narratively interrupted by the mob-rush to see Peter and John after the miracle is made known (3:11).

10. The above comment will perhaps suffice to indicate the (only) limited sense in which I endorse the temple vs. household paradigm suggested by John Elliott for Acts.

of Acts 1–7. Additionally, his eventual disclosure that the attempt to localize God's presence to Jerusalem and its Temple amounted to idolatry may be an attempt to explain the failure of this centripetal movement to materialize. Here the logic would seem to run: Jerusalem's envisioned role as the gravitational center for God's eschatological purposes has been frustrated (permanently? temporarily?) by its opposition to God's purposes and God's agents and above all by the fact that its Temple has, alas, become an idol.

STRENGTHENING THE IMPRESSION (ACTS 8–28)

Jerusalem and its Temple largely drop from sight as the narrative of Acts pushes on—away from Jerusalem and into the foreign missionary work of Paul. As many have noted, however, Acts' movement away from Jerusalem is cyclical, and not straightforwardly dispersive, and things have a way of circling back around. The most significant reappearance of the sacred city occurs with Paul's fateful arrival there in Acts 21.

Here, quite curiously, Luke shines the spotlight on the Temple's ongoing cultic role—the first time he does such (by my count) since the opening pericope of his Gospel![11] What can this mean? Several points deserve consideration. Though rather obvious, it needs saying that Luke here acknowledges the Temple's ongoing cultic significance specifically in order to portray Paul's participating in a vow taken by four Jewish Christians.[12] Luke frames the taking of this vow as a concession: as suggested by James, Paul is to take this vow with four other Jewish Christians in order to demonstrate the falsehood of rumors that he was teaching Jews to abandon Moses, circumcision, and other Jewish identity markers (21:21–25). Luke thus depicts the Temple's cultic role here as holding specifically (and only) cultural significance and in doing so considerably diminishes its importance. Absent are any hints of the Temple's cosmic significance, its architectural and cultic correspondence to ultimate heavenly reality; on the contrary, Paul participates in the vow simply as a matter of Jewish custom, to edify his brothers.

---

11. Luke's highlighting of the JT's ongoing cultic role in Acts 21 is foreshadowed by his note in 20:16 that Paul was hurrying to get to Jerusalem before Pentecost. If an earlier verse in Acts 20 implies Paul's observance of the Passover Feast (v. 6—so Parsons, *Acts*, 303), any implied reference to the JT is muted by the fact that Paul partakes of the feast well away from Jerusalem.

12. Whether Paul himself also partakes in the vow is up in the air; see Parsons, *Acts*, 303.

APPENDIX

As things play out, however, Paul does not in fact complete the purification ritual, for misinformed and belligerent Asiatic Jews seize him in the Temple before the rite is completed (21:27-29). Once again, in a favorite Lukan plot-twist, a scene that begins with a cultic rationale reorients rather drastically when the cultic action is itself interrupted. Several differences apply here in comparison to earlier scenes following this pattern, however, not least of which are that the cultically-inclined character (here Paul) never gets to finish the rite and that this is so precisely because the characters who claim surpassing zeal for the Temple prevent him from doing so!

These are facts upon which any attempts to rehabilitate the Temple as a proper cultic site within Luke's theology on the basis of the sacerdotal/cultic elements of Acts 21 must ultimately founder. Indeed Luke here gives narrative illustration to the theological points made earlier regarding the Temple. Once again it serves as both the hub of opposition to God's will and proves to be an idolatrous stumbling block. Though Luke does not specifically raise the charge of idolatry here, intratextual connections—a favorite pastime of Luke especially in Acts—strongly point in this direction.

Indeed several parallels suggest a connection (taken together, a rather strong one in fact) between this scene and an earlier scene in Acts.[13] This earlier scene also centers around zeal for a temple, the Artemis Temple in Ephesus. As the Asiatic rabble-rousers stir up themselves and other members of the mob-to-be, their rationale hinges on the dubious claim that Paul has brought a Gentile into the Temple (21:27-28). Luke provides a semi-parenthetical note explaining that they had previously seen an Ephesian, Trophimus, in the city with Paul and had (rather wildly) inferred his presence also in the Temple. The identification of the man's city of residence as Ephesus serves as a verbal cue that recalls the earlier riot scene. Further links between the Ephesian riot (19:21-40) and Jerusalem riot scenes are ample and instructive (21:27—22:29). Both scenes of course share the general feature of narrating a mob scene that occurs surrounding a temple. More than this, in each scene a Jew attempts to address the mob—Alexander in 19:33 and Paul in 21:49. This Jew motions to the crowd and attempts to speak (19:33; 21:40). In both cases as the speaker begins to address the mob, his ethnic identity becomes a focal point of attention[14] and has an

---

13. I certainly do not deny connections also between this scene and other scenes in Luke's writings, especially between this scene and Acts 7 and between this scene and Jesus's passion. The accusations against Paul here and Stephen in Acts 6, e.g., are notably similar.

14. The crowd simply learns, through unidentified means, that Alexander is a Jew

immediate effect upon the crowd—re-igniting the crowd at Ephesus but further silencing the Jerusalem mob. Despite their divergent initial reaction, the Jerusalem mass ultimately re-ignites, demanding Paul's death (22:22) and is, like the Ephesian mob (19:35–40), dispelled only by the intervention of a Roman official (22:24). Also connecting the two scenes is that fact that, in narrating the Ephesian riot, Luke makes the surprising choice of describing the ringleader of the riot, Demetrius, as a maker of ναός (19:24)—the very word applied to the JT in Luke 1:9, 21, 22; 23:45; and often in the LXX.[15] The only other occurrence of ναός in Acts also refers to foreign temples or idols and also emphasizes their composition by human hands (17:24). These uses of ναός echo against Stephen's description of the JT as something "made by human hands" and thus insinuate an implicit identification and criticism of the JT—hence, working to connect the Ephesian and Jerusalem riot scenes.

These several similarities work to link the Jerusalem riot scene with the Ephesian riot scene in the minds of Luke's auditors. The divergent response to Paul's speaking in Aramaic, then, likely injects an element of hope into the latter scene (22:2). Here the parallelism seemingly breaks down: unlike the rioting idolaters of Acts 19, perhaps the crowd in Acts 22 will listen to Paul's message. But this hope proves vain, and the Jerusalem worshipers follow the pattern of the Ephesian heathen—despite Paul's cultically-appropriate worship and despite the fact that the offensive elements of his speech consisted of a revelation mediated while praying in the JT itself (22:17–18). Thus Luke, in narrative confirmation of the closing words of Stephen, shows the Jerusalemites, when faced with a threat to their Temple "made with hands," behave exactly as Luke's ideal readers/auditors should expect idolaters to act.

The closing of the Temple doors (ominously narrated in Acts 21:30) bears ambiguous symbolic import. It probably represents a final indication of both the intractability of Jerusalemite opposition to God's purposes and the sealing of the fate of the Jerusalem Temple and its idolatrous

---

(19:34), whereas Paul emphasizes his own heritage by speaking in Aramaic (21:40—22:2) and by other means, such as describing the law as τοῦ πατρῴου νόμου (22:3).

15. As indicated in chapter 3 of this study, I generally follow Taylor's view on this (see "Jerusalem Temple," 472), that Luke employs ναός polemically, in ways designed to stress God's abandonment of the JT. He does this in the Third Gospel by shifting away from acknowledging the cultic/sacerdotal role of the Temple and by using the term to detail the rending of the veil and in Acts by applying the term exclusively to human-made temples/idols (Acts 17:24; 19:24).

Appendix

worshipers,[16] in particular anticipating, likely by allusion to Mal 1:10, the cessation of the Temple's cultic activities.

---

16. On this latter point, I am in line with the view of Bruce, "The Church of Jerusalem," 659, though I do not share his overall assessment of the question of Jerusalem and the Temple in Luke's writings.

Bibliography

Ahl, Frederick. "The Art of Safe Criticism in Greece and Rome." *American Journal of Philology* 105 (1984) 174–208.
Alexander, Loveday. *Acts in Its Ancient Literary Context*. London: T. & T. Clark, 2005.
Allison, Dale C., Jr. "Matt. 23:39 = Luke 13:35b as a Conditional Prophecy." *Journal for the Study of the New Testament* 18 (1983) 75–84.
Arai, Sasagu. "Zum 'Tempelwort' Jesu in Apostelgeschichte 6:14." *New Testament Studies* 34.3 (1988) 397–410.
Aune, David E. "Enthymeme." In *The Westminster Dictionary of New Testament and Early Christian Literature and Rhetoric*, edited by David E. Aune, 150–57. Louisville: Westminster John Knox, 2003.
Ayuch, Daniel Alberto. "Jesús y el Templo de Jerusalén en Lucas: Entre Narración e Historia." *Revista Bíblica* 67, no. 3–4 (2005) 179–92.
Bachmann, Michael. *Jerusalem und der Tempel: Die geographisch-theologischen Elemente in der lukanischen Sicht des Jüdischen Kultzentrums*. Beiträge zur Wissenschaft vom Alten und Neuen Testament 109. Stuttgart: Kohlhammer, 1980.
Bailey, Kenneth E. *Poet and Peasant through Peasant Eyes: A Literary-Cultural Approach to Parables in Luke*. Combined ed. Grand Rapids: Eerdmans, 1983.
Baltzer, Klaus. "The Meaning of the Temple in the Lukan Writings." *Harvard Theological Review* 58, no. 3 (1965) 263–77.
Bauckham, Richard. "Apocalypses." In *Justification and Variegated Nomism*, edited by D. A. Carson, Peter T. O'Brien, Mark A. Seifrid, 1:135–87. Wissenschaftliche Untersuchungen zum Neuen Testament 2/140. Tübingen: Mohr/Siebeck, 2001.
———. *The Jewish World around the New Testament*. Wissenschaftliche Untersuchungen zum Neuen Testament 233. Tübingen: Mohr/Siebeck, 2008.
———. "The Two Fig Tree Parables in the Apocalypse of Peter." *Journal of Biblical Literature* 104, no. 2 (1985) 269–87.
Beale, G. K. "The Descent of the Eschatological Temple in the Form of the Spirit at Pentecost—Part 1: The Clearest Evidence." *Tyndale Bulletin* 56, no. 1 (2005) 73–102.
———. "The Descent of the Eschatological Temple in the Form of the Spirit at Pentecost—Part 2: Corroborating Evidence." *Tyndale Bulletin* 56, no. 2 (2005) 63–90.
Beck, Richard, and Sara Taylor. "The Emotional Burden of Monotheism: Satan, Theodicy, and Relationship with God." *Journal of Psychology and Theology* 36, no. 3 (2008) 151–60.
Black, Allen. "'Your Sons and Your Daughters Will Prophesy . . .': Pairings of Men and Women in Acts." In *Scripture and Traditions: Essays on Early Judaism and Christianity*

Bibliography

in Honor of Carl R. Holladay, edited by Patrick Gray and Gail R. O'Day, 193–206. Leiden: Brill, 2008.

Blenkinsopp, Joseph. "The Servant and the Servants in Isaiah." In *Writing and Reading the Scroll of Isaiah: Studies of an Interpretive Tradition*, edited by Craig C. Broyles and Craig A Evans, 155–75. Leiden: Brill, 1997.

Blomberg, Craig. *Interpreting the Parables*. Downers Grove, IL: Intervarsity, 1990.

Boase, Elizabeth. "Constructing Meaning in the Face of Suffering: Theodicy in Lamentations." *Vetus Testamentum* 58 (2008) 449–68.

Bock, Darrell L. *Proclamation from Prophecy and Pattern: Lucan Old Testament Christology*. Journal for the Study of the New Testament Supplement Series 12. Sheffield: JSOT Press, 1987.

Bonaventure, St. *Commentary on the Gospel of Luke*. Vol 1. Translated by Robert J. Karris. St. Bonaventure, NY: Franciscan Institute, 2001.

Bovon, François. *Das Evangelium nach Lukas*. Evangelisch-katholischer Kommentar zum Neuen Testament 3. Zürich: Neukirchener, 2002.

———. *Luke: A Commentary on the Gospel of Luke 1:1—9:50*. Hermeneia. Minneapolis: Fortress, 2002.

Brawley, Robert L. *Luke-Acts and the Jews: Conflict, Apology, and Conciliation*. Society of Biblical Literature Monograph Series 33. Atlanta: Scholars, 1987.

———. *Text to Text Pours Forth Speech: Voices of Scripture in Luke-Acts*. Bloomington: Indiana University Press, 1995.

Broadhead, Edwin K. "Mk 1,44: The Witness of the Leper." *Zeitschrift für die neutestamentliche Wissenschaft und die Kunde der älteren Kirche* 83 (1992) 257–65.

Brodie, Thomas L. "The Departure for Jerusalem as a Rhetorical Imitation of Elijah's Departure for the Jordan (2 Kings 2)." *Biblica* 70, no. 1 (1989) 96–109.

———. *Luke the Literary Interpreter: Luke-Acts as a Systematic Rewriting and Updating of the Elijah-Elisha Narrative*. Rome: Pontifical University of St. Thomas Aquinas, 1987.

———. "Luke-Acts as Imitation and Emulation of the Elijah-Elisha Narrative." In *New Views on Luke and Acts*, edited by Earl Richard, 78–85. Collegeville, MN: Liturgical, 1990.

———. "A New Temple and a New Law: The Unity and Chronicler-Based Nature of Luke 1:1—4:22a." *Journal for the Study of the New Testament* 5 (1979) 21–45.

———. "Towards Unraveling Luke's Use of the Old Testament: Luke 7:11–17 as an *Imitatio* of 1 Kings 17:17–24." *New Testament Studies* 32, no. 2 (1986) 247–67.

Brooke, George J. "Isaiah in the Pesharim and Other Qumran Texts." In *Writing and Reading the Scroll of Isaiah: Studies of an Interpretive Tradition*, edited by Craig C. Broyles and Craig A Evans, 609–32. Leiden: Brill, 1997.

Brown, Raymond E. "The Annunciation to Mary, the Visitation, and the Magnificat (Luke 1.26–56)." *Worship* 62, no. 3 (1988) 249–59.

———. *The Birth of the Messiah: A Commentary on the Infancy Narratives in Matthew and Luke*. Garden City, NY: Doubleday, 1977.

———. *Death of the Messiah: A Commentary on the Passion Narratives in the Four Gospels*. 2 vols. Anchor Bible Reference Library. New York: Doubleday, 1994.

———. "Finding of the Boy Jesus in the Temple: A Third Christmas Story." *Worship* 51, no. 6 (1977) 474–85.

———. "The Presentation of Jesus (Luke 2:22–40)." *Worship* 51, no. 1 (1977) 2–11.

Bruce, F. F. "The Church of Jerusalem in the Acts of the Apostles." *Bulletin of the John Rylands University* 67, no. 2 (1985) 641–61.

———. *Commentary on the Acts of the Apostles*. New International Commentary on the New Testament. Grand Rapids: Eerdmans, 1956.

———. "Stephen's Apologia." In *Scripture: Meaning and Method: Essays Presented to Anthony Tyrrell Hanson for His Seventieth Birthday*, edited by Barry Thompson, 37–50. Hull, UK: Hull University Press.

Brueggemann, Walter. "Some Aspects of Theodicy in Old Testament Faith." *Perspectives in Religious Studies* 26, no. 3 (1998) 253–68.

Caird, G. B. *Saint Luke*. Pelican Gospel Commentaries. New York: Seabury, 1963.

Carroll, John T. *Response to the End of History: Eschatology and Situation in Luke-Acts*. Society of Biblical Literature Dissertation Series 92. Atlanta: Scholars, 1988.

Chance, J. Bradley. *Jerusalem, the Temple, and the New Age in Luke-Acts*. Macon, GA: Mercer University Press, 1988.

Charlesworth, James H., ed. *The Old Testament Pseudepigrapha*. 2 vols. Peabody, MA: Hendrickson, 1983.

———. "Theodicy in Early Jewish Writings." In *Theodicy in the World of the Bible*, edited by Antti Laato and Johannes C. de Moor, 470–508. Leiden: Brill, 2003.

Coggins, R. J. *Samaritans and Jews: The Origins of Samaritanism Reconsidered*. Oxford: Blackwell, 1975.

Collins, John J. "The Sibylline Oracles: A New Translation and Introduction." In *Old Testament Pseudepigrapha*, edited by J. H. Charlesworth, 1:317–472. Peabody, MA: Hendrickson, 1983.

Conzelmann, Hans. *The Theology of St. Luke*. Translated by Geoffrey Buswell. Philadelphia: Fortress, 1961.

Crenshaw, James L. *Defending God: Biblical Responses to the Problem of Evil*. Oxford: Oxford University Press, 2005.

———. "The Problem of Theodicy in Sirach: On Human Bondage." *Journal of Biblical Literature* 94, no. 1 (1975) 47–64.

———. "The Sojourner Has Come to Play the Judge: Theodicy on Trial." In *God in the Fray: A Tribute to Walter Brueggemann*, edited by Tod Linafelt and Timothy K. Beal, 83–92. Minneapolis: Fortress, 1998.

———. "Theodicy in the Book of the Twelve." In *Thematic Threads in the Book of the Twelve*, edited by Paul L. Redditt and Aaron Schart, 175–91. Beihefte zur Zeitschrift für die alttestamentliche Wissenschaft 325. Berlin: de Gruyter, 2003.

———. *Theodicy in the Old Testament*. Philadelphia: Fortress, 1983.

———. *A Whirlpool of Torment: Israelite Traditions of God as Oppressive Presence*. Philadelphia: Fortress, 1984.

Croatto, J. Severino. "Jesus, Prophet Like Elijah, and Prophet-teacher Like Moses in Luke-Acts." *Journal of Biblical Literature* 124, no. 3 (2005) 451–66.

Culpepper, R. Alan. *Anatomy of the Fourth Gospel: A Study in Literary Design*. Philadelphia: Fortress, 1983.

Culy, Martin M., Mikeal C. Parsons, Joshua Stigall. *Luke: A Handbook on the Greek Text*. Baylor Handbook on the Greek New Testament. Waco, TX: Baylor University Press, 2010.

Danker, William. *Jesus and the New Age: A Commentary on St. Luke's Gospel*. Rev. ed. Philadelphia: Fortress, 1988.

Darr, John A. *Herod the Fox: Audience Criticism and Lukan Characterization*. Journal for the Study of the New Testament Supplements Series 163. Sheffield: Sheffield Academic Press, 1998.

BIBLIOGRAPHY

Davidson, Richard M. *The Typology in Scripture*. Andrews University Seminary Doctoral Dissertation Series 2. Berrien Springs, MI: Andrews University Press, 1981.

Dawsey, James M. "Confrontation in the Temple: Luke 19:45—20:47." *Perspectives in Religious Studies* 11, no. 2 (1984) 153–65.

———. *The Lukan Voice: Confusion and Irony in the Gospel of Luke*. Macon, GA: Mercer University Press, 1986.

———. "The Origin of Luke's Positive Perception of the Temple." *Perspectives in Religious Studies* 18, no. 1 (1991) 5–22.

Demetrius: On Style. Translated by W. Rhys Roberts. Cambridge: Cambridge University Press, 1902.

Denaux, Adelbert. "The Delineation of the Lukan Travel Narrative within the Overall Structure of the Gospel of Luke." In *The Synoptic Gospels: Source Criticism and the New Literary Criticism*, edited by Camille Focant, 359–92. Bibliotheca ephemeridum theologicarum lovaniensium 110. Leuven: Leuven University Press, 1993.

———. "The Parable of the King-Judge (Lk 19,12–28) and Its Relation to the Entry Story (Lk 19,29–44)." *Zeitschrift für die neutestamentliche Wissenschaft und die Kunde der älteren Kirche* 93, nos. 1–2 (2002) 35–57.

———. *Studies in the Gospel of Luke: Structure, Language and Theology*. Tilburg Theological Studies 4. Berlin: Lit, 2010.

Derrett, J. Duncan M. "The Lucan Christ and Jerusalem: τελειοῦμαι (Lk 13:32)." *Zeitschrift für die neutestamentliche Wissenschaft und die Kunde der älteren Kirche* 75, no. 1–2 (1984) 36–43.

Eco, Umberto. "The Author and His Interpreters." Lecture at The Italian Academy for Advanced Studies in America, 1996. http://www.themodernword.com/eco/eco_author.html. Accessed 2-12-13.

Edwards, O. C. *Luke's Story of Jesus*. Philadelphia: Fortress, 1981.

Eliade, Mircea. *Cosmos and History: The Myth of the Eternal Return*. New York: Harper & Row, 1959.

Ellingworth, Paul. "Forgiveness of Sins." In *Dictionary of Jesus and the Gospels*, edited by Joel B. Green and Scot McKnight, 241–43. Downers Grove, IL: Intervarsity, 1992.

Elliott, John Hall. "Household and Meals versus the Temple Purity System: Patterns of Replication in Luke-Acts." *Hervormde Teologiese Studies* 47 (1991) 386–99.

———. "Temple versus Household in Luke-Acts: A Contrast in Social Institutions." In *Social World of Luke-Acts*, edited by J. H. Neyrey, 211–40. Peabody, MA: Hendrickson, 1991.

Esler, Philip Francis. *Community and Gospel in Luke-Acts: The Social and Political Motivations of Lucan Theology*. Society of New Testament Studies Monograph Series 57. Cambridge: Cambridge University Press, 1987.

Evans, C. F. *St. Luke*. Philadelphia: Trinity, 1990.

Evans, Craig A. "From Gospel to Gospel: The Function of Isaiah in the New Testament." In *Writing and Reading the Scroll of Isaiah: Studies of an Interpretive Tradition*, edited by Craig C. Broyles and Craig A. Evans, 651–92. Leiden: Brill, 1997.

———. "The Function of the Elijah/Elisha Narratives in Luke's Ethic of Election." In *Luke and Scripture: The Function of Sacred Tradition in Luke-Acts*, edited by Craig A. Evans and James A. Sanders, 70–83. Minneapolis: Fortress, 1993.

———. "'He Set His Face': On the Meaning of Luke 9:51." In *Luke and Scripture: The Function of Sacred Tradition in Luke-Acts*, edited by Craig A. Evans and James A. Sanders, 93–105. Minneapolis: Fortress, 1993.

———. *Luke*. New International Biblical Commentary. Peabody, MA: Hendrickson, 1990.

———. "Luke's Use of the Elijah/Elisha Narratives and the Ethic of Election." *Journal of Biblical Literature* 106, no. 1 (1987) 75–83.

———. "Prophecy and Polemic: Jews in Luke's Scriptural Apologetic." In *Luke and Scripture: The Function of Sacred Tradition in Luke-Acts*, edited by C. A. Evans and J. A. Sanders, 171–211. Minneapolis: Fortress, 1993.

Evans, Craig A. and Lidija Novakovic. "Typology." In *Dictionary of Jesus and the Gospels*, edited by Joel B. Green, 986–90. 2nd ed. Downers Grove, IL: Intervarsity, 2013.

Farris, Stephen. *The Hymns of Luke's Infancy Narratives: Their Origin, Meaning, and Significance*. Sheffield: JSNT Press, 1985.

Fay, Ron. "The Narrative Function of the Temple in Luke-Acts." *Trinity Journal* 27, no. 2 (2006) 255–70.

Fisk, Bruce N. "See My Tears: a Lament for Jerusalem (Luke 13:31–35; 19:41–44)." In *Word Leaps the Gap*, edited by J. Ross Wagner, C. Kavin Rowe, A. Katherine Grieb, 147–78. Grand Rapids: Eerdmans, 2008.

Fitzmyer, Joseph A. *The Acts of the Apostles*. Anchor Bible Commentary 31. New York: Doubleday, 1998.

———. *The Gospel according to Luke: Introduction, Translation, and Notes*. Anchor Bible Commentary 28–28a. 2 vol. Garden City, NY: Doubleday, 1981–1985.

Fleddermann, Harry T. *Q: A Reconstruction and Commentary*. Leuven: Peeters, 2005.

Fowler, Robert M. *Let the Reader Understand: Reader-Response Criticism and the Gospel of Mark*. 2nd ed. Valley Forge, PA: Trinity, 2001.

Garland, David E. *Luke: An Exegetical Commentary*. Grand Rapids: Zondervan, 2011.

Gaston, Lloyd. *No Stone on Another: Studies in the Significance of the Fall of Jerusalem in the Synoptic Gospels*. Leiden: Brill, 1970.

Gaventa, Beverly Roberts. *The Acts of the Apostles*. Abingdon New Testament Commentaries. Nashville: Abingdon, 2003.

———. "Interpreting the Death of Jesus Apocalyptically: Reconsidering Romans 8:32." In *Jesus and Paul Reconnected*, edited by Todd D. Still, 125–45. Grand Rapids: Eerdmans, 2007.

Gaylord, H. E., Jr. "3 [Greek Apocalypse of] Baruch: A New Translation and Introduction." In *Old Testament Pseudepigrapha*, edited by J. H. Charlesworth, 1:653–79. Peabody, MA: Hendrickson, 1983.

Giblin, Charles Homer. *The Destruction of Jerusalem according to Luke's Gospel: A Historical-Typological Moral*. Analecta Biblica 107. Rome: Biblical Institute Press, 1985.

Goppelt, Leonard. "Typos, antitypos." Translated by G. W. Bromiley. In *Theological Dictionary of the New Testament*, edited by G. Kittel and G. Friedrich, 8:246–59. Grand Rapids: Eerdmans, 1972.

———. *Typos: The Typological Interpretation of the Old Testament in the New*. Translated by D. H. Madvig. Grand Rapids: Eerdmans, 1982.

Gregory, Andrew F. *The Reception of Luke and Acts in the Period before Irenaeus: Looking for Luke in the Second Century*. Wissenschaftliche Untersuchungen zum Neuen Testament 2/169. Tübingen: Mohr/Siebeck, 2003.

Gregory, Andrew F., and C. Kavin Rowe, eds. *Rethinking the Unity and Reception of Luke and Acts*. Columbia: University of South Carolina Press, 2010.

Bibliography

Green, Joel B. "The Demise of the Temple as a 'Cultural Center' in Luke-Acts: An Exploration of the Rending of the Temple Veil (Luke 23:44–49)." *Revue Biblique* 101 (1994) 495–515.

———. "Discourse Analysis and New Testament Interpretation." In *Hearing the New Testament: Strategies for Interpretation*, edited by Joel B. Green, 175–96. Grand Rapids: Eerdmans, 1995.

———. *The Gospel of Luke*. New Internationl Commentary on the New Testament. Grand Rapids: Eerdmans, 1997.

———. "The Problem of a Beginning." *Bulletin for Biblical Research* 4 (1994) 61–85.

———. *The Theology of the Gospel of Luke*. Cambridge: Cambridge University Press, 1995.

Gurtner, Daniel M. "LXX Syntax and the Identity of the NT Veil." *Novum Testamentum* 47, no. 4 (2005) 344–53.

Haacker, Klaus. "Lukas 18:7 als Anspielung auf den *Deus absconditus*." *Novum Testamentum* 53 (2011) 267–72.

Hamm, Dennis. "Praying 'Regularly' (Not 'Constantly'): A Note on the Cultic Background of *Dia Pantos* at Luke 24:53, Acts 10:2 and Hebrews 9:6, 13:15." *Expository Times* 116, no. 2 (2004) 50–52.

———. "The Tamid Service in Luke-Acts: The Cultic Background Behind Luke's Theology of Worship (Luke 1:5–25; 18:9–14; 24:50–53; Acts 3:1; 10:3, 30)." *Catholic Biblical Quarterly* 65, no. 2 (2003) 215–31.

———. "What the Samaritan Leper Sees: The Narrative Christology of Luke 17:11–19." *Catholic Biblical Quarterly* 56, no. 2 (1994) 273–87.

Hartley, John E. *Leviticus*. Word Biblical Commentary 4. Dallas: Word, 1992.

Hays, Richard B. "Can the Gospels Teach Us How to Read the Old Testament?" *Pro Ecclesia* 11, no. 4 (2002) 402–18.

———. *Echoes of Scripture in the Letters of Paul*. New Haven: Yale University Press, 1989.

———. "Torah Reconfigured: Reading Scripture with Matthew." Speech delivered at 2011 Winter Pastor's School, Truett Seminary, Baylor University.

Hays, Richard B., and Joel B. Green. "The Use of the Old Testament by New Testament Writers." In *Hearing the New Testament: Strategies for Interpretation*, edited by Joel B. Green, 223–35. Grand Rapids: Eerdmans, 1995.

Heath, Malcolm. "Pseudo-Dionysius *Art of Rhetoric* 8–11: Figured Speech, Declamation and Criticism." *American Journal of Philology* 124 (2003) 81–105.

Hempel, Charlotte. "The Laws of the Damascus Document and 4QMMT." In *The Damascus Document: A Centennial of Discovery*, edited by J. M. Baumgarten, E. G. Chazon, and A. Pinnick, 69–84. Leiden: Brill, 2000.

Herzog, William. *Parables as Subversive Speech: Jesus as Pedagogue of the Oppressed*. Louisville: Westminster John Knox, 1994.

Hjelm, Ingrid. *The Samaritans and Early Judaism: A Literary Analysis*. Journal for the Study of the Old Testament Supplement Series 303. Sheffield: Sheffield Academic, 2000.

Holmås, Geir Otto. "'My House Shall Be Called a House of Prayer.'" *Journal for the Study of the New Testament* 27, no. 4 (2005) 393–416.

Huddleston, Jonathan. "What Would Elijah and Elisha Do? Internarrativity in Luke's Story of Jesus." *Journal of Theological Interpretation* 5, no. 2 (2011) 265–82.

Huffard, Everett. "The Parable of the Friend at Midnight: God's Honor or Man's Persistence?" *Restoration Quarterly* 21, no. 3 (1978) 154–60.

Hultgren, Arland J. *The Parables of Jesus: A Commentary*. Grand Rapids: Eerdmans, 2000.

Bibliography

Hutcheon, Cyprian Robert. "'God Is with Us': The Temple in Luke-Acts." *St. Vladimir's Theological Quarterly* 44, no. 1 (2000) 3–33.

Jeremias, Joachim. *The Parables of Jesus*. 2nd rev. ed. Translated by S.H. Hooke. New York: Scribners, 1972.

Jervell, Jacob. "God's Faithfulness to a Faithless People: Trends in Interpretation of Luke-Acts." *Word and World* 12, no. 1 (1992) 29–36.

———. *Luke and the People of God: A New Look at Luke-Acts*. Minneapolis: Augsburg, 1972.

Johnson, Luke T. *The Acts of the Apostles*. Sacra Pagina. Collegeville, MN: Liturgical, 1992.

———. *The Gospel of Luke*. Sacra Pagina. Collegeville, MN: Liturgical, 1991.

———. "Literary Criticism of Luke-Acts: Is Reception History Pertinent?" *Journal for the Study of the New Testament* 28, no. 2 (2005) 159–62.

———. "The Lukan Kingship Parable (Luke 19:11–27)." *Novum Testamentum* 24.2 (1982) 139–59.

Jones, Kenneth R. *Jewish Reactions to the Destruction of Jerusalem in 70 A.D.: Apocalypses and Related Pseudepigrapha*. Leiden: Brill, 2011.

Just, Arthur, Jr., ed. *Luke*. Ancient Christian Commentary on Scripture. New Testament 3. Downers Grove, IL: Intervarsity, 2003.

Karris, Robert J. "The Gospel according to Luke." In *The New Jerome Biblical Commentary*, edited by Raymond E. Brown, Joseph A. Fitzmyer, and Roland E. Murphy, 675–76. London: Chapman, 1995.

———. *Luke: Artist and Theologian—Luke's Passion Account as Literature*. New York: Paulist, 1985.

Keathley, Naymond H. "The Temple in Luke and Acts: Implication for the Synoptic Problem and Proto-Luke." In *With Steadfast Purpose: Essays in Honor of Henry Jackson Flanders, Jr.*, edited by N. H. Keathley, 77–105. Waco, TX: Baylor University Press, 1990.

Keener, Craig S. *Acts: An Exegetical Commentary*. Vol 1. Grand Rapids: Baker Academic, 2012.

Kingsbury, Jack Dean. *Conflict in Luke: Jesus, Authorities, Disciples*. Minneapolis: Fortress, 1991.

———. "The Plot of Luke's Story of Jesus." In *Gospel Interpretation: Narrative-Critical and Social-Scientific Approaches*, edited by Jack D. Kingsbury, 155–65. Harrisburg, PA: Trinity, 1997.

———. "Reflections on 'the Reader' of Matthew's Gospel." *New Testament Studies* 34, no. 3 (1988) 443–60.

Kinman, Brent. "Jesus' Royal Entry into Jerusalem." *Bulletin for Biblical Research* 15, no. 2 (2005) 223–60.

———. "Lucan Eschatology and the Missing Fig Tree." *Journal of Biblical Literature* 113, no. 4 (1994) 669–78.

———. "Parousia, Jesus, 'A-Triumphal' Entry, and the Fate of Jerusalem (Luke 19:28–44)." *Journal of Biblical Literature* 118 (1994) 279–94.

Klauck, Hans-Josef. "Die Heilige Stadt: Jerusalem bei Philo und Lukas." *Kairos* 28, nos. 3–4 (1986) 129–51.

Klein, Hans. *Das Lukasevangelium*. Kritisch-exegetischer Kommentar über das Neue Testament 10. Göttingen: Vandenhoeck & Ruprecht, 2006.

BIBLIOGRAPHY

Knibb, Michael. "Isaianic Tradition in the Apocrypha and Pseudepigrapha." In *Writing and Reading the Scroll of Isaiah: Studies of an Interpretive Tradition*, edited by Craig C. Broyles and Craig A Evans, 633–50. Leiden: Brill, 1997.
Koet, Bart J. "Isaiah in Luke-Acts." In *Isaiah in the New Testament*, edited by Steven Moyise and Maarten J. J. Menken, 79–100. London: T. & T. Clark, 2005.
———. "Simeons Worte [Lk 2,29–32.34c-35] und Israels Geschick." In *The Four Gospels 1992: Festschrift Frans Neirynck*, edited by Frans van Segbroeck et al., 2:1549–69. Louvain: Peeters, 1992.
Kurz, William S. *Reading Luke-Acts: Dynamics of Biblical Narrative*. 1st ed. Louisville: Westminster John Knox, 1993.
Laato, Antti, and Johannes C. de Moor. "Introduction." In *Theodicy in the World of the Bible*, edited by Antti Laato and Johannes C. de Moor, vii–liv. Leiden: Brill, 2003.
Laato, Antti, and Johannes C. de Moor, eds. *Theodicy in the World of the Bible*. Leiden: Brill, 2003.
Larsson, Edvin. "Temple-criticism and the Jewish Heritage: Some Reflections on Acts 6–7." *New Testament Studies* 39, no. 3 (1993) 379–95.
Laurentin, Rene. *Structure et Théologie de Luc I–II*. Paris: Lecoffre, 1964.
Le Donne, Anthony. "The Improper Temple Offering of Ananias and Sapphira." *New Testament Studies* 59, no. 3 (2013) 346–64.
Levine, Lee I. A. "Judaism from the Destruction of Jerusalem to the End of the Second Jewish Revolt: 70–135 C.E." In *Christianity and Rabbinic Judaism: A Parallel History of Their Origins and Early Development*, edited by Hershel Shanks, 125–50. Washington, DC: Biblical Archaeology Society, 1992.
Liefeld, Walter L. "Parables on Prayer (Luke 11:5–13; 18:1–14)." In *The Challenge of Jesus' Parables*, edited by Richard N. Longenecker, 240–62. McMaster New Testament Studies 4. Grand Rapids: Eerdmans, 2000.
Litwak, Kenneth Duncan. *Echoes of Scripture in Luke-Acts: Telling the History of God's People Intertextually*. Journal for the Study of the New Testament Supplement Series 282. London: T&T Clark International, 2005.
Llewellyn, Peter. "The Consolation of Israel and the Redemption of Jerusalem." *St Mark's Review* 188 (2002) 8–13.
Lohfink, Gerhard. *Die Himmelfahrt Jesu: Untersuchungen zu den Himmelfahrts- und Erhöhungstexten bei Lukas*. Munich: Kösel, 1971.
Longenecker, Bruce W. *2 Esdras*. Guides to Apocrypha and Pseudepigrapha. Sheffield: Sheffield Academic, 1995

———. *Eschatology and the Covenant: A Comparison of 4 Ezra and Romans 1–11*. Journal for the Study of the New Testament: Supplement Series 57. Sheffield: Sheffield Academic, 1991.
———. "Good News to the Poor: Jesus, Paul, and Jerusalem." In *Jesus and Paul Reconnected: Fresh Pathways into an Old Debate*, edited by Todd D. Still, 37–66. Grand Rapids: Eerdmans, 2007.
———. *Hearing the Silence: Jesus on the Edge and God in the Gap—Luke 4 in Narrative Perspective*. Eugene, OR: Cascade, 2012.
———. "Locating 4 *Ezra*: A Consideration of Its Social Settings and Functions." *Journal for the Study of Judaism in the Persian, Hellenistic, and Roman Periods* 28, no. 3 (1997) 271–93.
———. "Rome's Victory and God's Honour: The Jerusalem Temple and the Spirit of God in Lukan Theodicy." In *The Holy Spirit and Christian Origins: Essays in Honor of*

James D. G. Dunn, edited by G. N. Stanton, B. W. Longenecker, and S. C. Barton, 90–102. Grand Rapids: Eerdmans, 2004.

Macdonald, John. *The Theology of the Samaritans*. New Testament Library. Philadelphia: Westminster, 1964.

Maile, John F. "The Ascension in Luke-Acts." *Tyndale Bulletin* 37 (1986) 29–59.

Malbon, Elizabeth Struthers. *Mark's Jesus: Characterization as Narrative Christology*. Waco, TX: Baylor University Press, 2009.

Mallen, Peter. *The Reading and Transformation of Isaiah in Luke-Acts*. Library of New Testament Studies 367. London: T. & T. Clark, 2008.

Mare, W. Harold. "Acts 7: Jewish or Samaritan in Character?" *Westminster Theological Journal* 34, no. 1 (1971) 1–21.

Marguerat, Daniel. "Luc-Actes Entre Jérusalem et Rome. Un Procédé Lucanien de Double Signification." *New Testament Studies* 45, no. 1 (1999) 70–87.

Marshall, I. Howard. *The Acts of the Apostles: An Introduction and Commentary*. Grand Rapids: Eerdmans, 1980.

———. *The Gospel of Luke: A Commentary on the Greek Text*. New International Greek Testament Commentary 3. Exeter: Paternoster, 1978. 1st American ed. Grand Rapids: Eerdmans, 1978.

Martens, Allen W. "'Produce Fruit Worth of Repentance': Parables of Judgment against the Jewish Religious Leaders and Nation (*Matt. 21:28—22:14, par.; Luke 13:6–9*)." In *The Challenge of Jesus' Parables*, edited by Richard N. Longenecker, 151–76. Grand Rapids: Eerdmans, 2000.

Matera, Frank J. "The Death of Jesus according to Luke: A Question of Sources." *Catholic Biblical Quarterly* 47, no. 3 (1985) 469–85.

———. "Jesus' Journey to Jerusalem (Luke 9.51—19.46): A Conflict with Israel." *Journal for the Study of the New Testament* 51 (1993) 57–77.

McComiskey, Douglas S. *Lukan Theology in the Light of the Gospel's Literary Structure*. Paternoster Biblical Monographs. Bletchley, UK: Paternoster, 2004.

McConnell, James R. *The Topos of Divine Testimony in Luke-Acts*. PhD diss., Baylor University, 2009.

McKnight, Scot. *Jesus and His Death: Historiography, the Historical Jesus, and Atonement Theory*. Waco, TX: Baylor University Press, 2005.

Merenlahti, Petri, and Raimo Hakola. "Reconceiving Narrative Criticism." In *Characterization in the Gospel: Reconceiving Narrative Criticism*, edited by David Rhoads and Kari Syreeni, 37–46. Journal for the Study of the New Testament Supplements 184. Sheffield: Sheffield Academic, 1999.

Metzger, Bruce M. "The Fourth Book of Ezra: A New Translation and Introduction." In *Old Testament Pseudepigrapha*, edited by J. H. Charlesworth, 1:517–59. Peabody, MA: Hendrickson, 1983.

Metzger, James A. *Consumption and Wealth in Luke's Travel Narrative*. Biblical Interpretation Series 88. Leiden: Brill, 2007.

———. "God as F(r)iend? Reading Luke 11:5–8 & 18:1–8 with a Hermeneutic of Suffering." *Horizons in Biblical Theology* 32 (2010) 33–57.

———. "Where Has Yahweh Gone? Reclaiming Unsavory Images of God in New Testament Studies." *Horizons in Biblical Theology* 31 (2009) 51–76.

Meynet, Roland. "Dieu Donne Son Nom à Jésus: Analyse Rhétorique de Lc 1:26–56 et de 1 Sam 2:1–10." *Biblica* 66, no. 1 (1985) 39–72.

Bibliography

Moessner, David P. "The Meaning of Kathexēs in the Lukan Prologue as a Key to the Distinctive Contribution of Luke's Narrative Among the 'Many.'" In *The Four Gospels 1992: Festschrift Frans Neirynck*, edited by Frans van Segbroeck et al., 2:1513-28. Louvain: Peeters, 1992.

Munck, Johannes. *The Acts of the Apostles*. Revised by William F. Albright and C. S. Mann. Anchor Bible Commentary 31. Garden City, NY: Doubleday, 1967.

Myers, Jacob M. *I and II Esdras*. Anchor Bible. Garden City, NY: Doubleday, 1974.

Nickelsburg, George W. E. *Jewish Literature Between the Bible and the Mishnah: A Historical and Literary Introduction*. 2nd ed. Minneapolis: Fortress, 2005.

Nolland, John. *Luke*. Word Biblical Commentary. 3 vols. Dallas: Word, 1989.

Pao, David W. *Acts and the Isaianic New Exodus*. Wissenschaftliche Untersuchungen zum Neuen Testament 2/130. Tübingen: Mohr/Siebeck, 2000.

Pao, David W., and Eckhard J. Schnabel. "Luke." In *Commentary on the New Testament Use of the Old Testament*, edited by G. K. Beale and D. A. Carson, 251-414. Grand Rapids: Baker Academic, 2007.

Parsons, Mikeal C. *Acts*. Paideia Series. Grand Rapids: Baker, 2008.

———. *The Departure of Jesus in Luke-Acts: The Ascension Narratives in Context*. Journal for the Study of the New Testament Supplements 21. Sheffield: JSOT Press, 1987.

———. *Luke*. Paideia Series. Grand Rapids: Baker, 2015.

———. "Luke and the *Progymnasmata*: A Preliminary Investigation into the Preliminary Exercises." In *Contextualizing Acts: Lukan Narrative and Greco-Roman Discourse*, edited by T. Penner and C. Vander Stichele, 43-63. SBL Symposium Series 20. Atlanta: Scholars, 2004.

———. "Narrative Closure and Openness in the Plot of the Third Gospel." In *SBL Seminar Papers, 1986*, edited by Kent H. Richards, 201-23. Atlanta: Scholars, 1986.

———. "The Place of Jerusalem on the Lukan Landscape: An Exercise in Theological Cartography." In *Literary Studies in Luke-Acts*, edited by Richard P. Thompson and Thomas E. Phillips, 155-72. Macon, GA: Mercer University Press, 1998.

Parsons, Mikeal C., and Richard I. Pervo. *Rethinking the Unity of Luke and Acts*. Minneapolis: Fortress, 1993.

Pervo, Richard I. *Acts: A Commentary*. Hermeneia. Minneapolis: Fortress, 2009.

Pokorný, Petr. *Theologie der Lukanischen Schriften*. Forschungen zur Religion und Literatur des Alten und Neuen Testaments 174. Göttingen: Vandenhoeck & Ruprecht, 1998.

Powell, Mark Allan. "Toward a Narrative-Critical Understanding of Luke." In *Gospel Interpretation: Narrative-Critical & Social-Scientific Approaches*, edited by Jack D. Kingsbury, 125-31. Harrisburg, PA: Trinity, 1997.

———. *What Is Narrative Criticism?* Guides to Biblical Scholarship, New Testament Series. Minneapolis: Fortress, 1990.

Price, Jonathan J. "The Provincial Historian in Rome." In *Josephus and Jewish History in Flavian Rome and beyond*, edited by Joseph Sievers and Gaia Lembi, 101-19. Supplements to the Journal for the Study of Judaism 104. Leiden: Brill, 2005.

Progymnasmata: Greek Textbooks of Prose Composition and Rhetoric. Translated by George A. Kennedy. Atlanta: Society of Biblical Literature, 2003.

Pseudo-Cicero. *Ad Herennium*. Translated by Henry Caplan. LCL. Repr., Cambridge, MA: Harvard University Press, 1954.

Pummer, Reinhard. *Early Christian Authors on Samaritans and Samaritanism: Texts, Translations and Commentary*. Texts and Studies in Ancient Judaism 92. Tübingen: Mohr/Siebeck, 2002.

———. *The Samaritans*. Iconography of Religions. Leiden: Brill, 1987.
Quintilian. *Institutiones Oratoriae*. Edited and translated by H. E. Butler. Cambridge, MA: Harvard University Press, 1920.
Ravens, David. *Luke and the Restoration of Israel*. Journal for the Study of the New Testament Supplement Series 119. Sheffield: Sheffield Academic, 1995.
Resseguie, James L. *Narrative Criticism of the New Testament: An Introduction*. Grand Rapids: Baker Academic, 2005.
Rhoads, David. "Narrative Criticism: Practices and Prospects." In *Characterization in the Gospel: Reconceiving Narrative Criticism*, edited by David Rhoads and Kari Syreeni, 264–85. Journal for the Study of the New Testament Supplements 184. Sheffield: Sheffield Academic, 1999.
Rice, Peter H. "The Rhetoric of Luke's Passion: Luke's Use of Common-place to Amplify the Guilt of Jerusalem's Leaders in Jesus' Death." *Biblical Interpretation* 21, no. 3 (2013) 355–76.
Richard, Earl J. "Acts 7: An Investigation of the Samaritan Evidence." *Catholic Biblical Quarterly* 39, no. 2 (1977) 190–208.
Robbins, Vernon K. "From Enthymeme to Theology in Luke 11:1–13." In *Literary Studies in Luke-Acts: Essays in Honor of Joseph B. Tyson*, edited by R. P. Thompson and T. E. Phillips, 191–214. Macon, GA: Mercer University Press, 1998.
Robinson, James, et al., eds. *The Sayings Gospel Q in Greek and English: With Parallels from the Gospels of Mark and Thomas*. Minneapolis: Fortress, 2002.
Robinson, Timothy J. "In the Court of Time: The Reckoning of a Monster in the *Apocolocyntosis* of Seneca." *Arethusa* 38 (2005) 223–57.
Rowe, C. Kavin. *Early Narrative Christology: The Lord in the Gospel of Luke*. Grand Rapids: Baker, 2009.
———. "Literary Unity and Reception History: Reading Luke-Acts as Luke and Acts." *Journal for the Study of the New Testament* 29, no. 4 (2007) 449–57.
Runia, David T. "Theodicy in Philo of Alexandria." In *Theodicy in the World of the Bible*, edited by A. Laato and J. C. de Moor, 576–604. Leiden: Brill, 2003.
Rusam, Dietrich. *Das Alte Testament bei Lukas*. Zeitschrift für die Neutestamentliche Wissenschaft und die Kunde der Älteren Kirche 112. Berlin: de Gruyter, 2003.
Russell, D.A. "Figured Speeches: 'Dionysius,' Art of Rhetoric *VIII–IX*." In *The Orator in Action and Theory in Greece and Rome: Essays in Honor of George A. Kennedy*, edited by Cecil W. Wooten, 156–68. Mnemosyne. Leiden: Brill, 2001.
Sanders, Jack T. "The Parable of the Pounds and Lucan Anti-Semitism." *Theological Studies* 42, no. 4 (1981) 660–68.
Sanders, James A. "A Hermeneutic Fabric: Psalm 118 in Luke's Entrance Narrative." In *Luke and Scripture: The Function of Sacred Tradition in Luke-Acts*, edited by Craig A. Evans and James A. Sanders, 140–53. Minneapolis: Augsburg, 1993.
———. "Isaiah in Luke." In *Luke and Scripture: The Function of Sacred Tradition in Luke-Acts*, edited by Craig A. Evans and James A. Sanders, 14–25. Minneapolis: Fortress, 1993.
Schultz, Brian. "Jesus as Archelaus in the Parable of the Pounds (Lk 19:11–27)." *Novum Testamentum* 49, no. 2 (2007) 105–27.
Septuaginta: Id Est Vetus Testamentum Graece Iuxta LXX Interpretes Edidit Alfred Rahlfs. Repr. Germany: Deutsche Bibelgesellschaft Stuttgart, 1979.
Septuaginta: Vetus Testamentum Graecum Auctoritate Academiae Scientarum Gottingensis editum. 23 Vols. Göttingen: Vandenhoeck & Ruprecht, 1931–.

Bibliography

Serrano, Andrés García. *The Presentation in the Temple: The Narrative Function of Lk 2:22–39 in Luke-Acts.* Analecta Biblica 197. Rome: Gregorian & Biblical, 2012.

Simson, P. "The Drama of the City of God: Jerusalem in St. Luke's Gospel." *Scripture* 15 (1963) 65–80.

Snodgrass, Klyne R. "*Anaideia* and the Friend at Midnight (Luke 11:8)." *Journal of Biblical Literature* 116, no. 3 (1997) 505–13.

———. *Stories with Intent: A Comprehensive Guide to the Parables of Jesus.* Grand Rapids: Eerdmans, 2008.

Snook, Lee E. "Interpreting Luke's Theodicy for Fearful Christians." *Word and World* 3 (1983) 304–11.

Spencer, F. Scott. *Journeying through Acts: A Literary-Cultural Reading.* Peabody, MA: Hendrickson, 2004.

Squires, John T. *The Plan of God in Luke-Acts.* Society for New Testament Studies Monograph Series 76. Cambridge: Cambridge University Press, 1993.

Sterling, Gregory E. *History and Self-Definition: Josephos, Luke-Acts, and Apologetic Historiography.* Supplements to Novum Testamentum. Leiden: Brill, 1992.

Stone, Michael E. *Fourth Ezra.* Hermeneia. Minneapolis: Fortress, 1990.

———. "Reactions to Destructions of the Second Temple: Theology, Perception, and Conversion." *Journal for the Study of Judaism in the Persian, Hellenistic, and Roman Periods* 12, no. 2 (1981) 195–204.

Strauss, Mark L. *The Davidic Messiah in Luke-Acts: The Promise and Its Fulfillment in Lukan Christology.* Journal for the Study of the New Testament Supplements Series 110. Sheffield: Sheffield Academic, 1995.

Sylva, Dennis D. "The Temple Curtain and Jesus' Death in the Gospel of Luke." *Journal of Biblical Literature* 105, no. 2 (1986) 239–50.

Talbert, Charles H. *Literary Patterns, Theological Themes, and the Genre of Luke-Acts.* Cambridge, MA: Society of Biblical Literature, 1974.

———. *Reading Acts: A Literary and Theological Commentary on the Acts of the Apostles.* Rev. ed. Reading the New Testament. Macon, GA: Smyth & Helwys, 2005.

———. *Reading Luke: A Literary and Theological Commentary on the Third Gospel.* New York: Crossroad, 1982.

———. *Reading Luke-Acts in Its Mediterranean Milieu.* Supplements to Novum Testamentum 107. Leiden: Brill, 2003.

Tannehill, Robert C. "'Cornelius' and 'Tabitha' Encounter Luke's Jesus." *Interpretation* 48, no. 4 (1994) 347–56.

———. "Israel in Luke-Acts: A Tragic Story." *Journal of Biblical Literature* 104 (1985) 69–85.

———. *The Narrative Unity of Luke-Acts: A Literary Interpretation.* Foundations and Facets 1. Philadelphia: Fortress, 1986.

Taylor, Nicholas H. "The Destruction of Jerusalem and the Transmission of the Synoptic Eschatological Discourse." *Hervormde Teologiese Studies* 59 (2003) 283–311.

———. "Jerusalem and the Temple in Early Christian Life and Teaching." *Neotestamentica* 33 (1999) 445–61.

———. "The Jerusalem Temple in Luke-Acts." *Hervormde Teologiese Studies* 60, nos. 1–2 (2004) 459–85.

———. "Luke-Acts and the Temple." In *The Unity of Luke-Acts*, edited by J. Verheyden, 409–21. Leuven: Peeters, 1999.

———. "Stephen, the Temple, and Early Christian Eschatology." *Revue Biblique* 110 (2003) 62–85
Thiselton, Anthony C. *Hermeneutics: An Introduction*. Grand Rapids: Eerdmans, 2009.
Tiede, David Lenz. *Luke*. Minneapolis: Augsburg, 1988.
———. *Prophecy and History in Luke-Acts*. Philadelphia: Fortress, 1980.
Tyson, Joseph B. *Images of Judaism in Luke-Acts*. Columbia: University of South Carolina Press, 1992.
———. "The Birth Narratives and the Beginning of Luke's Gospel." *Semeia* 52 (1990) 103–20.
Van der Waal, C. "The Temple in the Gospel according to Luke." In *Essays on the Gospel of Luke and Acts*, edited by W. C. van Unnik, 49–59. Neotestamentica 7. Pretoria: University of Pretoria Press, 1973.
Van Eck, Ernest. "When Neighbours Are Not Neighbours: A Social-Scientific Reading of the Parable of the Friend at Midnight (Lk 11:5–8)." *Harvard Theological Studies* 67, no. 1 (2011) 1–14.
Van Stempvoort, P. A. "The Interpretation of the Ascension in Luke and Acts." *New Testament Studies* 5 (1958–1959) 34–37.
Vanhoye, Albert. "L'Interete de Luc pour la Prophetie en Lc 1,76; 4,16–30 et 22,60–65." In *The Four Gospels 1992: Festschrift Frans Neirynck*, edited by Frans van Segbroeck et al., 2:1529–48. Louvain: Peeters, 1992.
Vegge, Ivar. *2 Corinthians: A Letter about Reconciliation: A Psychagogical, Epistolographical and Rhetorical Analysis*. Wissenschaftliche Untersuchungen zum Neuen Testament 239. Tübingen: Mohr/Siebeck, 2008.
Walker, Peter W. L. *Jesus and the Holy City: New Testament Perspectives on Jerusalem*. Grand Rapids: Eerdmans, 1996.
Weinert, Francis. "Luke, Stephen, and the Temple in Luke-Acts." *Biblical Theology Bulletin* 17, no. 3 (1987) 88–90.
———. "Luke, the Temple and Jesus' Saying about Jerusalem's Abandoned House (Luke 13:34–35)." *Catholic Biblical Quarterly* 44, no. 1 (1982) 68–76.
———. *The Meaning of the Temple in the Gospel of Luke*. PhD diss., Fordham University, 1979.
———. "The Meaning of the Temple in Luke-Acts." *Biblical Theology Bulletin* 11, no. 3 (1981) 85–89.
———. "Parable of the Throne Claimant (Luke 19:12, 14–15a, 27) Reconsidered." *Catholic Biblical Quarterly* 39, no. 4 (1977) 505–14.
Whitlark, Jason A. "'Here We Do Not Have a City that Remains': A Figured Critique of Roman Imperial Propaganda in Hebrews 13:14." *Journal of Biblical Literature* 131, no. 1 (2012) 161–79.
Wolter, Michael. *Das Lukasevangelium*. Handbuch zum Neuen Testament 5. Tübingen: Mohr/Siebeck, 2008.
Wüthrich, Serge. *Le Magnificat: Témoin d'un Pacte Socio-politique dans le Contexte de Luc-Actes*. Christianismes anciens 2. Bern: Lang, 2003.
Zarrow, Edward M. "Imposing Romanization: Flavian Coins and Jewish Identity." *Journal of Jewish Studies* 57, no. 1 (2006) 44–55.
Zeitlin, Solomon. "The Hallel." *Jewish Quarterly Review* 53 (1962) 22–29.

Index of Scripture

Genesis
11:32	80n75
23:17–20	80n75
33:19	80n75
49	147, 148
49:11	126
50:13	80n75
50:24, 25	127n21

Exodus
3:16	127n21
13:19	127n21
32:11–14	107n63
32:30–34	107n63
34:9	107n63

Leviticus
4:20–35	93
5:10–18	93
5:26	93
9	148n102, 149
9:22	147n97
9:22–24	146
13:49	96n21
14	95, 96n23, 117
19:22	93
26:1	159n7
26:30	159n7
28:10	150n106
28:15	150n106
28:23	150n106
28:24	150n106
28:31	150n106
29:6	150n106
29:11	150n106
29:16	150n106
29:19	150n106
29:22	150n106
29:25	150n106
29:28	150n106
29:31	150n106
29:34	150n106
29:38	150n106

Numbers
14:13–19	107n63
15:25–28	93

Deuteronomy
16:16–17:17	109n69
22:4	76n66
33	147–48

Joshua
6:15–21	76n65
7:10	76n66

Judges
4:14–16	76n65
4:16	76n67
7:13–15	76n65
13:2–7	62

Ruth
1:4	127n21

Index of Scripture

1 Kingdoms

1–4	62
1:1	62n14
1:6	63n20
1:9–15	62
1:10–11	63n20
1:11	62, 62n14, 65
1:13–14	63n20
1:19–20	62, 62n14
1:20	63n20
2	64n27
2:1	64
2:1–10	64
2:4–5	64
2:5	64
2:5–8	64n28
2:7	64
2:7–8	64n28
2:10	65n32
3:20	63n20
4:18	77
12:17–18	108n63
14:3	80, 86
17:47–49	76n65
21:9–14	76n65
31:4–5	76n68

2 Kingdoms

3:29	76n67
6:2–11	63
9:7	150n106
9:10	150n106
9:13	150n106
22:39	76n66

3 Kingdoms

1:50–52	76n65
2:27	80, 87
8:30	93
17:17–24	26, 27n73
19:19–21	26

4 Kingdoms

1:10–12	26
2:9–10	26
4:9	150n106
9:13	126n19
25:29	150n106
25:30	150n106

1 Chronicles

16:11	150n106

2 Chronicles

9:7	150n106
24:17–22	109n71

Job

7:18	127n21
10:12	127n21
24:12	127n21
28	33
29:4	127n21
31:14	127n21
34:9	127n21

Psalms [LXX]

2	114n88
15:5	42n51
42:9–11 [41:10–12]	46
59:4–5 [58:5–6]	46
74[73]:10–11	46
74:1–11 [73:1–11]	46
77:7–9 [76:8–10]	46
77:60	87n101
88 [87]	46
99:6	71n47
105:23	107n63
[117]	126n19
[117:26]	126
[131:17]	65n32

Isaiah

2:1–4	53, 54n89, 55
2:2–3	53, 158
2:18	159n7
5	103, 104, 105, 105n57, 106n58, 107, 108, 119, 153
5:1–7	103, 104, 104n55, 106n59

5:2	104	56	130n33, 131n37
5:3	104, 113	56:3	54n92
5:6	104, 105	56:7	53, 128, 129, 130, 131, 133
5:7	113	57:13	53
5:15	104n54	58:6	91
6:1–7	53n87	59:9	82
7:13	113	60	53, 158n4
8	78n71	60:3	158
8:14	113	60:10	158
8:14–18	78n71	61:1	91
8:17	113	61:1–7	53
8:18	113	61:5	158
10:3	127n21	62	53
10:11	159n7	62:2	53n89
11:9	53n89	63	83, 83n86, 83n87
11:9–16	53	63:4	82, 153
11:10–16	54n89	63:10	83
14:1	113	65:11	53
16:12	159n7	65:17–25	53
17	113	65:20–23	54n89
17:1	74n60	66:12–13	82, 82n80
19:1	159n7	66:20	53
21:9	159n7		
23:17	127n21		
24:22–23	127n21		

Jeremiah

29:6	127, 127n21	3:12	100n40
31:7	159n7	3:21	133
35:6	54n92, 158n5	6:15	74n60, 127, 127n21
40	91	7	27, 131
40–66	82, 158n4	7:11	128, 131n39
40:1	82, 82n80	7:12	87n101
40:5	82	7:14	79, 87, 87n101
42:1–7	73n55	7:16	108n63
42:6	82	8:13	27, 106n58
46:6	159n7	9	79, 87, 87n101
46:13	82	9:16–19	138n66
49:1–9	73n55	10:15	127n21
49:6	25, 54n92, 82, 157	11:22	109n69
51	82n81	12	111n80, 112n80, 114n90
51:17	74n60, 76n66	12:7	111n80, 112n80
51:22	74n60	15:1	71n47, 108n63
52:7–10	53	15:19	42n51
52:9–10	82	16:15	42n51
52:10	54n89	19:45–46	128
53	34	21:10	100n40
54	138n67	22	112n80, 112n83, 113n84, 114n90
54:1	138, 138n67		
54:10	138n67		

Index of Scripture

Jeremiah (continued)

22:1–8	111n80
22:1–9	112, 112n83, 113
22:5	111, 111n80
23:8	42n51
30:2	127n21
33	113, 112n80, 113, 113n84, 113n85, 114, 114n88, 114n90, 115, 116, 119
33:1–19	114
33:6	79, 87, 87n101, 115, 115n91
33:8	113
33:19	113n85
33:20–24	114n88
51:12	76n67
51:13	127, 127n21

Ezekiel

5:12	76n67
6:2	100n40
6:11	76n67
6:12	76n67
7	127n22
7:22	127, 127n22
8–11	132
10:18	132n42
11:10	76n67
11:23	132n42
13:17	100n40
14:8	133
14:17	73n57, 78n71
15:7	133
16:55	42n51
17:21	76n67
17:24	139
21:2	100n40
21:7	100n40
21:7–11	100n38
24:21	76n67
25:13	76n67
26:15	74n60
26:18	74n60
27:27	74n60
31:13	74n60
31:16	74n60

32:10	74n60
34:11	127n21
34:11–12	127n21
34:16	127n21
38:2	100n40
43	132
43:8–9	132

Hosea

7:16	76n67
10:8	139
11:11	42n51

Amos

5:25–27	159
7:17	76n67
9:10–11	76n65
9:11	76n66

Micah

7:1	105n57, 106n58
7:6	105n57

Nahum

3:3	74n60

Zephaniah

2:7	127n21

Zechariah

9:9	126
10:3	127n21
12	138
12:10–14	138
14:12	74n60
14:15	74n60
14:18	74n60

Malachi

1:10	164

Matthew

1	13n26

3:4–6	91	1:18–20	63n20
16:21	92n7	1:21	84n93, 142, 163
21:12–13	128	1:22	63n20, 84n93, 142, 163
21:33	104	1:24	63n20
21:33–46	103	1:24–25	63
23:37–39	42, 108	1:25	63n20
23:39	110, 114n90	1:26–38	61, 63
		1:26–56	61n12

Mark

		1:35	133n45
		1:36	64n23
1:5–6	91	1:39–44	63n19
1:44	95n19	1:39–56	61, 61n13, 64
2:23–28	141n79	1:41	61n13
2:27	93n11	1:43	58n98, 61n13
3:7–12	141n79	1:46–47	64
4:3–9	141n79	1:47	65
8:31	92n7	1:48	65, 74
11:8	126	1:52–53	64, 64n29, 65, 74–77
11:12	128n25	1:56	63n19
11:12–14	126n20, 128n25	1:57–66	61
11:15–16	130	1:57–80	65
11:15–19	128	1:67–79	65, 72
11:17	27	1:67–80	61
11:20–25	126n20	1:68	133n45, 137, 137n56
12:1	104, 105n56	1:69	65–66n32,
12:1–12	103	1:76	65
12:6	93n12	1:78	133n45
12:11	105n56	1:80	60, 65, 66, 67, 68, 69, 70,
13	135		75n63
13:3–4	135	2:1–11	61
13:14	136n53	2:1–21	66
14:3–9	141n79	2:7	66n34
14:58	114n87	2:21–28	144
15:29–30	139	2:22–24	72n51, 84
15:33	140	2:22–40	57, 58, 61, 66, 71–85,
			152, 158n2

Luke

		2:22–52	60, 71, 71–88, 154
1–2	24n60, 25, 58, 59–89, 98,	2:23–24	24
	105, 115, 119–20, 143,	2:25	54n92, 80, 81, 82
	152, 153, 154, 157	2:25–28	72
1:5–7	62	2:26	71n47
1:5–25	61, 61n12, 63, 95n20,	2:27	84
	144	2:28	66
1:8–11	84, 84n91	2:29–32	72, 82, 145
1:9	84n93, 142, 163	2:33–35	71n47, 73, 134
1:9–22	84n93, 143n84, 152	2:34–35	100, 119
1:13	63n20	2:36–38	61, 66, 71
1:15–16	62	2:37	67

183

Index of Scripture

Luke (continued)

2:38	42, 54n92, 55n93, 80–83, 88, 95n17, 101, 124, 137, 137n56, 137n60, 153, 154
2:39	84n91, 85
2:40	66, 67, 68, 69, 75n63
2:40–52	60
2:41	68, 85, 86
2:41–52	58, 59, 60, 61, 61n13, 67, 69, 71, 72, 73, 75n63, 85–88, 129, 144, 149, 152
2:42	86
2:46–47	86, 129
2:46–50	85
2:49	85, 85n97, 86, 132
2:49–50	67n40, 83n88
2:52	66, 68, 75n63
3–9	26
3–19	90–120
3:1–20	90–91, 134
3:1—4:13	90n1
3:1–9:51	90–98, 99, 100
3:4–6	24, 54n92, 82
3:6	137n56
3:7–9	91n4, 107
3:8–9	99
3:18–20	91n4
3:21–28	91
4–9	91
4:1–13	24, 58n97, 91, 94
4:9	83n88
4:14–30	91
4:18–19	24, 54n92, 91
4:18–21	55
4:24–27	26, 69n43, 69n45, 78n72, 91
4:28–30	91
4:30	8n4
4:31–33	92
4:33–37	92n5
4:38–41	92n5
4:42–44	92
5:1–11	133n45
5:3	92
5:4–7	92
5:8	95, 95n17
5:12	95, 95n19, 96
5:12–16	58, 92n5, 94–98, 116, 120, 143, 149, 152
5:14	95n19, 116n96
5:16	92
5:17–26	92n5, 93
5:20	93n9
5:20–21	92
5:21–22	74n62
5:27–32	92
5:36–39	92
6:1–5	92, 93n11, 141n79
6:3–5	24
6:6–11	92
6:8	74n62
6:12–16	92
6:17–19	92, 92n5, 141n79
6:20–26	74
6:20–49	92
7:1–10	92n5
7:11–17	26, 92n5
7:14–15	27n73
7:16	133n45
7:22	54n92, 55, 91, 92, 96
7:24–28	69n45
7:27	24
7:29–30	91n4
7:33–35	92
7:36–50	92, 141n79
7:48	93n9
8:1–3	92
8:4–18	92
8:5–8	141n79
8:10	24, 54n92
8:12	94n15
8:19–21	92
8:22–25	92
8:26–39	92n5
8:40–42	92n5
8:43–48	92n5
8:49–56	92n5
9:1–6	92
9:9	109n68
9:10–11	92
9:12–17	92
9:18–22	92
9:22	50, 98n29

Index of Scripture

9:23–27	92	13:1	102
9:28–36	58n97, 92	13:1–5	48–49, 49n13, 105, 106, 106n59
9:31	26, 93n11, 132	13:1–9	102–8, 145, 154
9:32	93n11, 132	13:2–3	103
9:34	93n11, 133n45	13:4	104
9:46–47	74n62	13:4–5	103
9:46–48	92	13:6–9	54n92, 103–8, 109, 111, 112, 116, 119, 153, 154
9:48	99		
9:51	26, 69n45, 83n86, 92, 100–101, 116n95, 119, 132–33, 153	13:8	104, 105, 106n59, 111n75
9:51—19:27	80n75, 98–120	13:10–17	99, 108
9:52–56	26, 79n75, 101–2, 116n95, 119	13:16	94n15, 102n45, 155
		13:18–21	108
9:61–62	26	13:22	108, 109n67
10:16	99	13:22–30	108, 109, 110
10:17–20	102n45	13:31	109, 109n67, 109n68, 110
10:18	94n15		
10:18–19	155	13:31–35	58, 58n97, 83, 84n88, 103, 105, 106, 108–16, 119, 127, 145, 153
10:30–37	79n75, 101		
11:1–13	43–44		
11:5–8	43–44, 44n59, 45, 45n63, 154n2	13:33	42, 50, 58, 109, 144n87
		13:33–35	88, 139
11:8	43n54, 44	13:34	107, 109, 138n70
11:13	45n63	13:34–35	27, 42, 101, 108
11:14–26	102n45	13:35	83n88, 86n97, 110–16, 127, 143, 152, 153, 154
11:18	94n15		
11:23	99	14:1	114n88
11:27–28	102n46	14:15	102n46
11:37–44	99	14:15–24	99
11:37–54	99, 102	15:1–3	99
11:43	130	15:11–32	99, 103n50
11:45	102n46	16:14	99, 130
11:48	99	17:11	116, 116n95, 118
11:49–51	58, 88, 101, 109, 110, 116, 139, 145, 153	17:11–19	58, 79n75, 97, 97n27, 99, 101, 116–19, 120, 133n45, 143, 145, 148, 149, 152
11:51	112n81		
12:1–3	99, 102		
12:1—13:9	102n47	17:14	116, 116n96, 117
12:13–21	102	17:16	150
12:17	74n62	17:17–19	117–19
12:41	102n46	17:20–35	46n64
12:49–53	99, 102	17:22–37	45, 47, 47n71
12:49–59	102	17:25	50
12:53	105n57	17:33	47
12:54–59	103	18:1–8	43, 43n54, 45, 45n63, 46, 46n64, 47, 47n70, 48, 107n61, 154n2
12:57–59	101		
12:58	102n47		

Index of Scripture

Luke (continued)

Reference	Pages
18:9–14	95n20, 99–100
19–24	121–51
19:10	127n21
19:11	121, 122, 123, 124, 124, 124n12, 125, 125n17, 154
19:11–27	42, 55n93, 58n97, 107n61, 121–25, 154
19:11–48	121–33
19:27	123n9
19:28	121–22, 125
19:28–36	126
19:28–40	58n97, 116
19:28–44	121n2
19:28–48	132–33
19:39–40	126
19:41–44	42, 58, 58n97, 81n78, 101, 107, 108, 110, 111, 116, 126–28, 128n24, 128n25, 139, 145, 153
19:41–48	133
19:44	127–28, 133, 133n45
19:44–45	42
19:45	125
19:45–46	128–33
19:45–48	58, 58n97, 128–32, 143, 152
19:46	54n92, 115n92, 152
19:47	125
19:47–48	135
19:47—21:38	99, 129, 130, 149
20:1	125, 128, 129
20:1–8	134
20:1—21:4	129n28
20:6	129
20:7	129
20:9	129
20:9–18	58n97, 103, 105, 106n59, 107n61, 134
20:14	74n62
20:19	129, 134
20:20–26	129, 134
20:27–38	129
20:27–40	134
20:40–44	129, 134
20:45–47	99n35, 130, 134
21	115n92
21–24	134–50
21:1–2	128
21:1–4	134, 135
21:5–6	128, 135
21:5–38	81n78, 135–37
21:9	135n52
21:9–19	146
21:20–22	42, 111
21:20–24	108n64
21:24	49–50, 83n87, 111, 136–37, 155
21:27	132n43
21:28	137
21:37	128, 135
21:37–38	134
21:38	129, 129n26
22–23	134
22:1–6	102n45, 134
22:2	134
22:3	94, 134
22:4–6	134
22:24–27	125n16
22:28–30	122, 130
22:31–32	107
22:37	50, 54n92
22:53	102n45
23:2	113n87, 125
23:6–12	114
23:13	113n87, 114n88
23:13–25	138
23:18	113n87
23:23–25	113n87
23:26	138
23:27–31	42, 58, 108, 111, 138–39, 145, 153
23:28	138n70
23:29	54n92
23:31	139n69
23:34	139
23:35	114n88, 139
23:38	125
23:39–43	139
23:44	140, 141
23:44–47	144–45
23:45	58, 80n75, 84n93, 85, 111, 115, 139–46, 152, 163

23:45–46	140, 141n79	5:28	158
24	50, 115n93, 148, 157	5:33–39	158
24:20	114n88	6–7	95n20, 139n73
24:25–27	50	6:12—8:1	158
24:38	74n62	6:13–14	114n87
24:44–53	146–50	7	5, 26n72, 80n75, 149, 159
24:48	96		
24:50–53	95n20, 146–50, 152	7:2	93n12
24:53	144n87	7:42–43	24, 159
		7:48	131n35, 159

Acts

		7:49–50	24, 54n92, 159
1–5	115n93	7:55	93n12
1–7	157–61	8	119, 130n33
1:4–9	148	8–28	161–64
1:6	42	8:1–3	159
1:6–8	4n11, 49–50, 55n93, 125, 136, 154, 157	8:26–39	54n92
		8:32–33	24, 54n92, 91
1:8	25, 54n92, 96, 118n103	10	149n104
1:13–14	55n92	10:2	150n106
2	158, 158n3, 160n9	10:3	95n20
2:17	53	10:24	117
2:17–18	55n92	10:30	95n20
2:23	50	13:33	24
2:24	50	13:34	54n92
2:25	150n106	13:35	24
2:43–47	160	13:41	24
2:46	144n87	13:47	24
3–7	145n94	13:47	25, 54n92
3:1	95n20, 144n87, 160n9	15	145n94
3:1–10	158n5	15:16–18	24
3:2	158n5	17:24	84n93, 85, 143n85, 163, 163n15
3:8	54n92, 158n5		
3:11	115n93, 160n9	19:21–40	162–63
3:11–26	130	19:24	84n93, 85, 143n85, 163, 163n15
3:14	50		
3:15	50	20:6	161n11
3:22–23	71n47	20:16	161n11
3:22–26	26, 70	21	95n20, 143n85, 144n87, 161–62
4:1–22	158		
4:23–31	130n34	21–22	115n93, 143n85, 145n94, 161–64
4:25–26	114n88		
4:28	50	21:2	144n87
4:32–37	160	21:21–25	161
5:1–11	55n92	21:27–29	162
5:14	55n92	21:27—22:29	162–63
5:17–42	158	21:28	131n38
5:20–26	130	21:30	163
		24:16	150n106

Index of Scripture

Acts (continued)

28:25–27	54n92

Romans

11:10	150n106

1 Corinthians

10	26n72

2 Thessalonians

3:16	150n106

Hebrews

2:15	150n106
2:17	76n68
9:6	150n106
13:15	150n106

Sirach

15:12	66n32
35:11–24	47–48n71
48:22–25	54
48:24–25	53, 53n87
50	147, 148n101, 148n102, 150
50:20–23	146–50

Baruch

2:26	114n90

1 Maccabees

4:15	76n67
4:46	71n47
7:38	76n67
7:46	76n67
9:27	71n47

4 Ezra (2 Esdras 3–14)

32n8, 33, 33n17, 34, 35n22, 35n23, 36, 36n30, 37–38, 39, 41n50, 46, 56

Visions I–III

33n17, 37, 50, 56

3:14	49n74
3:20–27	37
3:27–28	36n30
3:28–36	37
4:1–21	37
4:21	49n74
4:22–25	37
4:26–32	37
4:33	49n74
4:33—5:13	49
5:21–30	37
5:25	36n30
6:7	49
6:7–10	49n74
6:19	36n30
6:55–59	37
7:14–16	37n33
7:26–28	36n30
7:62–69	38

Vision IV

36n30

Visions IV–VII

33n17, 37

9:38—10:59	36n30

Vision V

37n31

Visions V–VI

37

13:36	36n30

www.ingramcontent.com/pod-product-compliance
Lightning Source LLC
Chambersburg PA
CBHW051742230426
43670CB00012B/2126